DISCOVER THE WAY OF LOVE, HEALING, AND HOLY FIRE

MAGDALENE
Unveiled

Compiled by Jane Astara Ashley
with 33 Contributing Authors
Foreword by Elayne Kalila Sophia Doughty

FLOWER *of* LIFE PRESS

"Mary Magdalene was and is an extraordinary revolutionary. Dr. Nicola Amadora captivates her essence deeply, in this 'real to the bone' story. She takes you on a riveting journey to experience how gutsy, all-encompassing, and timeless Mary's way truly is. Guiding women to come alive, stand in love, and to embody boldly the holy grail in the streets of our shaken world."

—**Dr. Sue Morter,** Author of *The Energy Codes*

"Amanda Alappat's chapter rings true as a sacred reclamation—an invocation of Mary Magdalene's ancient wisdom, the sovereign rite of free birth, and the timeless magic of women gathering in sacred circle. Her words are laced with spiritual remembrance and embodied knowing, stirring something primal, holy, and deeply feminine within the reader. This is more than a chapter—it's a portal for any woman ready to return to her inner oracle and rise in the power of sisterhood."

—**Latha Jay,** Spiritual Strategist, Bestselling Author of *Shadow Work for Self Love* and *Law of Attraction Manifestation Journal*

"In 'The Wise Web of the Red Thread,' Alessandra Mary offers more than a personal story—she extends a thread to every woman who has ever felt lost, called, broken open, or reborn. Her words carry the pulse of the Magdalene, the ache of becoming, and the truth that our path is never walked alone. This chapter is a luminous reminder that your red thread is already weaving through you. All that's left is to listen, follow, and let yourself be led."

—**Kelly Taveras**

"Sarah Devereux offers us profound wisdom and soulful guidance on what it means to live authentically. In these pages, she emerges as a luminous heroine—one who dares to step beyond the traditional roles of child, daughter, and mother to reclaim her true essence. Sarah is an edge-walker, a woman deeply attuned to the rhythms of change and the call of transformation. Rather than be bound by routine or expectation, she moves with the currents of life, ever seeking what is real and alive. A gifted storyteller and masterful wordsmith, Sarah writes with the kind of honesty and beauty that stirs the soul. Her words take flight, and in doing so, they awaken the longing within us to do the same—to rise, to choose, to listen to what our own hearts are crying out for. This is not the retelling of the old Martha and Mary tale we've heard in church pews—it is the revelation of the sacred third, the one who births the Muse. Through Sarah's voice, we are invited to remember her, to embody her, and to dance with her into the light of our own becoming."

—**Diana DuBrow,** Scent Priestess, Founder of The Emerald Temple

"Elsa Alegria's 'Reclaiming Womb Rose Codes' is a sacred scroll of remembrance—tender, unflinching, and alight with ancestral fire. Each word is an invocation, guiding us through the spiral of loss, reclamation, and ecstatic rebirth. With the serpent and rose as her companions, Elsa weaves a living testament to the power of the feminine body as oracle, altar, and threshold. This is not just a story—it's a transmission for all who are remembering the holiness of their womb-space, whether it remains within or has been released to the Earth."

—**Rebecca Cavender,** Writer, Oracle, Guide

"Leyolah Antara is an epic and deeply embodied high priestess. And it is rare I use the words 'high priestess,' yet for her it feels so fitting. Read her words and be transported into the bridal chamber, as she reminds all of us of the beating sacred heart of love and holy union. The birthright we all are here to reclaim. We all need a guide like Leyolah to remind us of the depths and heights of High Tantra. Read her words and receive the remembrance."

—**Kiya Ankara,** Author of *Egyptian Tantric Secrets* and *Magdalena's Tales*

"In this powerful contribution, Dionisia Hatzis invites us into a sacred journey of feminine reclamation with Mary Magdalene as the ultimate Guide through Death and Rebirth. With a uniquely compelling and evocative voice, she weaves her personal pilgrimage with the universal longing for bodily sovereignty, soul healing, and wholeness, transforming her own courageous descent and emergence into medicine for all."

—**Stella Stathi, M.A.,** Jungian/Somatic Psychotherapist, Midlife & Transitions Guide, Mentor

"Reading this chapter was a balm for my soul! Connie Viglietti shares the powerful story of her personal healing journey and how it led her to step onto the path of the scent priestess with detail, depth, and grace. Her words brought goosebumps to my skin and tears to my eyes. Connie has gifted us with a grounded and inspiring transmission about the power of remembering and embodying Mary Magdalene's essence. May it be shared far and wide, inviting as many of us as possible to wake up to the truth of love."

—**Melinda Scime,** Priestess, Author of *My Sacred Pause* and *Badass Self-Care*

"In this stunning remembrance, Elizabeth Brett walks us through an initiation as ancient as time—one that begins in the salt of the sea and ends in the sacred blood of lineage reclaimed. What unfolds is a resurrection story. Through raw survival, ancestral visitation, sacred oils, and womb blood offered to the Earth, Elizabeth offers herself—and us—back to sovereignty. Written with fierce tenderness, her words spiral like a prayer. I am deeply honored to have walked beside her on part of this journey. Magdalene Unveiled *is her hymn of return.*"

—**Rebecca Cavender,** Bestselling Author, Oracle, Guide

"Reading Dianne Chalifour's chapter was like hearing a long-forgotten song of the soul, one that speaks directly to the heart of every woman who has ever doubted her worth or silenced her own knowing. This is more than a personal story. It's a sacred offering and a call to remembrance. Dianne's voice is both fierce and tender as she walks us through the pain of disconnection and the courage it takes to reclaim our sacred power, over and over again. Her line, 'the pattern of choosing to remain stuck in victim consciousness... simply because we didn't believe it was possible,' resonated deeply. I see this hurt mirrored every day in women who've been taught they are unworthy of love, softness, or power. This chapter reminds us that if we quiet the noise and truly listen, the Divine Feminine will speak, and She will guide us back home to ourselves. Dianne's journey as a Priestess of Love is a luminous example of what it means to rise, not in spite of the wounds, but through them. Her story is a gift, one that has the power to awaken the collective heart of herstory and birth a new future grounded in fierce compassion, embodied truth, and the undeniable power of love."

—**Reid Bickley,** Business Development Specialist, Writer, and Community Advocate

"Sandra Corcoran is one of the forerunners in a massive resurrection of the lost and hidden teachings of Mary Magdalene and Jesus the Christ. Her reminder that Mary's job was to activate high-frequency energy—love and light—as a necessary pathway through the union of the physical body to open and actualize the light body is an essential guiding principle in our reframing of relationship as a path to experience unity with the Divine. Sandra's time spent in the crucible clearly bears gold in the wisdom she shares of deep, esoteric concepts taught in so many priestess lineages that trace back to the Magdalene codes. Bless Sandra for her courageous and curious spirit to bring these mysteries forward into the light of consciousness."

—**Rev. Dr. Stephanie Red Feather,** Author of *The Evolutionary Empath* and *Empath Activation Cards*

"Having known Molly Douglas for years, I have witnessed not only her devotion to healing and truth but also the way she lives what she teaches. Her presence alone carries the frequency of love, remembrance, and fierce grace. Reading Magdalene Unveiled and the chapter 'Initiation: The High Priestess Path' is like stepping into a sacred temple of transformation, each word an invocation, each memory a mirror, each ritual a doorway into our collective remembrance (built from Love). This chapter is not just a personal account, it is a map for anyone on the path of reclaiming the Divine Feminine within. It guides us through the layers of ancestral wounds, societal shame, and spiritual suppression, gently yet powerfully inviting us to return home to the wisdom of the body, the voice of the soul, and the sacredness of our sensual, intuitive nature. To read this is to remember who you truly are. To walk with her in these pages is to awaken your own light. And as it ALWAYS is with Molly, what a magical walk it is."

—**Harrison Meagher,** Author of *Your Cosmic Love Antenna*, Mentor, Heart Leader

"This reading felt like sitting at the feet of an ancient soul, whispering secrets of the sacred feminine into my heart. Hallie Lifson's words are a transmission… raw, devotional, and deeply activating. This piece is not just a story; it's a remembrance. A love letter to every woman who has ever felt the call to walk the priestess path. These words are sure to invite countless women to remember who they are."

—**Leola Watkins,** Author of *Sacred Sex Ed*

"Kathy Forest is one of most deeply grounded spiritual transmitters I've had the pleasure of working with. I love sitting in her circles because she not only 'gets it,' she knows how to share it. So, it came as no surprise to me that Kathy's chapter is filled with juicy nuggets of truth. But more than that, Kathy is tracking a key aspect of what every modern-day mystic needs to know to navigate these challenging times: Transcending crisis opens a portal to joy. As she writes, 'It is sometimes a very strange place to be: to feel so much joy in the face of so much suffering.' If you're ready to follow the lead of the Magdalene, who survived the unthinkable to launch a movement, step into Kathy's world and she'll show you the path to a heart-centered reality that is emerging in front of our eyes, if only we can see it."

—**Dr. Rima Bonario,** Author of *The Seven Queendoms: A Soul Map for Embodying Sacred Feminine Sovereignty*

"AnuMa Jackie Heydemann's chapter is nothing short of a sacred transmission, a transmission of healing, wisdom, and wild grace. It's a living prayer, each word infused with the essence of Mary Magdalene. Her poetry, her raw honesty, and the profound recounting of her near-death experience moved me to tears. Every word felt like a blessing from the Divine Mother herself. Her words carry the frequency of feminine devotion, raw, real, and holy. I felt the Divine Feminine moving through her story, guiding us all back to our truth, our power, and our deep remembrance of the Mother's love."

—**Beverley Holt,** Reiki Master, Mediation Teacher and Atomic Empowerment Coach, Collaborative Author of *LadyX*

"In 'Womb Wisdom, Moon Magic,' Lara O'Neil's captivating, profound, and heartfelt writing reveals the true depth of womanhood. Her eloquent account of what it is to be a daughter, woman, and mother in the context of matriarchal death transmits an energetic path for navigating this life passage with grace and authenticity, serving as a portal of possibility. In a world where women are conditioned to suppress their innate depth, I feel it is a significant contribution to the Magdalene Legacy of feminine embodiment, a true gift to humanity."

—**Martha Langer,** Feminine Embodiment Coach and Author of *Embrace Your Vibrance: Practices for Vibrancy Activation*

"'My Priestess experiences were the most glorious thing that have ever happened to me in my life,' says Christy Michaels in her chapter, 'Peek Behind the Veil.' I had a first-hand view of her remarkable transformation beginning on 10/10/10 and continue to be curious about that unseen, mystical, and alluring energy… It's a compelling force that captivated and took us on a quest that radically changed the direction of our lives. It's intellectually hard to name or speak about, but it is an undeniably compelling force. I call it 'A Magdalene Calling.' However you want to name it, it's real, and She is calling many of us, for there is much work to accomplish. Christianity is incomplete without Magdalene standing in her rightful place next to Jesus in the Christian Mystery, and Christy Michael's Magdalene Moonrise Easter Celebrations ask us to see Easter through the eyes of Mary Magdalene. We are all aware that our world is out of balance. Women are needed to rise up, speak out, and stand as co-equals with men if we are to bring about greater harmony, balance, and Peace on Earth."

—**Elizabeth Kelley,** Priestess of Mary Magdalene and Hierophant of the Lyceum of the Holy Sophia

"After reading Anaïs Theyskens' story, my whole body was tingling with aliveness. I could feel the truth in every word she shared, and the generosity of her spirit woven throughout. Her journey is nothing short of pure inspiration. The courage and power it must have taken to choose herself and to be guided by the teachings of Mary Magdalene is awe-inspiring. I came away from her words feeling deeply inspired, empowered, and a full-bodied yes to the beauty and sacredness of life."

—**Chloe Isidora,** Author, Sacred Womb Facilitator

"In Sarah Alissandra Nomngomas 'The Rose,' I was transported into the mythical and profound landscape that follows a mother and daughter through the mythic journey of Demeter and Persephone. Sarah allows us to feel the profound and complex love shared between a mother and daughter. I was deeply moved and inspired by her journey as a single mother, raising a daughter and allowing her to become herself, even through painful choices and outcomes, and never wavering in her belief that, like Demeter, her daughter would return and they would be united. Wonderful!"

—**Mari Dreamwalker,** Author of *The Sacred Shawl*

"Jacquie Eva Rose Shenton manages to put words to experiences that very often evade them—her writing on her experiences of grief serves as a beautiful opener and a call back to the part of the Magdalene within each of us that is the Grief Walker. Grief can so often be an isolating experience, but Jacquie's message here is a reminder of the alchemy that comes from when we are willing to surrender into—and express—the fullness of our hearts."

—**Ellie Cleary,** Initiative Astrologer, AstroCartographer & Guide

"Sometimes, the story of a journey demands another thousand words—if not more. In Crystal Steinberg's essay, we witness the evolution of a life marked at times by brutality, yet always driven by curiosity and a warrior's spirit. As we follow her path, we're gifted with glimpses of her work—her voice, her artistry, her reflections. The journey culminates in a sense of hard-won joy, one that feels both personal and universally resonant. Crystal's journey is not just an essay; it's a testament."

—**Rosie Hartmann,** Artist, Author, and Advisor

"Tears are falling from my eyes, and my heart is bursting with electricity! As I read Stellar's pages of the Blue Rose, they ignite something in me that I can't explain with human words, it feels so sacred and so pure that it resonates with every part of my being like sacred codes embedded in the written words activating my own inner codes. It feels like an ocean of truth hitting my soul at once, expanding my consciousness into the infinity of Divine love."

—**Ligia Grande,** Author of 13 Sacred Initiations from Divine Mother of Dragons

"Elisha Tichelle is a powerful writer, a priestess from the ancestral realm, and an embodiment of Mary's essence. And that is all revealed through this chapter. It is raw and refined at the same time. It is a revealing and a remembrance. In this writing, she takes the reader through the journey into the mystical depths of her becoming, and it is an honour to witness it. Once I started, I couldn't stop reading it! Thank you for sharing these words with us."

—**Pallak Arora,** Nervous System Healing Coach, Sacred Life Wayshower

"A heartfelt and potent sharing of the deep work across generations of healing. In sharing her story, Lettie Sullivan shows us how our own healing journeys contribute to the reclaiming of Divine Feminine power, authority, and unconditional love, through which she becomes the Matriarch who holds the family and community together, as did her Mother before her. Lettie's story touched my heart, brought tears to my eyes, and inspired me to keep up the work for my own family and community."

—**Alana Betzold**

"I read 'Magdalene Maverick' and felt like I was reading through a true disciple of Mary Magdalene teachings. Rose Wilder was able to translate stories of Mary Magdalene and modernize them through the frequency of abundance and certainty. She reminded me multiple times to trust my inner guidance system, trust the feminine way of exchange, and value my gifts, my voice, and my unique expression in business. She brought me back to life. All the 'maybe I should…' have been evaporated, dissolved, and extinguished! It's like they don't even exist anymore… and the only thing that's left is me trusting me and my 'limitations.' This should be a handbook in every priestess's medicine bag. To remind ourselves that our greatest currency is our love. Thank you, Maverick Rose!"

—**J Muenz,** Unmuted Creatrix, Spiritual Teacher, Humor Priestess aka Hypnotherapist + Multi-6 fig Biz Woman

"Wow. wow. wow. Reading Marin Bach-Antonson's chapter was a whole transmission! Her words have true frequency. Her writing feels encoded. For me, it was a tsunami of remembrance! I had chills and tears in my eyes, and I wasn't even halfway through reading the piece. It is so good. So many women are going to feel so seen and be so activated by these words."

—**Dani Frederick,** Divine Feminine Mystic

"Magnificent! Shardai Moon shares deep wisdom in her own struggle to reclaim her feminine power [and heal from hidden abuse]. Hers is a magical, poetic tale filled with the grit of real life and the grace of a spiritual journey that is so relevant to women around the world. The grace woven into this women's healing path is a gift to all who encounter it."

—**Claire Sierra,** MA, Arts Therapist, Priestess, Author of *The Magdalene Path*

"In these years of troubling suppression of so many people with differences, I found Lin Murphy's story full of wisdom, hope, and comfort. Our humanity depends on the transformative power of love, and Lin's words honor its history and its possibilities."

—**Kittie Coffey Bintz,** Author of *Everyday Altars*

FLOWER of LIFE PRESS

Copyright © 2025 Flower of Life Press

All rights reserved. No part of this book may be used or reproduced by any means, graphic, electronic, or mechanical, including photocopying, recording, taping, or by any information storage retrieval system without the written permission of the publisher except in the case of brief quotations embodied in critical articles and reviews.

Because of the dynamic nature of the Internet, any web addresses or links contained in this book may have changed since publication and may no longer be valid.

The views expressed in this work are solely those of the authors and do not necessarily reflect the views of the publisher, and the publisher hereby disclaims any responsibility for them.

Published by Flower of Life Press
www.floweroflifepress.com

Flower of Life Press books may be ordered through online retailers, booksellers, or by contacting support@floweroflifepress.com

Cover and interior design by Jane Astara Ashley
Cover Art by Sue Ellen Parkinson

Library of Congress Control Number: Available upon request.

ISBN: 979-8-9987870-1-0

DEDICATION

*To the ones who are remembering—
Those who have walked through fire,
carried sorrow as sacred offering,
and chosen to rise in love, again and again.*

*To Mary Magdalene—
Apostle of the apostles, keeper of the Rose,
embodiment of the Way of Love.
Your voice echoes through these pages,
a balm, a fire, a call to awaken.*

*To Yeshua, the Christ—
Bearer of holy compassion,
Divine One, Beloved, and Bringer of Light.
You, who reminds us
that healing is born through the fusion of love and truth,
of presence and surrender.*

*To the daughters and sons of the future,
may these stories open your hearts,
restore your faith,
and return you to the knowing
that your story is sacred,
your heart is a sanctuary,
and Love is the path home.*

Contents

Magdalene Blessing
by Diana DuBrow 1

Artist's Statement
by Sue Ellen Parkinson, Cover Artist 5

Foreword: A Threshold of Remembrance
by Elayne Kalila Sophia Doughty 9

Introduction: Remembering Love Beneath the Veil
by Jane Astara Ashley, Publisher 13

Chapter 1: Birthing into Power
by Amanda Alappat 19

Chapter 2: Reclaiming Womb Rose Codes
by Elsa Alegria 31

Chapter 3: She is Here—Mary Magdalena's Revolutionary Way
by Dr. Nicola Amadora 41

Chapter 4: Magdalene Revealed—A Love Story Never Told
by Leyolah Antara 51

Chapter 5: The Call to Divine Embodiment—A Sacred Trinity of Magdalene Initiations
by Marin Bach-Antonson 65

Chapter 6: Reclaiming My Sacred Blood
by Elizabeth Brett 83

Chapter 7: Chief Magdalene Officer
by Beth Cavagnolo 95

Chapter 8: Bridging the New Paradigm—Resurrecting the Sacred Temple of Unconditional Love
by Dianne Chalifour 105

Chapter 9: What Would Love Do?
by Sandra Corcoran 117

Chapter 10: The Unwritten Path—Neither Martha, Nor Mary
by Sarah Devereux 129

Chapter 11: The Magdalene Apocalypse
by Elayne Kalila Sophia Doughty 139

Chapter 12: Initiation—The High Priestess Path
by Molly Douglas 151

Chapter 13: The Passion of the Magdalene
by Kathy Forest 165

Chapter 14: The Desert Within—Grief, Grace, and the Magdalene Path of Rebirth
by Dionisia Hatzis 177

Chapter 15: Reborn, Here I Am—A Woman's Homecoming Journey to the Mother Through the Very Guidance of the Magdalene
by AnuMa Jackie Heydemann 189

Chapter 16: The Magdalene Path—Re-Birthing the Priestess
by Hallie Lifson 201

Chapter 17: The Wise Web of the Red Thread
by Alessandra Mary 213

Chapter 18: Peek Behind the Veil
by Christy Grace Michaels 223

Chapter 19: Midwifed by the Magdalene—Resurrecting the Holy Woman
by Shardai Magdalena Rose Moon 235

Chapter 20: Mary Magdalene and Me
by Lin Murphy 251

Chapter 21: The Rose
by Sarah Alissandra Nomngoma 259

Chapter 22: Womb Wisdom, Moon Magic
by Lara O'Neil 271

Chapter 23: Compassion Remembered—Getting Intimate with Grief, Death, and Loss
by Jacquie Eva Rose Shenton 281

Chapter 24: Unveiled Creative Expression
by Crystal L. Steinberg 297

Chapter 25: The Blue Rose
by Stellar 311

Chapter 26: Becoming Big Mama—From Daughter to Matriarch, Initiated by Love and Guided by Magdalene
by Lettie Sullivan 323

Chapter 27: Mary Magdalene—Death Doula and Priestess of Resurrection
by Anaïs Theyskens 335

Chapter 28: Who is your Truth for? A Journey of Embodiment with a Magdalene
by Elisha Tichelle 347

Chapter 29: My Voice is Medicine
by Connie Viglietti 359

Chapter 30: Magdalene Maverick—The Art of Achieving Wild Success Through Divine Love
by Rose Wilder 371

The Magdalene Blessing

by Diana DuBrow

May all who receive this offering be anointed with the scent of truth that stirs the heart, and awakens the fire of love, kindness, and justice that lives within us all.

The Magdalene walks with us now—in every breath, in every act of courage, in every step toward wholeness and healing. She rises not as myth, but as living presence—a flame within the sacred heart of humanity.

She speaks with the voice of the Divine Feminine, and lives in every faith, every culture, as the heart of longing for equality, justice, compassion, and awakening. She reminds us that no one walks alone, communion is our calling, and we are here to lift one another in the spirit of sacred love.

Come, you who hunger for truth. Come, you who carry the weight of injustice. Come, you whose dreams are filled with light. Be anointed now in the spirit of the Magdalene, she who came with the alabaster jar—the woman who poured her love as sacred oil upon the Beloved. Let her presence meet you here. Open your heart to receive her anointing: feel the warm oil touch your brow, awaken your soul, and flow forth as a blessing to the world.

This is the blessing: That we become the way of love. That we honor the holy in one another. That we remember who we truly are—and act from that knowing.

Blessed be the awakening.

Blessed be the anointing of love.

Blessed be the return of the Sacred Heart in every one of us.

Diana DuBrow

Diana DuBrow is a devoted Scent Priestess and the visionary founder of The Emerald Temple, a sanctuary for the sacred art of anointing and a multi-generational apothecary dedicated to crafting holy oils as allies for healing, awakening, and remembrance. Rooted in the wisdom of the ancient temples, her life's work is to restore the path of the Scent Priestess, returning anointing to its rightful place as a sacred healing modality.

Diana's journey began with a profound sacred dream, a vision in which she was initiated into an ancient priestess lineage and called to reclaim the lost temple traditions of holy oils. This dream awakened a deep remembrance within her, guiding her to create Emerald Temple Holy Oils, hand-crafted anointing blends that carry the vibrational imprint of devotion and divine communion.

Through the Rosa Mystica Mystery School, Diana trains modern-day anointers, guiding them to form a living bond with the oils and awaken their own priestess lineage. Her teachings weave scent, spirit, and sacred ceremony, offering a transformative path for those called to reclaim anointing as an embodied practice of healing, initiation, and divine connection.

Diana's work is a bridge between the ancient and the modern, a call to those who feel the remembrance of walking the Way of Love. Through her teachings, courses, and handcrafted anointing oils, she invites seekers to step into the lineage of the Scent Priestess and bring the wisdom of anointing back into the world.

Learn more:
https://www.emeraldtemple.com
https://pp.priestesspresence.com/rosa-mystica-mystery-school

MOTHER OF MYSTERIES
Acrylic on wood

The Cover Art—
"Mother of Mysteries"

Artist: Sue Ellen Parkinson

When I first began painting Mary Magdalene, I had no expectations or intentions past a desire to honor womankind. I felt that Magdalene, like so many other women, had been misrepresented and marginalized. It seemed to me that she was the perfect iconic representation of "all women." If I could help to raise her up through my imagery, all of us would be lifted.

It seemed the truth of who she was had been rendered nearly invisible by the endless and boring projections of the patriarchy. I had wept over that and longed to know who she truly was. As I began painting her, I remember asking, over and over again, "Who are you?" To my surprise, I was answered with a profound sense of her loving presence. This mysterious Magdalene energy has flooded my life and has been so restorative to my soul that I now feel life would be unbearable without my connection to Her.

Mary Magdalene has been interpreted in many ways, but today, no one really knows what she looked like. Yet, as I've continued to paint her, I've begun to see her in every woman that I meet. I know that any woman could be a suitable model for Magdalene! As long as I paint her with deep respect, I feel that I have her blessing to explore her many faces.

In the south of France, where Magdalene lived and died, hundreds of statues of the Black Madonna have been found. Some scholars have speculated that these statues could be representations of Magdalene. The statues are often found buried at the roots of Oaks or hidden in their hallows. Keeping with that history, I painted the Black Madonna that graces this book cover, with acorns around her nimbus. I also gave her the manifestation of honeycombs, as Magdalene was beloved and is said to have been called "The Queen of the Honeybees" because her words were so sweet.

The title of this painting is "Mother of Mysteries." The model for "Mother of Mysteries" is the daughter of one of my dearest and oldest friends. Her name is Rachel, and at the time she modeled for this painting, she was a very hip, modern-looking twenty-year-old. She had dreadlocks and shredded jeans, and her head was half shaved. I told her about my feelings for the Black Madonna and then draped the white veil over her head. I stepped back to look at her in the light. I could barely breathe with the beauty of what was before me. I was stunned by her instant embodiment of the Divine Feminine. I remember thinking, "It's just that close, right there, just beneath the veil." The Divine exists everywhere, in every moment, and in every person. This is one of the many mysteries that the Magdalene reveals to us.

Sue Ellen Parkinson

Sue Ellen Parkinson is a contemporary American artist and mystic, renowned for her evocative paintings that celebrate the Sacred Feminine. Her painting, "Mother of Mysteries," adorns the cover of *Magdalene Unveiled*.

She paints traditional religious iconography through a feminist lens. Her work always seeks to honor women by replacing patriarchal narratives with images that reflect women's truth, wisdom, and innate spiritual connectivity. Parkinson describes her creative process as a form of prayer, stating, "It is my sanest response to the world. It keeps me whole and connects me to the mystery."

She also co-hosts a weekly podcast with her granddaughter, Savanna Wonderwheel, called "Little Gifts."

Learn more:
www.sueellenparkinson.com

Foreword—
A Threshold of Remembrance

by Elayne Kalila Sophia Doughty

There are moments in history when the world shifts, when the old ways can no longer hold, and something ancient begins to rise through the cracks. We are living in such a moment. A time of rupture and rebirth. A time of great unraveling, sacred remembering, and fierce emergence.

Across the globe, the systems that once defined our lives—politically, spiritually, culturally—are being deconstructed. Truth is rising like smoke from the ashes of what once was. And in the midst of this global transformation, a long-veiled presence is stirring.

She is the Magdalene.

Not as myth or symbol alone, but as a living current, an embodied wisdom, a sacred flame re-igniting in the hearts of those who are ready to remember.

She is the voice that was silenced.

The love that was buried.

The power that was hidden in plain sight.

And now, she is unveiling.

A Tapestry of Remembrance

This book, *Magdalene Unveiled*, is born from that unveiling. It is not merely a collection of essays—it is a sanctuary of soul stories, a sacred vessel of thirty-three voices, each one bearing witness to a personal encounter with her presence. These stories are not simply about the Magdalene; they are her, speaking through the lived experiences of women who have walked through fire, who have knelt at the altar of grief, who have remembered love as a revolutionary force.

Some met her in dreams scented with roses and starlight. Others found her in the dark night of the soul, when everything else had fallen away. For some, she came as fierce protector, urging the reclamation of truth and voice. For others, she appeared as a gentle balm, a hand on the heart whispering, Beloved, rise.

What you will find here are not just stories—they are living transmissions. Each one carries a thread of the greater tapestry of the Feminine's return. You may feel yourself reflected in these words. You may be stirred, undone, nourished, activated. This is her work. This is her way.

The Call of the Feminine

For too long, the Sacred Feminine has been relegated to the margins—dismissed, distorted, forgotten. The Magdalene, once named Apostle to the Apostles, was recast as sinner, silenced as lover, erased as teacher and priestess. But she has never truly left us. Her voice lives on in the body, in the blood, in the silence between heartbeats.

She is the mirror of the Feminine in all of us, not passive, not soft alone, but wild, sovereign, undivided. She is love as truth-telling. Devotion as fire. Embodiment as a spiritual path.

This book is a response to her call. A living testament to the many ways she appears to us in this time of awakening. Through these stories, we remember that the Magdalene is not here to be worshipped—she is here to be embodied.

An Invitation to the Mystery

As you journey through these pages, I invite you to enter as you would a sacred sanctuary. Come with reverence. Come with curiosity. Come as you are.

Some stories will arrive like soft whispers, inviting you into the mystery. Others will blaze through you with fire, breaking open old patterns and calling forth your truth. Let it all move you.

Perhaps you will feel a memory you cannot name awaken in your bones. Perhaps you will find a thread of your own voice, your own longing, your own story within these words. Perhaps you will feel the Magdalene stir within you.

Trust what arises. She does not come without purpose. If you are holding this book, there is something here for you.

This Is Our Time

The unveiling of the Magdalene is not happening in isolation. It is part of a larger collective awakening, a return to what has been exiled, a reweaving of what was torn. We see it in the rise of women's voices. In the dismantling of outdated structures. In the hunger for a more embodied, heart-centered, and sovereign way of being.

This moment is not simply a crisis—it is an invitation. A crossing into the unknown. And the Magdalene stands at the threshold, whispering: Come. You are ready.

To walk with her is to walk into wholeness. Into the wild beauty of your own soul. Into a remembrance that is older than time.

A Final Blessing

May this book be a sanctuary.
May it nourish the parts of you that are ready to rise.
May it soften what is brittle and ignite what is true.
May you remember who you are.
And may you know that you are not alone.
You are part of something vast and ancient—
something sacred, unfolding even now.
The Magdalene is unveiling herself in you,
in me,
in all of us.
This is her time.
This is our time.

With Devotion and Love,
Elayne Kalila Sophia Doughty

for Elayne's bio and sacred gift to you, see pages 147-148

Introduction—
Remembering Love Beneath the Veil

by Jane Astara Ashley, Publisher

I didn't think I was going to make it.

This isn't a dramatic metaphor. It's just the truth.

Two years ago, I was plunged into a season of life that cracked me open from the inside out. My father died. My dog, Kona, and I were viciously attacked by a Rottweiler. Kona survived—but only after multiple surgeries, a shredded haunch, and weeks of trauma care. I came out of it with a torn ear and PTSD that lived in my body like a ghost.

Then came the move—across the country, across everything I had known as stable for twenty-five years. We landed in North Carolina to be close to my mom. And with the move came a deep, unfamiliar stillness as our last daughter headed off to college. With the empty nest came more grief.

I had a plan before all of that, to write my book and launch my podcast. But when the waves came crashing, all of that went under. And I did, too.

I stopped creating. I stopped trying. I let go of the vision I'd been gripping and focused on the only thing that made sense: healing. Getting out of bed. Feeding my body. Sleeping through the night. Daily walks along the Haw river trails near my new North Carolina home. I felt the forest, the Earth herself, holding me, womb to womb. Slow and steady. One breath at a time.

And that's where Magdalene found me.

She met me in the mess of my recalibration—quiet, steady, present. She came while I was scribbling in my Morning Pages. Three longhand pages a day, no filter, no expectations. It was the only spiritual practice I could keep. I wrote through the fog, through the pain, and through the long ache of becoming undone. And slowly, through that daily rhythm, she came.

She didn't talk much at first. Just sat with me. Just witnessed. And then, one morning, she whispered something that changed everything:

"Come sit with me under the veil. Find your black veil—bring it to me."

That was it. That was the whole message. And yet—it was everything.

And so I draped my black lace veil over my head, and I sat.

I felt myself wrapped in an ancient veil—soft, gauzy, weightless. I saw her next to me, not rushing, not fixing. Just being. Just grieving with me. Magdalene knew the underworld. She wasn't afraid of it. She was formed by it. And she invited me to sit there with her, not to escape it, but to learn from it.

In that sacred space behind the veil, a new vision started to take root. Not a strategy, but a stirring. A sacred remembering. She began to show me something—a book. A circle. A gathering.

And so I kept sitting under my veil, and I kept writing. Every morning, for months, I met her under that veil and on the page like clockwork. She gave me the blueprint. Not of how to build something grand, but how to hold something sacred. She asked me to create a new container for stories. For truth. For women like me who had walked through the fire and were ready to speak.

At first, I designed it the way I always had. With tiers. Featured authors. More visibility for more investment. It made sense—until it didn't.

Because Magdalene stopped me.

"This is not about hierarchy," she said. "This is about synarchy. No thrones. No ladders. Only circles. Only sisters."

I sat with that for a long time. I cried, honestly. Because I had been trained to climb. To hustle. To elevate. And here was Magdalene, calling me back to the Way of Love. To the fecundity and humility of the ground.

So I deleted the tier. I let the whole project recalibrate around a different center. And that's when *Magdalene Unveiled* began to come to life.

A few months later, I traveled to Glastonbury, England for an anointing training with my teachers Elayne Kalila Sophia Doughty and Diana DuBrow. I found myself lying on the anointing table inside the Magdalene Rose Chapel—a stunning sanctuary steeped in mystery and memory. I was being anointed with holy oils by three dear sisters... reconsecrated, purified, loved back to wholeness.

And then—they came.

Magdalene at one shoulder. Christ at the other. Their presence was real, visceral, undeniable. Magdalene leaned in, placed her mouth near my ear, and said:

"It is time, beloved. We are here with you. You are to plant the seeds of the Way of Love. Call in the voices of the Magdalene. As you sit in your own holy fire, know that you ARE love. There is only love. Beloved, step up to the edge, and take the leap. Surrender to the mystery of your ministry. Release your ego. Release all expectations. Know you are held in the Sacred Heart of Christ."

Her words ignited something deep within me—something older than memory and truer than blood.

This book, this sacred anthology, is that ignition made manifest.

It is a vessel for the voices of women who have said yes to the path of love, healing, and embodied divinity. Women who have walked through death, through initiation, through awakening, and who are now rising—not to shout, but to reveal. Women who desire to serve and release the cloak of personality—release the old identities of being "someone" in order to be some of the ONE.

Magdalene Unveiled is not a performance. It is not a brand. It is not another notch in one's spiritual belt.

It is a sacred circle. A living text. A resurrection of truth.

This book is for the ones who have sat behind the veil and for those who have yet to venture in.

It's for the ones who know that the underworld is not punishment—but initiation, and who are willing to risk going down and in.

It's for the ones who are here to walk the Way of Love with bare feet and open hands.

It's for you.

Each chapter is a petal of the living rose, each story a testament to the courage it takes to walk the Way of Love.

This is our unveiling.
If you are reading this, welcome. You are part of the unveiling.
This is our collective adventure.
This is the holy fire we were born to walk through—together.

Welcome to the altar.
Welcome to the mystery.
Welcome to *Magdalene Unveiled.*

Jane Astara Ashley, M.A.

Before founding Flower of Life Press in 2009, I walked the path of a Transpersonal Psychotherapist, Art Therapist, Brand Strategist, and Creative Director within a major international publishing house. It was there that my high standards of excellence and finely-tuned intuition for midwifing women's voices first came alive. This foundation now fuels my mission: to uplift and amplify the voices of women within a sacred, judgment-free container of creative expression and deep truth.

As an author advocate, I've had the honor of speaking on podcasts, telesummits, and stages including New York City's Lincoln Center. I bring the heart of a priestess and the clarity of a professional to everything I do. As an ordained Priestess of the 13 Moon Mystery School and a Scent Priestess trained in the Rosa Mystica Mystery School, I guide women to embody their sovereignty, elevate their consciousness, and break through internal limitations to access a depth of presence, passion, and power they may have never known was possible.

Today, my team and I spend our days supporting visionary writers to birth their books and become bestselling authors. Together, we preserve the soul of your message and ensure you are presented to the world in your fullest, truest expression.

As your book midwife, I'm here to walk beside you—to witness your evolution, hold your process with reverence, and offer you a platform that elevates your voice and supports you in making the impact you were born to make.

Join me in the fall of 2025 as we launch our Magdalene Unveiled Podcast!

Learn more:
www.floweroflifepress.com
www.instagram.com/floweroflifepress
www.facebook.com/janescottashley

The Magdalene Channel Sacred Writing Bundle
Awaken Your Divine Voice with Automatic Writing

This sacred bundle of tools is designed to help you connect with the presence of Mary Magdalene and open your channel to divine wisdom through the art of automatic writing. Whether you're feeling called to write, create, or simply receive guidance, this gift offers a beautiful entry point to deepen your spiritual connection and hear the voice within.

Your free gift includes:

- **Guided Audio Visualization** to meet Magdalene and activate your heart channel.
- **Video Lesson** on the Magdalene Automatic Writing Technique.
- **Digital Workbook** with prompts, rituals, and tools to support your writing practice.
- **Printable Magdalene Altar Card** to anchor your intention and remind you of your sacred voice.

This practice will help you quiet the noise, attune to divine love, and write from your soul—with clarity, confidence, and compassion. Perfect for writers, seekers, and Magdalene devotees ready to receive and share the light within.

Access here:
https://magdaleneunveiled.com/jane_free_gift

CHAPTER 1

BIRTHING INTO POWER

by Amanda Alappat

Giving birth to my third child was the peak moment of my life. I pushed my baby out in the same bed she was conceived in, on a whim, after some oysters and a hot date with my husband. We joked about "making a baby," and here I was 10 months later, giving birth with the same passionate energy. I moved through this pregnancy much differently than my previous two, mostly because I chose not to hire a medical provider in any capacity and also because I had developed a deep connection to Mary Magdalene. I wanted to experience a completely sovereign birth, devoid of an OB or midwife or anyone who could exercise authority and power over me. But more than that, I wanted to meet Mary in the depths of labor, in the darkness of the great cosmic void, the liminal space before my baby's emergence earthside, where my power was matched by that of all creation.

I had two previous homebirths that left me feeling powerful and accomplished, but were so hard in many ways. They were grueling and tested my limits. But I wanted more for this third time, likely my last baby. I felt deeply, strongly, intuitively that there had to be a better way. A less painful way. I didn't want to fight my way through each contraction, suffer through the pain as punishment, feeling like I might die from the intensity of each surge. I wanted to experience a blissful, pain-free, perhaps even orgasmic birth. *Was that even possible?* I didn't know, but I was willing to go all in on trying. Plus, I knew Mary Magdalene would have my back, and part of my work was opening up to her divine guidance and support.

Here's the thing, though. I wasn't always connected to Mary Magdalene. In fact, it was only recently that I started to feel her presence, listening to the whisperings in my ear and longings in my heart. I grew up Catholic and mostly heard she was a whore who washed Jesus' feet. Glossed over and forgotten, she was entirely downplayed. In my twelve years of religious education, women were barely mentioned—except in May. I lived for this spring month because it was when we held the May crowning for Mother Mary. I was never picked to be a part of the procession, but I would watch wide-eyed in awe as fellow classmates carried large, colorful bouquets of flowers, the smell of lilies saturating the large auditorium, to be placed all around the towering statue of the Great Mother. Draped in cloaks of gentle blue, eyes lifted toward the heavens, her face struck me somewhere between sorrow and surrender. Year after year, as the one chosen student climbed the step stool and lovingly placed the flower crown on her head, I yearned for it to be me. I wanted to touch her and experience the motherly warmth she exuded, but instead, all I could do was sing the hymns dedicated to her. Hail, Holy Queen, indeed.

I didn't know it then, but that's where the red thread started, the link that connected me to my matrilineal ancestry, to all women and the womb of our collective origin. Mother Mary was my first memory of the Goddess in any form, expression, or archetype. The May crowning woke up my body, bringing me feelings of familiarity and aliveness, a sense of knowing and belonging that I had never felt in Church or the countless Bible parables I read. I felt nothing when receiving the Eucharist and going to confession in a strange, dark room with a strange man. Telling him all the ways I was bad and wrong felt scary and awful. But this was different. This was relatable and comforting. This was a mother, a woman, a female. This was me.

I spent years searching and studying spirituality once Catholicism lost its pull on me, and once I grew enough courage to tell my parents I was going to look elsewhere. They were supportive, albeit slightly disappointed, especially after spending thousands on private school tuition. I was on a mission to find that same connection I felt to Mary. Out in the big, wide world at 17 years old, I unknowingly was seeking Her. I was still so deeply programmed into male-centered, patriarchal religions that I could not even fathom God being a woman. I tried non-denominational Christian churches; I dated a born-again Christian and tried to jump on to his enthusiasm as Jesus being his personal savior. I dabbled in Buddhism and learned how to meditate. Yoga became my movement practice, and I dove headfirst into teacher trainings, vegetarianism, and the Sutras. That satiated me for a while, but it just wasn't "it."

Becoming a doula was what really put me on the path to eventually finding Magdalene. I had always been drawn to birth and witnessed my first one at 15 years old when my aunt was gracious enough to invite me to attend hers. She was a nurse and had a very graphic birth book that I would secretly pour over when no one was looking. I was curious, eager, and willing, and although she had a typical hospital birth, it left a deep impression that women were powerful beyond measure. It was also a pretty potent form of birth control—I certainly picked up a bit of a fear that is so common around birth.

I continued to follow that red thread as a personal trainer and yoga instructor. I worked with pregnant women at the gym, holding space as they shared their struggles and secrets. It was only when a dear friend asked me to be her doula that I even considered it as a career.

"But I'm not a doula," I responded quite matter-of-factly to her request for me to attend her birth during a yoga retreat in Costa Rica.

"You are to us," she replied.

"But I'm not certified," I said, my words coated with a mix of excitement and resistance. My heart thumped in my chest.

"So?" she responded with a smile.

So, I did what any perpetual A+ student would do and began researching doula certifications. There was a weekend training a month before her due date. I immediately signed up and started what is now a decade-long career in deep devotion to women, their babies, and their families. In the beginning, I would support any and all births, and in the process, I gathered a lot of firsthand experience for what I would want whenever the day came when I would have my own children. But more than that, through witnessing, supporting, and observing birth, I began to recognize the power of women—not just in others but within myself. Up until this point, I thrived in hyper-masculine energy. I had to in order to survive in New York City. That version of me was a personal trainer and champion boxer, a very rigid, self-proclaimed hustler, and a constant overachiever who loved control. I ate clean and was rigid with my routine. I wore tight clothes, checked the boxes, and lived in my perfectly organized apartment. But when I attended a birth, I melted. I felt a softening. AWE. I saw women surrender. Own their power. Straddle the veil between life and death. Touch the source of creation. Breathe their babies from their yonis in full power and authority. And though I wasn't ready to have my own family, I knew I wanted in.

While still a maiden, I continued to follow the subtle nudges and started holding women's "gatherings" in my backyard. I felt the call to hang with women outside of just socializing but wasn't yet anchored into any form of the sacred feminine. I would weave together yoga with a delicious meal and then a circle for us to talk about a specific topic. I didn't realize it at the time, but this was the beginning of my life as a ceremonialist and women's circle facilitator. My connection to Magdalene hadn't become real, alive, or embodied yet, but the gentle whisper to deepen with women was undeniable.

Things really began to shift when I had my first daughter after a three-day, seventy-hour homebirth and then my son three years later during the peak of the pandemic. Both births were midwife-assisted; both rocked my world and birthed me anew. I was forced to soften despite my resistance. I was cracked open, my rigidity no longer able to fortify my heart because the purity of my babies' faces unfroze parts of me that I had tucked away in neat little boxes. I began to morph and shift. I stopped personal training but continued to hold circles, attend and host retreats, and found myself increasingly drawn to the Goddess—opening to the idea that my spirituality could be anchored in Her, on Her, and with Her. I felt a strong pull toward "the sacred feminine" but often felt like a fraud. I didn't feel "feminine" enough. I judged myself for those masculine tendencies, for feeling tight in my hips, for not having enough floral dresses in my closet. But I could not ignore the pull, that red thread dangling in front of my face, asking me to trust and continue to follow it.

With intention, deep inner work, a steady diet of circling, a budding community of sisterhood, and a daily morning practice, I began to feel into and find my feminine essence. I consulted Goddess oracle cards and learned about the different archetypes of the 13 Moon Mystery School. I read books, took courses, and spent time in meditation, asking for the Goddess to awaken in me. I changed my wardrobe and how I moved in the world, untangled my worth from productivity, moved with my family from the city to the country, and took up gardening. I knew I would find her in nature, but I just had to get myself *IN* nature. Hyper-masculine culture, be gone!

It was then that Mary Magdalene became front and center. She was the Goddess I felt most intrigued by. Cloaked in confusion, I began to read her gospel and quickly realized the depth of her understanding and involvement in Jesus' ministry. I was floored to reconsider her as his wife, his equal, the counterpoint to create a sacred union. Reading how they kissed on the mouth felt so scandalous and yet so humanizing. I never realized the significance of her anointing, evidence of her role as a Priestess, and her connection to the temples of ancient Egypt. Her teachings about the interconnectedness of all beings and how power lives within struck a chord of resonance in me. *YES*, my body would respond as I poured over the words, feeling as though I had discovered a truth purposely hidden from us. Her invitation to embodiment and how we must be fully present in our bodies to have a direct experience with the divine left me in chills. Never had I experienced such a felt sense of truth.

When I lived in the city, I walked everywhere, but life was much more sedentary in the country. To compensate and recreate my urban lifestyle, I often went out for walks around the neighborhood. On one particular day, I stumbled upon a property I had never seen before. It stopped me in my tracks. I stood there, mouth open, as it literally sparkled in the sunlight. I immediately got a full-body instant and intense download—a loud and clear command with a tone that made me feel like I better listen. *You need to buy this house.*

The property was alive with beauty. A small, two-story deep red house with black shutters and white trim sat next to a quaint red garage with the most dazzling pond tucked behind it. A smaller red shed on the far end of the property laid adjacent to a charming wooden bridge. The property was meticulously manicured, teeming with bursts of bright flowers and stone borders intentionally placed along a babbling stream. A dead tree overtaken by a bounty of ivy stood as a stunning piece of art. There were birds and trees and a sense of aliveness that left me utterly captivated.

What? I thought to myself. We didn't need to buy a house! We had a huge barn house not one minute up the road and were still paying to rent our apartment in Manhattan. Not only could we not afford to purchase another piece of land, but to my rational Virgo mind, it didn't make any sense.

But I couldn't shake the feeling—the longing. The undeniable *knowing* that this particular piece of land belonged to us—was yearning to come to us. I gushed to my husband Sebastian, who, bless him, is always willing to indulge my crazy, whimsical ideas. But this property wasn't even for sale, so what did it matter, anyway? It's not like we were going to knock on their door and make an offer. One house in Kunkletown felt like plenty, right?

Later that day, my father-in-law sent us a real estate listing for an ordinary, outdated, gaudy house nearby. He had been in the market to purchase a lake house close to us to enjoy the grandkids and spend time out of the city. The house was nothing special, but Sebastian curiously started looking at other options in our area, hoping that something might jump out at him to suit his dad's taste.

"Hey babe, come here. Look at this cute house," he called out to me as I was playing with our daughter. As I peered over his shoulder, I couldn't believe my eyes. It was the small red house down the road. It went on the market THAT

DAY. What are the chances?! One might call it a coincidence, but I knew better. This was fate! Destiny! I took it as a sign and stalked the agent until I was able to set up a viewing. We were the first ones to see it.

My heart was just bursting the whole time, and inside, I felt a deep, resounding *YES*. It didn't make any sense because the house was too small for us to live in, and the township didn't allow short-term rentals. So what then? Why was the pull so strong? As we were checking the detached, two-story garage, I walked up those narrow white steps into the upstairs room, and I got that same kind of download, that same knowing. It was Mary Magdalene whispering in my ear, *This will become a temple dedicated to the Sacred Feminine. The Red Rose Temple.*

I didn't disclose that to my husband immediately because even then, I wasn't sure exactly what it meant. But I felt like this could be a space where I could write, dream, teach, and maybe even hold women's circles. I would figure out the temple part later. But despite keeping it to myself, my husband saw the potential, the beauty, and the magic and was eager to go for it. So, with some convincing, lots of prayer, and holding the vision that this home would be ours, we put in an offer and waited. In my bones, I knew we would get it, but still, the anticipation grew in my belly. I was worried and anxious because I wanted it so badly. *Magdalene wouldn't lead me to this point and not come through, right?* I pondered over and over again. Then we got the call that our offer was accepted, and I suddenly felt the weight of having to make good on this gift.

A few months later, The Red Rose Temple was birthed into the world. I wasn't sure how a space dedicated to centering the Sacred Feminine would be received in rural Pennsylvania, but I had to try. I started small, low-key, testing the waters. I canceled the first circle and rebranded it as a yoga class because I was afraid of how it would be received. Yoga felt edgy enough, and I worried small-minded townspeople would judge a New York witch. But as the months passed, I grew in courage and trust alongside my growing belly, pregnant with my third child. I began to find women who were hungry for connection and sisterhood, looking to fill their spiritual cups, desperate for time and space away from their roles and responsibilities. Women who were ready to explore taboo and touchy subjects like money and polarity, experience their range, collaborate and heal collectively, honor the earth-based holidays, and reclaim themselves as wild, primal, passionate, and purposeful. Those who were committed to circling for years to come through different stages and phases. It felt risky at first, and I feared backlash and being ostracized. I was met instead with joy, willingness, support, and friendship. The Red Rose has been one of my most profound and meaningful offerings. She has served as a huge catalyst for so many women to step into their unique paths and share their medicine and offerings with our growing community. Even more than that, the Red Rose was crucial for preparing me for my sovereign birth while strengthening my connection to Mary Magdalene.

During my pregnancy, the Red Rose Temple became an anchor and expression of my prenatal care. Sitting with women in meditation, during vulnerable shares, as we danced, moved, and breathed together, I felt a web of support that I could lean on as I approached the portal of birth. The permission field to be real, raw, and messy was expanded every time a woman revealed her heart openly. Through a special circle called a Village Prenatal, I gathered with other pregnant mamas as we were witnessed in speaking our deepest fears and dream births. My daughter drew on my belly as we sang songs, prayers pleading *Let it be easy*. I was also given a Mother's Blessing, where my closest friends and family were invited to celebrate and honor me and the gift of carrying new life. My feet were washed in warm waters. I was anointed and bestowed blessings and gifts, crowned with flowers, and laid at the center of the circle, where hands of peace and healing were placed all over my body. My mother apologized for the pain she caused me, and my wisest sisters spoke words of encouragement, inner strength, and belief in my ability to birth on my own terms, regardless of their own fears and projections. These circles and ceremonies became my monthly check-up, fortifying and strengthening my resolve and confidence that so many women trusted me and held the vision for my deepest desires around this birth.

I was 41 weeks +3 days pregnant in the last days of August, round, hot, and ready. I had been having surges for the past several days, but labor hadn't officially started. I was annoyed and agitated and spent most of the day in my room, alone. I was feeling overstimulated by my other two kids and needed to retreat. It was a super full moon the next day, and I was convinced I would have a baby soon. Since I was going "unassisted," there was no midwife to call. The only person outside my husband and daughter who would be present was my medicine woman friend, Alyssa. But because of that choice, there was no one to check how dilated I was, listen to the fetal heart tones, or tell me my baby was okay. I had to step into that role of ultimate authority.

Labor started to intensify. In my previous two homebirths, I resisted the surges, feeling like I had to survive them, tightening and constricting myself as the contraction would overtake me. I had stamina and mental fortitude from my boxing years, so I was able to endure the pain. But this time, whenever I would feel the energy building, I chose to meet it, opening my arms and legs wide to welcome it. Befriending it and swirling my hips, circling my body as I expressed gratitude. *Yes, thank you, more please.* Not in an egoic way, but with Magdalene in my heart, I roared *BRING IT*. I consciously decided to soften instead of fight, to be so available for all the sensations, welcoming them with a sense of joy. It required discipline as the option to suffer, to play the victim, to crumble within each wave was ever-present, so tempting, so available.

Because there was no external source of power or expertise in the room, I was profoundly present in my body. I could feel my baby descend, pressing along my sacrum, slowly. I was annoyed that there was no orgasmic bliss, that it still felt hard and heavy, but it was also simultaneously lighter and easier. I was, and always am, in choice of how I experience life. As I moved closer to meeting my baby, the intensity almost overtook me, and I remember feeling Magdalene and calling out, *Thank you, Jesus!*

As emergence drew closer, I was drawn to direct all of my energy straight down into my perineum, laser-focused on one single spot, and with all my might, all of the energy of the cosmic mother, I pushed, and my baby spiraled out of my body and onto the bed. I paused, breathless, and sat up carefully as my husband, daughter, and friend silently witnessed my beautiful, slick, and slimy baby utter her first cry, loud and immediate. She was surprisingly pristine as if just baptized by my holy amniotic waters. Naked and sweating, I scooped my baby into my arms, crying out in pure relief. I held her to my bare chest and looked to the heavens, sobbing tears of an oxytocin-induced high streaming down my flushed cheeks. Rocking back and forth, whispering, "I did it." A literal feeling of heaven on earth.

Here's where that red thread picks up again. I would have never had the courage, inner knowing, devotion, or confidence to give birth unassisted had I not come to know Mary Magdalene. She was the force that was missing in my previous two births: the deep connection to my womb, intuition, and pleasure. Magdalene expanded the permission field so that I could truly and wholly claim my power. I developed the capacity to handle being judged or misunderstood, possibly shunned and ostracized, or accused of making a dangerous decision. She gave me a sense of fortitude to prioritize my desires over what was expected and instead walk the path of pregnancy with deep reverence and trust, an embodiment of inner knowing that I could never outsource to anyone. Magdalene awoke in me true, pure, passionate power and a strength unlike any other. It was the spiritual high of a lifetime.

Amanda Alappat

Amanda Alappat is devoted to bringing the Sacred Feminine back into birth. All three of her children were born at home, the most recent being unassisted. Amanda walks with women during their pregnancies and guides them to weave ceremony, ritual, self-trust, and authority into their birth experiences.

In her former life, she was a personal trainer and champion boxer, holding a Master's Degree in Exercise Physiology from Columbia University. Currently, Amanda teaches forest school to children and yoga to her local community. She holds monthly women's circles at her sacred space, the Red Rose Temple, centering sisterhood, beauty, and the Goddess traditions. She's also been breastfeeding for close to 100 months, loves baking sourdough bread, working in her garden, and writing about motherhood.

Learn more:
https://www.amandaalappat.com
https://www.instagram.com/amanda_alappat
https://substack.com/@amandaalappat?

Sacred Pregnancy: How to Weave Ceremony and Ritual into Your Birth

Step into the sacred power of pregnancy with this gentle guide to honoring birth as a rite of passage. This mini-ebook is for the mother-to-be who craves a deeper, more meaningful path through pregnancy and birth. Inside, you'll find ways to help you slow down, listen deeply, and bring intention to every step of the journey.

Whether you're gathering your village, building an altar, or envisioning your dream birth, this mini-ebook invites you to remember that you are not just giving life—you are living a ceremony.

Access here:
https://www.amandaalappat.com/sacredpregnancy

CHAPTER 2

Reclaiming Womb Rose Codes

by Elsa Alegria

I'll never forget the doctor's words, "If you're in a relationship or planning to have babies, I suggest you do it now because you require a hysterectomy."

As I lay on the exam table, legs splayed, yoni open and exposed, a shockwave moved through that felt like a violent force thrust upon me.

What surprised me more than her prognosis was my initial reaction—an onslaught of self-judgment and fear about losing my womb at such a young age. But even more astonishing was how quickly those feelings were replaced by the absolute knowing that this was not what my body was asking for. A knowing that was coming from my body, not my mind.

In 1999, a month before my 30th birthday, I stood at this portal in a new state, job, and relationship. This move represented a newfound trust in my inner knowing and cutting ties to old patterns of co-dependency and people-pleasing. Now, I found myself being told I would need to remove my fibroid-riddled uterus to lead a "normal" life.

I'd only been in Seattle a few months and couldn't yet imagine a future with babies and my new partner simply to make "use" of my uterus before it was removed. Nor could I believe this doctor—a woman, no less—could be so quick to suggest this could be my only option.

I felt a ring of truth vibrating from within my rage, as if sitting in the center of a stillness I had only just rediscovered within me. NO, it was not yet time to release my womb!

As much as I'll never forget that doctor's words, I'll always remember that feeling of truth coming from the center of my being. That experience marked the beginning of a long healing journey for myself and my lineage. Twenty-five years later, that journey came full circle, with the choice to remove the density and calcification held within my womb to reclaim the codes that have always lived there.

Shortly after the initial shock of the diagnosis, I found another doctor who offered alternatives so I could keep my womb. I eventually married my beloved and became pregnant, albeit not without difficulty. The fibroids even seemed to disappear during the pregnancy, making me hopeful for a new relationship between my womb and body.

The journey hasn't been easy. A miscarriage a few years after my son's birth led to a hospitalization, a moment of reckoning, and a call from the Mother—the Dragon Mother, the Mother of all life. She called me out of my sleepwalking state, initiating me through the womb portal and onto the priestess path to break outworn patterns long before I even knew about the divine feminine mysteries or what it meant to be a priestess. She was calling me into wholeness after living a fragmented life of illusions and wearing masks.

In 2016, another gynecologist informed me that relief from my heavy bleeding and pain due to the fibroids would require a hysterectomy.

I could feel the lie of that word again: hysterectomy. "Hyster" means womb. The subsequent term "hysteria" was created by men in science to define uncontrolled emotions (or unwanted "difficulties") in women. There was an apparent convenience within this lie that the womb was the root of uncontrolled emotions or difficulties as defined by men who would remove (-ectomy) it for fear of the power of creation (and destruction) held within that womb portal.

The tension between what I was being led to believe and my inner wisdom revealed there was more healing for me to do with regard to the betrayal I felt from the patriarchy and men.

Between the initial directive to have a hysterectomy and the deep knowing that it was not yet time to release it, I felt an undeniable resistance. Amid the subsequent trials of pain, heavy bleeding, fatigue, and heaviness held within the calcified fibroids, I struggled to keep my uterus intact. I desired and fought to stay connected to the portal of the Goddess.

In the darkest moments, I would feel that ring of truth coming from the stillness of my center amidst whatever confusion, disappointment, fear, or rage was dancing around me. I didn't have the words yet, but I felt it—the wisdom of the womb priestesses, such as Magdalene and Mother Mary, calling me deeper into the mysteries of the feminine.

In 2018, I was led to the 13 Moon Mystery School and dove into divine feminine mysteries. Rediscovering the ways of the womb shaman and priestess within me was electrifying and catalytic, so much so that I felt drawn back to Mexico to reclaim lost codes of my priestess lineage on my ancestral lands.

In 2019, I took my husband and son on a pilgrimage to the temples of Teotihuacan to honor my 50th birthday and reconnect to my ancestors and the land. At the top of the Sun Temple, I reconnected to my body as a portal to the

God/dess—to all life—through my womb. I unexpectedly came upon a circle of women at the top of the pyramid who invited me to join them. We called in the power of the serpent—the kundalini—through the pyramid and into our yoni portal to fill us with the codes of activation we each came to hold and embody. These codes were now reawakened within me through my womb.

After that trip, I felt the Magdalene and Mother Mary with me all the time, renewing my connection to my sovereignty as a priestess. As I deepened into their wisdom, I noticed my womb space becoming more sensitive. The fibroids were growing, and I was experiencing more discomfort. I sought relief from various healers to energetically break up the fibroids, which I now understood held the density of the wounds of my mother line.

The healing journey I had started in 2018 was bringing more and more to the surface, revealing all the ways the women of my lineage and I had been suppressed and diminished despite our oracular abilities. These gifts had long been buried in the wombs of the women of my line.

I could feel the weight of their burden in *my* womb. I also felt a deep resentment for all the ways the men had not protected and revered the women. I felt centuries of deep-rooted shame for my body and womb and all the power it held, causing me to disconnect from its wisdom. It felt as though I could no longer trust my body as it revealed so much pain and suffering.

In meditations, Magdalene reassured me of my path of healing for my lineage into sacred sovereignty through the chrysalis of awareness and choice. *What would I choose now?* The only choice forward was to walk as love.

During my ordination ceremony as a priestess of the 13 Moon Mystery School, Magdalene came to offer healing light into my womb. I felt her hands through the hands of my beloved priestess mentors as they anointed me.

I was transported back to the top of the Sun Pyramid in Mexico from years before to reconnect with the serpent energy that had come through the deep womb of Mother Earth, through the temple, and into my womb. Snake emerged from the temple and wrapped herself around a beautiful holographic rose that felt like an invitation to come into a deeper connection with the beauty of all my life. It was as if I was the tightly closed bud that was being invited to open and bloom. The petals of the rose begin to turn brown and decay, falling back down into the earth, like the Snake shedding her skin, preparing to re-emerge. I felt these codes of regeneration and beauty as medicine for my healing.

For most of my life, I'd been ashamed of my body for its curves and fullness but also of a very deep oppression of the Sacred Feminine by the patriarchy.

Magdalene came to me to expand my perception, to be in deeper intimacy with my body, myself, my magic, and with Source that connects us through these portals.

She reawakened womb codes that had been dormant within me to bring me into deeper intimacy with my body, awakening my awareness of my body as an oracle and as the portal to clear ancestral lineage patterns of subjugation and shame into the reclamation of beauty and aliveness.

I deepened my devotion to Magdalene, inspired to learn and rediscover more about her, the way of the Rose, and womb wisdom. During that time, it seemed the more I devoted myself to her, the more I was being initiated into deeper feminine leadership in every aspect of my life, from the temples of the 13 Moon Mystery School to my most personal relationship with my beloved.

I was being called to reclaim the power of my womb and sovereignty while also honoring the healing that was occurring. At the age of 53, I was given a sliver of hope when my gynecologist suggested that because I was now in menopause, my fibroids should start to shrink. We decided to wait and see. As a priestess, I entered into my womb temple every day in hopes of bringing my pain and power into union, seeking the sacred third.

During this time, I felt called to visit Magdalene, where she had traveled in Avalon. While this made no sense to my logical mind, my body rang with the truth of the call. I was being led deeper into the mystery of the rose.

In 2023, holding so much pain and discomfort in my womb, I traveled to Avalon. I was instantly met with an electrifying remembrance of being in England. This made no sense to me as I have no English ancestors, yet I felt a connection to the land that I tried to play off as my imagination. As I walked out of the airport terminal to meet my driver, I was literally brought to my knees, crashing down onto the sidewalk, with my hands out to stop my fall, bowing to the land. I laughed at the immediacy of the call and offered a prayer of gratitude to the land and ancestors for calling me.

There were several beautiful moments of remembrance during the retreat. The most profound was on the day I was anointed. The temple space was punctuated by the smells of ancient oils and the sounds of holy songs, creating a beautiful sacred space where we could be held. As my beautiful sister began gently anointing my crown and third eye, I felt myself opened up to another dimension. As she moved from my feet up my body, I felt each energy center open up to receive more codes that came through me as ecstatic ripples of remembrance that I am more than the pain in my womb.

I found myself dancing on familiar waves of ecstatic bliss like the ones I had experienced years before at the Sun Temple and my ordination. Magdalene came to me again. This time, She was accompanied by Yeshua and my ancestors, who surrounded me on an astral plane with intricate mandalas of light and sound that moved through me, breaking up the energetic calcification in my womb. I felt like I was being pulled through my womb portal to the cosmos to receive new codes of light and energy.

As I received my codes, I became aware of sound emanating from me like a primal chant anchoring this ecstasy in my body. Magdalene reminded me of the ability to reconnect to the codes through my body and voice. I cried tears of release for all the years of feeling disconnected and ashamed of my body. I released the tears of trying to "fix" what I perceived as broken within me through so many modalities and healers, yet feeling like it wasn't enough or that I was doing it wrong. There was so much shame blocking me from my magic and my medicine through the density of the patterns that I'd been holding in my womb.

As I lay on the table in Avalon, I heard Magdalene whisper, "Beloved, it is time to let go of this story and pattern of brokenness and come back into sacred union within. It is time to release the heaviness; even if your womb is released, you are whole and holy. There is nothing they can take from you that you are not whole and holy."

I felt the reverberations of orgasmic ecstasy moving through me long after that anointing experience.

I returned reconnected to the beauty way that opened my heart to see and feel through the womb wisdom encoded within me. I felt a connection and intimacy with my beloved beyond what my mind could conceive. I felt the ecstasy of sacred union within and around me.

Six months after my pilgrimage to Avalon, I was confronted with another choice…

At my annual exam, my gynecologist informed me that despite being menopausal, the fibroids had not shrunk because of how dense they were. To my surprise, she suggested that since I had lived with them for so long, I should simply continue to do so!

Lying on yet another table, I felt the now familiar ring of truth bringing me to my center and the clarity that holding this physical manifestation of unhealed patterns was no longer mine to hold. With conviction in my voice and the knowing in my body, I told her it was time to release my womb. Feelings of deep peace washed over me like waves of light and sound as I spoke my truth.

Sensing my conviction, the gynecologist changed her approach to one of honoring my decision. In true Goddess fashion, the surgeon she referred me to was named Dr. Grace. Of course she was!

In the months leading to the surgery, I prepared for the release of my womb in daily ceremony by connecting with my ancestors, the land, and the Magdalene for guidance. Embodying the codes I had received in Avalon, I prepared myself by offering my voice through chanting, my hands through daily anointing of my body, and my heart through meditations to connect with my energetic womb temple. Throughout it all, I felt Magdalene calling me deeper into the mysteries of the holy of holies… the energetic womb that is always present.

When the day of the surgery arrived, I offered myself to Magdalene. I was overwhelmed by the immense love I felt from her, my family, my priestess sisters, and my medical team, including Dr. Grace. There was no fear, only grace.

As I was wheeled to the surgery wing, I was struck by how dark the corridor was, as if I were moving through another womb portal. Magdalene and Mother Mary were on either side of me. I felt immense peace as we moved through the doors and emerged on the other side in the light-filled chamber, met by Dr. Grace. I heard, "All will be well."

The surgery did go well, without major complications. As expected, my body was tender, and when I arrived home, I cried for what had been removed. I allowed space for all emotions to be held and healing to continue.

Three weeks after my surgery, I found myself in the throes of grief and sadness mixed with frustration over the physical pain I was still experiencing. I felt supported by the doctors as best as could be expected, yet I felt my body was showing me that physical healing was only one layer. I was being called into deeper connection to my energetic womb and trust in myself for having had the surgery and the ancestral healing that was still being integrated.

I invited a trusted priestess sister to hold a sacred ceremony with me, honoring the release of my womb. She took me on a journey to reconnect with my womb back through the portal that I'd traveled in Avalon.

In the portal, Magdalene led me to a cave to rest in stillness, to come back into myself through death (of my womb) to be reborn. In the darkness, I felt held in my energetic womb. The codes appeared like ribbons of light and sound, bathing me in love. After the ceremony, I continued communing daily with Magdalene, anointing myself and honoring my body as I integrated healing on all levels.

Nine weeks after my surgery, I felt a shift. I felt the remembrance of a wholeness that had always been there, calling me back. Magdalene reminded me that mysticism doesn't move through *me*. As a priestess, it moves through my *body* and my *energetic womb space*. My womb space is the temple to connect to that sacred mysticism. And though my physical womb is gone, it is never truly gone. Energetically, the connection feels stronger now that the density has been removed.

I'm grateful to be on the other side. To see and feel beyond the density and calcification that was held in the wound story of suppression and of voices being silenced in my own family and for all women who have been disconnected from their spiritual power.

Twenty-five years later, at the age of 55, came the clear knowing that the release of my womb would open the portal to embody the codes within me and the trust that it doesn't have to be in me to be *IN* me.

I now see how my life, my initiations, and the Magdalene have led me to the reclamation of my voice, my inner knowing, and the codes of my womb wisdom so that I could step into wholeness and sacred feminine leadership for myself and others. I could not have stepped into the roles I hold now while still holding onto that density.

You can take the "hysteria" out of the woman, but you can't take the womb out of the priestess.

And so, I step forward, whole and empowered, a living testament to the enduring power of the divine feminine, carrying the womb codes within my very being, forever.

Elsa Alegria

Elsa Alegria is an Ordained Priestess and Focalizer of the 13 Moon Mystery School and the temple keeper of The Radiant Heart Sanctuary. She offers womxn spiritual guidance, mentorship, and ceremony as a sacred feminine wisdom keeper.

Elsa Alegria is passionate about empowering womxn to live their most authentic lives. As a priestess, she helps them reconnect to their inner wisdom and codes to align with their heart's truth and reclaim their voice, power, and joy.

After 20 years in the corporate realm of architecture and interior design—that culminated in burnout—Elsa Alegria answered her soul's call to reimagine her life. She initially obtained a degree in nutrition and became a holistic dietitian nutritionist. Her mission was to guide womxn back to their inner knowing and vitality through holistic wellness. She practiced in this role for 5 years and quickly discovered that her work expanded beyond nutrition into the spiritual realm, as well as reconnection to the land and body wisdom.

Through her deep inner work with the divine feminine and reconnecting to her ancestral lineages, Elsa Alegria rediscovered her role as a priestess and sacred feminine wisdom keeper. Today, she weaves her gifts and learnings to create transformational spaces through one-on-one spiritual mentorship, cacao ceremonies, and sacred feminine temple circles.

Elsa Alegria bridges the worlds of spirit and form, bringing the etheric realm into embodied practice for everyday living that is both rooted and expanded.

Learn more:
www.elsaalegria.com

Sacred Gift

Womb Codes Meditation

Do you long to connect more deeply with the power within and around you—a power that is rooted in love—and encoded in you? Do you desire a connection to your womb codes to feel supported as you move through your daily life?

Journey with this meditation to deepen into greater connection to your womb codes. Be nourished by the power, wisdom, and love of the codes you carry.

This is how to awaken your radiant heart and sacred womb codes to reclaim your essence, joy, and power.

Access here:
https://www.elsaalegria.com/womb-codes-gift

CHAPTER 3

She is Here—Mary Magdalena's Revolutionary Way

by Dr. Nicola Amadora

In my wildest dreams, I could not have imagined such a *real-to-the-bone* journey.

Long ago, a relentless storm unleashed heavy rains as I arrived in the heart of Cathar land, France, seeking shelter in a tiny Madeleine chapel perched atop a hill. The wooden door creaked when I stepped into the dim sanctuary, lit by a few white candles. They softly illuminated the statues and paintings of women saints and our red lady. One man sat in the wooden pew, praying. Silence and thick stillness enveloped us. I joined in meditation, sensing her presence more and more deeply.

After a while, the man turned to me and introduced himself. As if we had known each other for lifetimes, we instantly connected, speaking about our shared bond with Mary Magdalene and the experiences we were having in this sacred place. It felt auspicious when Luic invited me to come with him to a secret cave—a four-hour journey away, somewhere in the mountains and hard to find. The kind of place you must feel called to and have a guide because it's a hidden, ancient power temple of the earth and Mary Magdalene—not a spiritual tourist attraction.

All hairs on my body rose up in recognition. Truth bumps. "Yes," I responded excitedly. How could I not when my soul and body felt in such resonance? But was I nuts? I had already learned as a child not to go with a stranger. Still, my gut reassured me—this kind Frenchman was genuine and safe.

After a long drive to Aix-en-Provence, we parked the car at the monastery and visited another chapel dedicated to Her. Immersed, I longed to stay forever, but Luic nudged me to leave since we had only a few hours left before nightfall. When we walked into the forest of Magdalena, my whole being quivered; my soul was singing with unencumbered joy. Yes, here she had lived, touched the ancient oak trees, and drank from pure springs that still flow today. I smelled her sweet rose scent wafting through the greens, welcoming us.

We made our way through thick brush, climbed over fallen trees and large boulders, and ascended the steep slopes of a majestic mountain range. There was no path, but Luic knew the way intimately edged into his soul. He was a protector of this hidden treasure I was about to experience. The air shifted as we passed through an unseen gateway into the other realm, and I felt the cave must be nearby. So much energy surged that I had to gallop up the rocky terrain.

When I suddenly came upon the temple entrance, my heart burst, tears streamed down my cheeks, and I shivered from head to toe. It was beyond anything I had ever seen. In awe, I could only get on my knees before this enormous yoni-shaped entrance formed by mighty rocks. There she appeared and beckoned me with a wave of her hand to slide down on my butt into her pitch-black cave. In the depths of this profound darkness, I received the gift of a lifetime. It was here that Magdalena revealed herself and the way of the feminine—so vastly different from what we have been taught.

I'll tell you what happened in this ancient goddess cave, but first, let me say this so you, too, can journey into it whilst reading the story:

She veils herself, covering her naked soul. Not to hide in fear of violence or in submission to oppression but for another reason—a deeper one. You see, you can't just rip her veils apart and march into her temple. You'll never find her, for she will not show herself that way. You must prepare yourself, leaving bags and stuff behind, dropping expectations and ideas, opening senses and the heart to touch each layer with reverence, adoration, and love. Only then will the petals of the rose within unfold, and she may grant you permission to enter this holy cave to receive what's hidden in plain sight.

She may offer you the Holy Grail, the sacred treasure sought since ancient times. And let you sip the exquisite red wine—an intoxicating nectar of everlasting life—that restores the weary, heals the broken, wakes the dead, and utterly enlivens your heart and belly down to your very bones.

Perhaps this is what salvation really means, *to truly come alive*. I realized there and then: Enlivenment is the feminine way.

Matter is sacred and Her way is about spiritual embodiment, incarnating the soul here on earth. This implies living in a way that honors all life as Her. Like not littering a cave with trinkets and trash, but being responsible and present in how we treat all living beings and our earth. She calls us to surrender into radical union between divine and human—to relate to our pain, joy, hands, and feet as sacred. Being truly human. For nothing is separate from the divine.

I assure you, you will not meet Her by transcending this form and world by disappearing detached into a faraway sky, but by immersing into the luminous dark unknown. Even if you must crawl on all fours into the cave. And then, in her innermost sanctuary, she'll strip you bare of all you imagined yourself to be, rip the control reins away from you, and reveal your worst fears and the clever ways you denied, silenced, and pushed Her and your own soul away. Sheer rage, grief, and terror may emerge as untamed power rises from the wet, musky ground below and takes hold of you.

Oh, yes, we are as frightened of the feminine as we are of love itself. Why are we so shaken by creation's power?

For centuries, we burned Her at the stake, repressed feminine wisdom and wildness, and tied women in shackles for the imagined crime of being Eve, the evil one. We desecrated the Earth—and our own human vulnerability—for a God we believed was beyond form. We poured asphalt over her breathing, living body. Even the common spiritual path treaded today is usually taught in a conceptual, whitewashed way, thereby denying her very existence—so vibrantly alive here on earth, in relationships, and beating in our hearts right now. We yearn for Her, this red pulse, this intimate connection with all beings, here in our bodies, at the kitchen sink whilst washing dishes, and as we meet each other in a coffee shop. To see with eyes that truly see, ears that truly hear, and a heart that truly feels.

Once I asked her: "Where are you? I have not felt you for a while." No answer came at first, until that same day, I drove along a small road in the Berkeley hills when, out of the blue, the car just stopped. My head turned to the side of the road. There, I saw what she was pointing to. Before me stood a human-sized, ancient painting of Her. Here she was, the gorgeous red one in full regalia. A dove is settled on top of her thick red hair, and in her hand, she holds a golden grail close to her heart. Her face and eyes express deep wisdom and surrendered bliss. The painting is draped in her colors—black, maroon, and gold. Funny, this synchronicity—the picture leaned against an electric pole. Of course, it's charged! I got out of the car, touched it to make sure it was for real, and heard her voice:

> *"You find me in the streets of humankind. You find me among the rich and poor, and you find me in nature among the wild. I am in this world—always, always loving you as my own."*

Just then, a guy who must have seen my mesmerized stare stepped toward me and asked, "You want the painting? If you do, it's yours." I happily nodded and he loaded it into my car, but half of Her hung out of the trunk. I laughed because that's just like Mary Magdalena. She doesn't fit into any box. She'll speak and appear to you in her own unique way. You sense and recognize when she does—her purity, mischief and feistiness, sanctity, intense loving, and wild, untethered and alive energy is unmistakable. So, invite Her to your kitchen table!

Mary is here, *siempre*. She won't be quieted and disappear, but keeps showing her face in the mirror and in your friend's embrace. The feminine power breaks through cement, just as ocean takes over land. The truth returns again and again; no matter how much we want to control, she has her own way.

Gentle as a dove, she caresses you one day and, with a feather-light kiss, dissolves your sturdy walls of defense and wounds into a flood of tears. And you might tremble as you hear her deafening, fierce lioness roar into a world that raped her: "This shall not pass!" That gal can kick ass and boldly stands up!

Veiled or in plain sight, she traverses the streets and wakes people from slumber. She uplifts the fallen ones and gathers the lost and outcast. And she rises with you and for all that's sacred, igniting us to show up for the great turning in action. Through this life-giving power, we can transform even the most horrific situations and help in this critical time when our survival hangs by a mere thread. You may have seen and heard Her more frequently on the streets, sparking a revolution, or you may feel her rumbling in your own belly and heart. Heed it!

Two thousand years later, Mary Magdalena, once cast aside from her significant role, is now rising in popularity and recognition. Why? She has experienced every single wound of the feminine and did not back down but walked barefoot through it all. This blood-and-flesh woman was fully embodied in her holy power and led a revolution in France in her time. And now she is rocking it on the world stage. With unabashed sensuality, vulnerable humanity, and true love, she is a fiery torch to show the way. And she is the tower of strength we so need today. Call on Her!

So much more was unveiled for me during these fatal initiation days in Mary Magdalene's cave, where she herself had guided women into the greater mysteries of the Tree of Life and this revolutionary feminine way during her walk on earth.

Beloved, come back into the story with me, so that I may reveal more to you.

Luic, my sturdy guide, was clear that I had to stay and declared he would pick me up in a few days. He gave me two bottles of water, some nuts and raisins, and an old scarf. I nodded my head. I knew that I had to be alone for three days and nights in this dark, freezing-cold womb cave and entrust myself entirely to nature and her hand. In the beginning, it was lovely and I enjoyed it. But she was not going to let me stay comfy for long. Nope, apparently she had more serious business with me. I shivered. The little candle wouldn't last for long, but for an hour, it gave a bit of warmth before the ordeal began.

Ruthless, she pulled me down and in, for this is Her way. She told me to strip, to give her everything I carried around, let all the knowledge from thirty years of intense spiritual practice and teaching depart, to throw out any beliefs and then some more. It was intense as if my skin was being peeled off layer by layer. I became so vulnerable and raw, and I wept for the children, the animals… and laid bare the excruciating suffering in my soul. Fury welled up, and she urged me to use the word "fuck" a lot (seems she likes that one). I must have roared for hours until I was so hoarse that no sound peeped out anymore. And then, I laughed until my belly hurt. Couldn't stop—don't even know what was so funny. Pearls of laughter touched the rocks, and I heard the whole temple with all the beings laughing, too.

When the candle had burned down, she pulled me toward the inner womb sanctuary. It was a steep drop into the below, and I didn't know if I would be able to ever climb out again. But if I should die there, it wasn't a bad place. A sliver of light from outside helped me see a few of the rocks to hold onto as I clambered down.

Barely had I touched the ground when I felt the incredible power in this womb center. Jolts upon jolts of energy surged through me. In rapture, I danced wildly barefoot on the rocks, taken by Her until I was utterly emptied, stood sweat-drenched and naked in the shining darkness, face to face with Her. That's when an immense transmission unleashed and surged through me from the ground up, rising like a snake through my spine. Words can't tell; I felt one in every way. After these immense waves had passed through, I curled up on the bare ground and must have slept for a while. When my eyes opened, she stood before me, and as I rose, she embraced me. Feeling my whole body in her arms, I heard the steady pulse of her heart and mine beating together. Such tender, fierce love infused every cell of mine, and as if the gates of heaven and earth opened, enormous grace flooded me. When love took a firm hold, I knew then and there what she had experienced herself. I won't tell you all of what happened, as some is far too intimate for words and remains deeply rooted in my soul.

I lost track of time, but probably on the second night, she revealed the original teachings and practices of her ancient feminine lineage to me. They were very specific and for different stages. How could I remember all this, as she talked for hours? I found a pen in my coat and wrote on my hands, arms, legs, and feet—not sure if I could read my scribbles later, as I could not see in the dark (some were readable, but most stayed strongly present in me).

She gave them to me with a profound, lasting transmission and guided me through each practice and teaching, so it would land as a felt experience and not stay mere head knowledge. This way, we learn best. Mary made it clear that the spiritual teachings, based on a male model, do not help women. Quite the opposite, they disconnect us from our femininity and the source. She kept insisting that the holy is whole, which means we unite what's human and divine, matter and spirit, pain and joy, instead of tearing them apart. That the "heart nous" is the gateway to all the treasures we seek, leading to the most intimate and vast connection with all living beings, to a profound love that embraces all. Which carries the living truth and life juice we so ache for, taking us home— body and soul. And then, of course, it's about walking and living it for real in the streets of our world.

I can affirm what she shared, as I experienced this liberation by opening all the way to merge with the primal life force, rising from below, through the spine, illuminating every part upon reaching the crown. And only oneness remained.

It must have been the last day when I felt moved to find my way by touch and sense into the sunlight. As I crawled out of the cave and my eyes tried to adjust from dark to light, I heard cooing. I looked up. A flock of doves circled above me, welcoming my birth. I wasn't the same person who had walked in. In ecstatic joy, I opened my arms and sang blessings into the wide, wide world. Mary stood right beside me. I felt Her as if you and I could touch, and we rejoiced together. But she wouldn't just leave it at that and commanded: "Guide my women home. Gather them from all over the world here in three months."

I didn't want to lead a retreat in these boonies and reveal the cave. How would they even know about it if I didn't market it? Nonchalantly, she said, "No worries. I will gather my own." I shrugged my shoulders and said, "Okay." I didn't bother, still immersed in the bliss realm and delighted to see Luic had arrived with a huge grin, knowing he had fulfilled his mission. Like a starving wolf, I devoured the food he had brought. Needless to say, within three months, a group of deep women gathered by word of mouth, and I had miraculously found a beautiful place for us to stay. Since then, I teach her way, guide devoted women into her embrace, and train those who are called to pass on the flame. She always opens her arms wide to each one who is willing to walk the way home for real.

I have seen it again and again. The yearning in our hearts is answered as we allow the dams and shackles to break, to weep all our tears and laugh all of our laughter. When we fully embrace our humanity and soul, we reunite what we've long tried to box apart—just as the women I've guided into the cave experienced. On their knees, they surrender to Her, embracing what's lost and split off, allowing this pure life power to ignite them. They are taken home through the fire of true love.

She beckons for us to recognize this simple truth—that she is made manifest through our bodies and luminous faces, the trees, the rivers… and that the holy wants to incarnate as your voice, hands, and feet. For real, to be lived in the mud and glory. To feel it. As you stroke your cat, dog, a friend, you are touching Her. Let Her take the lead in your life!

She will take you, shake and raise you into who you really are. She'll give you the courage to stand up and act for the benefit of all. This wild rose path is about walking the talk, acting with integrity, and living true to love, come what may. She is with you, and when she calls, follow her! I assure you, you can trust this down-to-earth rocking gal and sublime heavenly lady. Her gift to us is the revolution we urgently need for these wild times today. Rise with Her, beloved!

Mary Magdalena will show you a greater love than you may have ever known before.

> *"I have called you since before time. The hour is dawning, my beloved. Step into the unknown, I will meet you here and raise you up. Come unto me and I behold as you weep, laugh, and dance. I take you into my embrace all the way—as my only one. Fly on wings of grace, my love. Come home. And let me rise through you to bring forth a new dawn for humanity and this earth."*

Nicola Amadora, PhD

Nicola's work with women around the world has ignited a revolutionary movement for the feminine rising and Mary Magdalena. Nicola is renowned for her integrity, depth, and "real to the bone" teachings and transmissions that cut through illusion and open the heart wide.

With an illustrious career spanning over 30 years, she has guided thousands of people globally as a seasoned Spiritual Teacher, Holistic Psychologist, Women's Leader, Author, and Speaker.

She passionately lives and teaches the "Deep Feminine and Mary Magdalene's Way," ushering women towards the holy grail and to radically embody their soul in the streets of this world. Mary Magdalene called her by surprise a long time ago, and never let her go. After many years of rigorous training, Nicola was asked to initiate and guide women in this sacred path and train those who are called to carry forth the torch.

Both wildly mystical and down-to-earth practical, Nicola leads Mary Magdalene retreats, online courses, and professional training programs in her "Deep Feminine Wisdom School." Her work touches women as fiercely true, powerfully enlivening, and deeply authentic, emerging from the bedrock of ancient feminine wisdom and all-encompassing love.

She is the author of *Love Unleashed*, a groundbreaking book for embodied spirituality and a testimony to the power of the heart. It inspires profound transformations in readers worldwide.

Nicola is utterly devoted to the great turning we urgently need—for our lives, this shaken world, and our beloved earth.

Learn more:
https://www.nicolaamadora.com

SACRED GIFT

Enter the Sacred Egg Cave with Mary Magdalena

In this guided meditation, I invite you into the cave to meet Mary Magdalene, who already awaits you here. So you can experience, in a felt sense, that SHE is with you. To let down and be embraced as you are, by immense love. To drink from the grail and remember who you are.

With all your senses and feels, may you revel in the gift that is here for you. You can repeat this beautiful meditation often, and may find it goes deeper each time.

Access here:
https://www.nicolaamadora.com/mary-magdalene-gift-signup

CHAPTER 4

Magdalene Revealed— A Love Story Never Told

by Leyolah Antara

Bondi, Sydney, Early Summer 1988

It was a Sunday afternoon at the Bondi Pavilion in Sydney, and I was on the dance floor of a Latin music festival. My heart swelled with pure joy as I danced among 200 ecstatic bodies and smiling faces, celebrating life under a clear blue summer sky.

Then, amidst the crowd, I spotted him. Time seemed to stand still as our eyes met across the dance floor, and everything around us blurred and froze—leaving only him in sharp focus.

Then, suddenly he was dancing right next to me, within moments of that first glance. Our chemistry was electric, and our connection was undeniable. Our magnetism pulled us together like no one else occupied that dance floor.

It was just us.

We danced, laughed, and played until the music stopped. Then we walked on the beach, sat, watched the sunset, and shared snippets of our life stories.

This was how I met my first beloved soulmate, my first true love. A meeting that transformed the course of my destiny and initiated both of us into the alchemical arts of sacred union over the course of our seven-year marriage.

Sydney, House Party, Late Summer 1988

The Love Breath

One night, we discovered a unique way of breathing that took our lovemaking into the ecstatic realms of tantric union.

We were at a house party and decided to take some respite from the overcrowded basement dance floor, which didn't have much airflow. We went into the backyard and sat on the grass under the stars.

We sat facing one another in meditation posture, leaned our foreheads together, and nestled into the silence between us.

I felt so at home. We started to kiss softly, and then our kisses became a sipping breath through the mouth.

We brought our lips together and breathed in and out through the mouth, pursing our lips like we were sipping through a straw.

We allowed ourselves to anchor into the breath and stayed with it for some time. As we did this, our hearts opened wider, and we entered an ecstatic bliss state of consciousness.

No one taught us this breath, nor had I seen or heard it before.

But decades later, as I deepened my research into the mysteries of the bridal chamber of ancient beloveds who performed the rite of the Sacred Marriage, also known as the Hieros Gamos, I came to know it as the Nashakh. This sacred breath that entwines the souls of Beloveds.

We began to use the breath as an anchor when we made love.

Our synchronized breath connected our pleasure states and our orgasms, opening us into enchanted realms of sacred soul union.

The first time we made love, I felt my heart open in love like never before as my orgasmic energy found a new pathway—rising from my sexual gates, through my heart, up through my central channel, and out my crown chakra. I remember thinking, "This must be what a chakra is."

After making love, we would lay down and nest in, our hearts expanding in union, journeying into trance-like vision states. In these states, ancient and future timelines would come together in a pattern that revealed our karmic life lessons and soul gifts, catapulting us on an accelerated evolutionary journey.

This was the time when my memories of Mary Magdalene's life began. In those first months and years, flashes of that first-century timeline would flicker through my mind's eye, like a memory of a movie I had seen before.

Magdala, Galilee, 20 CE

That morning, Mother Mary came to visit me at my home. "He has returned from the mountains and knows it is your time to be together. He knows that his next training must come through the feminine, through you, his soulmate beloved. It is time for you to share your priestess training in the High Tantric Arts of Divine Union with him."

My heart soared and fluttered, simultaneously excited and afraid. I knew our time would come to be together as Beloveds, yet so soon?

It had been so hard to be apart from him all the years he had been away. I had to withstand my aloneness, my longing for union with him, my longing to fulfill the prophecy of the soul agreement we made before we were born earthside.

I felt a huge sigh of relief melt my heart. It was like a thousand years of longing rushing towards this moment. I have loved him since I first laid eyes upon him. I had loved him for eternity. I took a deep breath and gathered myself to respond.

"Tell him I am ready for him."

"That is so good to feel, Miriam; I will let him know. Great things will be born of your union. However, I must impress upon you that it is of the utmost importance that the two of you be discreet. Our people no longer covet the way of Sacred Union; the memory of the importance of this holiest of rites has been defiled through time, and your union could be potentially misunderstood as mere lust. Many will consider it unpure of him to lay with a woman; it could turn them against him and you."

"Well, you know whose fault that is; that has been the Roman Empire's way of controlling our people. They have done their best to exploit and defile sexual union to its lowest expression, keep the sacred couples separate, and outlaw the rites of the Sacred Marriage throughout all the lands they have conquered."

"Yes, Miriam, I know it is upsetting, and it has been the way for hundreds of years now. They have done what they can to destroy the remembrance of the template of sacred union and turn men and women from one another. That is why it is even more vital that you keep your union with Yeshua a secret. As if it is known, they will destroy you before you have had time to strengthen his light body and prepare him for his resurrection."

"I know, we will take care, Mother Mary, but that doesn't abate my anger about it."

Mary looked at me with deep compassion, melting the fire I was feeling inside my solar plexus. Although I was enraged, her presence always calmed me and helped me see the whole picture.

Mariam, the Mother of Yeshua, was a woman I adored above all others. I loved her like my own mother, yet she, too, was my mentor. I had never known a woman so pure of heart and so wise in the Way of Love. She was a high initiate of the temple and a central leader in our Essene community. She was the most revered elder of our Essene Order and was a leader of our movement to spread the Way of Love throughout the lands we walked.

She held my hand, and I was flooded with her warmth. Her words pierced directly into my heart: "My beloved Miriam, you are here to initiate him to open his inner luminous light pathways, bring him closer to the Divine Mother, and unify the love of God and the Goddess in his body. This will prepare him for his resurrection so he can continue his great work."

"I know, but let's get to know each other first. He also has so much to teach me. There is no brighter light and emanation of consciousness on this planet at this time. I am humbled."

"You have much to teach each other; the Feminine Mysteries are an important puzzle piece. Do not override what you carry with false humility."

"Yes, Beloved Mother. I do need to share that I have seen visions of the future, and I am also afraid that I must love him so fully and lose him."

"You will not lose him, my daughter. Your transmissions in the bridal chamber will assist him in awakening his Shakti fire to prepare him to resurrect his body, and he will continue to be with you and with all of us."

I shuddered at the thought, but I had seen what would come and knew my place in the design.

"As you know, your time is short. Please, my daughter, make the most of it."

We leaned in, hugged, touched our brows, and bowed as a symbol of respect, sealing the wisdom gleaned in this most important moment.

"I will go and share the good news with my son," said Mariam.

As she left, I knew her place in the prophecy was crucial, too. I knew we had work to do to support him together. She was so humble yet so powerful. I had no idea of the keys she held, but she knew everything about me.

Yeshua, too, looked up to her. It was beyond her role as his mother, but she was his guide and teacher in the Way of Love. Indeed, there was no one who held such purity in our community. I was grateful she was here, too—she brought a pillar of strength I would need to lean on again and again. She was the closest emanation of Divine Mother here. What a time we lived in. What a time.

The Love That Claimed Me

As the full moon rose, bringing light into the darkness, I heard a gentle knock on my bedroom door. As the door slowly opened, the deep, sultry tones of his voice whispered, "Miriam, it is I, Yeshua. May I enter?"

"Come in, Yeshua."

"My mother shared that you are ready to begin with my initiation into the ways of Sacred Union. I would be deeply honored if you would receive me into your beloved heart."

"You are already here and have been here for eternity," I whispered in his ear.

"Show me the way, Beloved. I am ready for your initiation," said Yeshua.

"We must come together, whole and complete. Two hearts fully inflamed by the union of God and Goddess. In our wholeness, we can unite," I said.

And with that, we embraced.

Our whole bodies pulsing, every cell tingling in a yearning to reunite. We looked into each other's eyes and synchronized our breaths. He was subtly following the rhythm of my breath, our energies entraining into a harmonic frequency whereby we could blend our consciousness.

The threads of our energy system began to weave and strengthen the tapestry of remembrance of our design as they wove together.

Our hearts melted into a vast golden ocean of light. There was no more he and no more me. There and then, we became we and dissolved in the divine dark light.

All was silent as we were held in the embrace of the Divine Mother. My womb was on fire, and I pressed my womb into his pelvic center.

In that moment, the inner flame of his holy womb chakra ignited. The ecstatic waves of Shakti began to ripple up through his chakra system, awakening the latent pathways of light.

The first part of the initiation had begun.

He had been linked into the womb of the Great Mother through his own body. He no longer would need the sexual fire of a woman to turn on his inner Shakti fire. The Goddess current had anchored in him.

He slowly pulled away from our embrace. As we held hands, our bodies pulsed in an ecstatic wave-like ripple that moved up our spines. It was like all the energy that linked us was returning to our sovereign energy systems.

"Why do you pull away?" I asked. The desire in me longed to continue to dive into the exquisite play of our energies dancing with one another.

"There are some things I must complete before we can fully merge. I must cleanse my energy system of some people and attachments before I merge with you again," he said.

"I understand. It is the way. Thank you for doing so."

He gently reached out, stroked my cheek, bowed, and left.

"See you soon, Beloved."

I fell back on my bed, awestruck by the magnitude of the love that passed between and through us.

My body felt like honey, as though every cell was puffed with light. He had such an incredible presence of love.

I thanked the Goddess for my blessings and knew of the cost to my own life, but it was a pain I would choose to bear for our mission to spread the teachings of the Way of Love, which was why I had incarnated.

I said yes. I chose him. At that moment, I chose our love.

My commitment had been sealed in the eyes of God-Goddess. There was no turning back.

So it was by day I followed him. By night, I led him gradually into the tantric mysteries of the bridal chamber to support his body's transfiguration and accelerate the activation of his rainbow-light body. Our practice together prepared him for his resurrection and strengthened his capacity to continue to be with us after his crucifixion. It was weird to know the future, but we had both seen that our time together in the physical was short; perhaps we had three years together at the most. So we needed to make the most of it. Ours was a true love, the most profound love I had ever known. A mystical romance where we remembered the highest possibilities for Sacred Union.

He came to my room each night for one moon cycle. The depth of reverence he shared with me was one I had never experienced with a man. We never made love or even kissed. Yet each breath was a prayer. His touch, a passage to a sacred paradise. To lay curled in his arms was a sanctuary for my soul.

The energy between us was so strong it required slow titrations. It was like getting used to a new kind of food or medicine, where you must gradually build up. Sometimes, he would get excited. I needed to pull away, knowing it was not time to merge.

"Why do you send me home so early?" he asked. "You know I want you fully and completely, the way a man desires a woman."

"Beloved, as we prepare for the rites of the bridal chamber, the energy that will pass through us is very strong. An immense power of love is preparing to pass through us, and if we open the gates too quickly, our systems can shut down. When we go slowly and open gradually, our system can expand to receive and allow this immense divine love to pour into the cup of our union," I explained.

On the 40th night, he came again. I had not seen him for one week as he had been traveling and had no idea when he would return. I had begun to shut down, feeling left and alone. Yet he came with a softness in his heart, inspiring me to allow the shield that had guarded my heart to soften and dissolve.

"You can trust me, you know."

"I know," I whispered. "But to open so far and then to have to let you go? I feel I must protect myself."

"I have seen the prophecy. It scares me, too," he said.

Feeling his vulnerability helped me to pull in my strength. The strength of love and gnosis within me made me trust this man.

It was my deepest knowing that we could create miracles when two souls came together in love and blended their energetic fields. I knew through our union, the teachings of the Way of Love would clarify.

Our First Time in the Bridal Chamber

So it was after three moon cycles of our courtship that we came together in the Bridal Chamber for the first time.

I ritually bathed, cleansing my body with water to receive him. I anointed my heart and sanctified my holy womb chakra as a crucible for the Goddess Isis with a blend of the sacred oils of Spikenard, Frankincense, and Rose. I combed the knots from my long hair, symbolizing the removal of the karmic knots that entwined me with past fears. I wrapped myself in my silk brocade robe.

He entered, and we sat before one another and called upon the great forces of light to bless and seal our sacred bridal chamber. So that no dark forces may feast on the light that we would generate through our tantric union. That we could meet in purity without external influences.

I could feel my heart pounding in my chest in anticipation of our closeness. I felt the hotness of desire overcome me, but I steadied my passions with my breath. Distributing the energy throughout my body.

We bowed, and as we looked into each other's eyes, I honored the indwelling flame of God in him, and he honored the spark of the Goddess in me. It was here we remembered that our bodies were the temples, and we learned how to pray with our breath and our touch.

He slowly removed the white cloth from my body and began to caress my skin, whispering praise and appreciation as he explored every nook and crevice of my body. My heart softened and opened to receive his sacred touch.

I looked deeply into his eyes, and without a doubt, I knew he was my true beloved. My soul flame. My vibrational match. The match to my holy flame.

I surrender. I am yours, beloved.

With that, he placed his lips upon mine, and we began to breathe the sacred breath of love, our breath swelling our bellies, our bodies touching and entwining our souls as one.

As we kissed, his mouth became a gateway to the holy of holies.

My mind was silent, and I was enveloped in a field of golden light.

He approached my body with reverence and innocence.

His touch, as light as a feather, ecstatically awakening my skin.

I emptied myself and surrendered to the waves of pleasure.

My body began to ripple as if waves of energy pulled upon my spine, full as the ocean tide during a full moon.

His body and my body merged as one ocean of starlight.

Black and silver, gold and blue hues enveloped my consciousness.

There were no more edges.

There was only light.

I spiraled into a territory unknown to my mind yet so known in my bones.

Then, as I began to lightly caress his spine, a sacred geometric light code appeared to be etched on his skin, revealing an ancient scripture, a language of love.

Then, I received a vision.

A Holy Book shimmered in golden light in my mind's eye.

A Sacred Codex of wisdom teachings for our times and beyond.

And from that moment, I knew.

Our love would give us access to the wisdom stream of love beyond the veil.

Our union would give us access to the Tantric Rose Mysteries, which are a portal to the rebirth of the Divine Human species on Earth.

Through our union, we would open the portal of remembrance so that humans would again reactivate the divine template held within their energy bodies and exist in harmonious union with each other and all of life.

I was shown that our love would be the silent power behind a great movement.

This would begin a journey that would take over two thousand years to fulfill. Two thousand years before, the fruits of our love would bear fruit.

We would be together in the physical dimension for now. And we would continue to assist humanity in the spirit realms for the next two thousand years, supporting the remembrance of the path of High Tantric Alchemy and the Alchemies of Divine Inner Union, Hieros Gamos, and the Mysteries of the Bridal Chamber.

Sacred technologies for couples to engage in a process that would birth the Divine Human species on earth.

The process of birth, death, and rebirth within one's lifetime.

Glastonbury, UK, 1994

I lay there curled up, nesting in his arms, after the most sublime lovemaking. It was the seventh year of our marriage, and our lovemaking had been a gateway to many shamanic journeys of remembrance.

"Did you see what I saw?" I asked him.

"Not sure, tell me what you saw and then I'll tell you what I saw," he said.

"I was in the bridal chamber with Magdalene and Yeshua. Their bed was like a cathedral with no ceiling. Just so much light pouring in. In the center of the chamber, I saw a sacred book, on a tripod. The book sat open, shimmering with golden text, an ancient codex of some kind."

"What was the book about?" he asked.

"I sense it is a book of knowledge of the keys of Divine Union. Technologies and wisdom teachings, a map of codes to awaken the Divine human."

"Wow, well, while you were seeing that, I was seeing a movie in my mind's eye of a ten-year-old boy running from a burning village with a book. He was running up a mountain path. I get a sense it was a Cathar Village in the Pyrenees in Southern France. The boy was running to escape the carnage and attack from the Roman Church. They were definitely after the book. Do you think the book still exists?" he asked.

"I think it has been destroyed but still exists in the ethers," I answered. "I wonder why we were shown the book?"

"You hold the treasure box within you," he said.

"And you are my key." As I said it, I heard a voice in my head saying, *You are bound to a promise to remain silent.* And with that, I turn to her. "Beloved Magdalena, help me to break the spell of silence that keeps the mysteries of sacred union out of reach."

As I am enveloped by the loving presence of the Magdalene, I hear her say, "The time has come, my sister."

After 7 years, that sacred soulmate relationship ended. It ended lovingly and consciously, and we are still friends. We just knew that we had lessons to learn outside the container of our marriage.

I'm grateful for the remembrance that was stirred through that relationship—one that still lives within me today, guiding my teaching, writing, and devotion to the Way of Divine Inner Union and Sacred Relationship as an alchemical path of transformation and spiritual awakening.

Leyolah Antara

Leyolah Antara is a compassionate guide dedicated to the embodied transformation field for over three decades. Widely recognized as a teacher of the tantric healing arts and an accomplished author with several impactful bodies of work, including Kundalini Dance Alchemy, Sexual Self-Healing, and Sacred Union - Healing the Barriers to Love.

Over the last decade, Leyolah has taught and trained priestesses in the alchemical arts in her Mystery School, where she has been dedicated to remembering and restoring the lost arts of Sacred Union and Tantric Alchemy.

Over the past three years, Leyolah has immersed herself in intensive studies and training in Hakomi Somatic Psychotherapy. Now having graduated, she specializes in experiential couples therapy, integrating this powerful system into her existing work with the Divine Feminine Mysteries of Sacred Tantric Union.

While Leyolah has a deep love for teaching groups, her most transformational work has emerged with her one-on-one clients. As a shamanic bodyworker, tantric coach, healer, and transformational guide, Leyolah has spent years offering private sessions to support and hold her clients to transform what was arising for healing through the tantric activations she offered in her Kundalini Dance workshops.

For couples seeking to take their relationship to the next level, please feel welcome to reach out and connect at Leyolah@leyolahantara.com.

Learn more:
www.leyolahantara.com

SACRED GIFT

Embodying the Inner Beloved
A Free Temple Offering from Leyolah Antara

Before sacred union with another, we are called to nourish the flame of love within. This free temple offering invites you to fill your own cup, tend to the inner sanctuary of your heart, and remember the divine love you already are.

Receive a guided audio meditation and a gentle embodiment practice to harmonize the inner masculine and feminine, awaken your Shakti, and root into the path of sacred union.

Let yourself be held. Let yourself remember.

Access here:
https://leyolahantara.com/embodying-the-inner-beloved-free-temple-practices

CHAPTER 5

The Call to Divine Embodiment
A Sacred Trinity of Magdalene Initiations

by Marin Bach-Antonson

> *I AM YOU*
> *YOU ARE ME*
> *WE ARE ONE*
> *WE ARE SHE*

These are the words Mary Magdalene transmitted to my consciousness the night my Magdalene codes were activated, and her presence was unlocked deep within me.

These four lines, which I would come to share with countless women to activate their own Magdalene rose remembrance, were an initiation. A rite of passage. A profound invitation to know the truth of my luminescence.

There was always a rhythm leading me back… back to the Temple of Magdalene.

Back to the knowing of my lineage.

Back to the kingdom of my heart.

There was always a voice whispering the way.

Not outside of me. But within me.

There were always words that resonated like a gong inside of my soul, giving me the clues and keys to my destiny.

Words like… Vesselhood. Sisterhood. Holy Grail. The Church of Love.

The path of becoming is often a spiral of soul-initiations.

For me, it all happened by way of three. A sacred trinity.

The Cracking.

The Coming.

The Call.

The Cracking

Every seeker will, at some point, make a passage through the velvet, dark petals of the Black Rose and stand at the threshold of the Dark Mothers.

Their presence upon the path of awakening is inevitable.

Kali Ma. Sekhmet. Hecate. Ereshkigal.

Even their names send a tremor through the bones.

One cannot prepare for descent. It arrives in divine timing, at the precise moment when, paradoxically, the soul is ready to rise.

The Dark Mothers do not come to destroy us cruelly, but with unwavering compassion they crack us open, unravel our illusions, and midwife us through death's portal—not to end us, but to birth us anew, again and again.

My first Black Rose initiation came in my mid-twenties.

It arrived like lightning, sudden and unforgiving. The moment my father found my younger brother's body in our garage.

He was gone.

Just 22 years old—athletic, charming, radiant with promise. Sensitive to the world, he was devastated by a breakup, unable to bear the weight of betrayal. In a single, irreversible moment, he chose to leave.

There was no warning. No signs. No note.

One instant, we were an ordinary family. The next, we were cast into an abyss that no heart should ever have to endure.

At the time, I was young and vibrant, full of dreams, obsessed with making it as an actress. Nothing could touch my fire—until grief extinguished it completely. Where once my belly pulsed with creativity, now there was only a leaden void.

I adored my brother. When he left, the world dimmed. My passion for the stage, my ambition, my drive—it all vanished in an instant. Like a switch flipped from on to off.

I became vacant. Gutted. Suspended in a liminal space of shock, rage, shame, and despair. For months, I lived there, melted and remolded by the inferno of loss.

I did not know it then, but his death was the crucible that would burn away everything false and birth me into something new.

Where I had once craved the stage, I now craved truth.

This was the moment my path shifted—from actress to seeker.

Suddenly, I saw the religion of my childhood differently. I no longer resonated with the God of Sunday Mass, Catholic school, and dry communion wafers.

I longed for the aliveness of the Divine.

So, I walked away—from the audition circuit, from religion, from the former scaffolding of my life that no longer fit—into the vast unknown.

Untethered.

Broken, yet open—a sacred coordinate I now know to be the doorway through which the Divine enters.

I didn't know it then, but I was being led.

I was broke, grieving, and in search of meaning.

I enrolled in a volunteer Seva program hoping to sit in the presence of yogis, shamans, and mystics—to soak in their teachings without the price tag—to be close to something inspiring, something true.

I was still in mourning, but the raw ache had begun to soften. I was slowly, cautiously, finding my way back to myself.

And that was when the light came through the crack.

One afternoon, after finishing my volunteer shift at the New York Open Center, I was offered a free pass to an evening workshop.

The choices? A Feng Shui event or an Autumn Equinox ceremony.

Looking back, it's almost comical—I didn't even know what *equinox* meant at the time. I had never attended a women's ceremony, never sat in a sacred circle, never stepped into the realm of the Divine Feminine.

And yet, with a nudge from something beyond logic—perhaps my higher self, perhaps destiny—I chose the equinox ceremony.

I planned to arrive early, but the subway had other plans. Delayed, frustrated, and hating to be late, I rushed to the venue, ready to burst through the door in a flurry of apologies.

But the moment I opened it, I *froze*.

What I saw on the other side would be seared into my soul forever.

A circle of women, dressed in their goddess best, gathered around a central altar. The room glowed in the soft flicker of candlelight, scented with incense and adorned with flowers and fall gourds. The air was thick with presence—something *ancient*, something *holy*.

At the center stood a woman unlike any I had ever seen—a Goddess, regal and radiant, holding a frame drum against her heart.

Ba, bum. Ba, bum. Ba, bum.

The beat thrummed through the space, through my soul, through *time itself*.

In an instant, I was no longer in a loft in New York City.

I was *between worlds*.

A thousand memories from nowhere and everywhere flooded my body. My cells popped and fizzled with recognition, unlocking something buried deep in my DNA.

I *knew* this. I *remembered* this.

Sisterhood. Circle. Ceremony and sacred space.

I remembered the temple.

The transfigurations and initiations.

I remembered the drum, the chanting, the rites, the tones.

I remembered it all in my belly, breath, being, and bones.

I. AM. HOME.

I stood there, trembling, lost in the enormity of it all. And yet, no one seemed to notice. Without a word, I slipped into the circle, taking my place as if I had always belonged.

The ceremony unfolded in waves of magic, and by the end, something inside me had *cracked wide open*.

I didn't choose this moment. *It chose me.*

Led by a force I couldn't name, I found myself moving straight toward the facilitator, my heart pounding, my hands shaking. Before I could think, the words tumbled out:

"I have to do what you do!"

She blinked, startled. And then, she smiled.

Over the next several weeks, over teas and long talks, she welcomed me into her world.

And then, she invited me to be her apprentice.

Years later, we would laugh about that night.

She would say I was bold.

I know I was broken but open. And the light led me to her.

Over the next two years, under her guidance, I was *re-womaned* in the ways of the ancient, sacred Feminine Mystery School.

I awakened to the harmony of my body, the power of my blood, the wisdom of my womb, and the dormant magic in my cells.

It was the beginning of my relationship with the Divine Mother. The unfolding of the petals of my heart.

That night, when I crossed the threshold into the Autumn Equinox ceremony, my priestess codes were activated, and my path of true becoming began.

By way of my brother's death, I was re-born—the great irony of the black rose.

During our darkest hours, we often believe we are in the tomb.

Yet, it's always the womb.

The *Priestess in me* emerged through loss. The *Magdalene* in me would be born through love.

The Coming

When a woman's Higher Self reveals to her that she is a Magdalene Rose Priestess, it is a profound awakening—a remembrance that shakes the very foundations of who she thought she was. In an instant, the illusion of powerlessness dissolves, and she stands at the threshold of her true spiritual potency.

She is no longer merely a seeker; she is a vessel, a living temple, a keeper of the sacred flame. This revelation is an inner initiation, unlocking the remembrance of her lineage, her past lives, and the holiness that has always been hers.

We all have our stories.

As for me and this second initiation, Magdalene came into my life entirely uninvited.

At the time, decades after meeting my spiritual mentor, the night of the Autumn Equinox circle, I was still a devoted disciple of the Goddess. *Women Who Run with the Wolves* was my bible. Viviane and Morgaine from *The Mists of Avalon* were my kindred. I was on an earth-priestess-pagan path, and Magdalene was nowhere on my radar.

And yet, there she was.

Her coming happened late at night as I was driving home from a retreat with Barbara Marx Hubbard. On the final evening, Barbara shared never-before-seen writings—biblical stories rewritten to restore the voices of the sacred feminine.

An assistant approached me in a flurry. "Marin, will you read Magdalene's part? Our reader had to leave."

I hadn't prepared, but I agreed. When the moment came, I took a breath and started the passage in the voice of Magdalene.

"I have been silenced for lifetimes. But now I speak…"

The words weren't mine, yet something ancient moved through me—a current of love and remembrance, a voice that had been waiting to be heard. The lines flowed through me like living water, quenching the thirst of women who longed across lifetimes to feel her again.

When I looked up, many had tears in their eyes. The moment was palpable.

Afterward, people approached me with excitement.

"You brought her through."

"You WERE Magdalene."

I shrugged off their words, figuring I'd simply nailed the reading. I had been a trained actress, after all.

But as I drove home under a star-strewn sky, something shifted.

The air grew thick, charged with an unseen presence—gentle yet immense.

I can't explain how I knew, only that I did.

It was her. It was Mary.

Somehow, I had the presence of mind to pull over before my consciousness catapulted into liminal space—somewhere between here, there, known, unknown, and what the fuck is happening?!

What unfolded was a full-blown mystical experience. With Magdalene. In my car. On a backcountry road.

My body felt as if it had been plugged into a cosmic current, every cell alive with an impossible voltage. I was pierced by her love—so sublime, it existed outside of time, space, and words.

Overcome and undone.

Baptized by light.

Brought to the glory of God through the gateway of her heart.

Lifetimes of forgetting loosened from my body as I was being shaken awake by what was coursing through me. I melted into her energy and opened to her mercy. With a diamond surge of crystalline knowing, I suddenly knew...

I was never my pain, my wounds, or my past. I was not the girl who thought she was a loser or believed she was ugly.

I just WAS.

We ARE.

ALL IS.

LOVE.

Everything dissolved into an ocean of oneness as I found myself ecstatically laughing and sobbing at the same time.

Truth be told, before the retreat, I had no real connection to Mary Magdalene. Growing up Catholic, she was a flat, supporting character in biblical lore.

But no more.

This Magdalene. This Mary. She was magnificent.

She appeared like a hologram to my consciousness—luminous, crystalline, wrapped in crimson robes that shimmered like liquid fire.

"You are home. You are whole. You are a daughter of the Rose."

Magdalene's words danced through me, lifting the veil, restoring the remembrance.

Then She reached out and passed a rose-gold flame from her heart into my own.

I AM YOU
YOU ARE ME
WE ARE ONE
WE ARE SHE

And just like that, Magdalene was no longer a stranger.

We were woven.

Sister to Sister.

Soul to Soul.

Hand to Hand.

Heart to Heart.

Holy Woman to Holy Woman.

Priestess to Priestess.

It was as if our circuits were reconnecting, like a key turning in an ancient lock, opening a long-forgotten door within.

Reading her passage at the retreat was more than a moment—it was a threshold. A miracle that redirected the river of my life.

That night, Magdalene came to me as pure love, inviting me to remember: *I am love.*

Beckoning me, once again, to walk with my lineage. Awakening the essence of the rose. Activating my Magdalene Codes.

It was the second initiation.

Pure exhalation.

Now, it was time to take up the mantle and answer the call.

The Call

Throughout time, women have felt an inner call—a summons from the soul to remember, resurrect, and serve. Some name it the call of the wild, the phoenix, the heroine's journey. But at its core, it is the immanence of the Feminine Christ rising within.

For centuries, holy women have heeded this call, acting as custodians of the divine feminine. They carried the white flame of the Mother Temple within the cauldron of their wombs, seeding the codes of the Lineage of Light.

They traversed cosmic portals and practiced loving with undefended hearts.

They embraced the catalyzing power of the dragon and the consecration of the dove.

They safeguarded secrets and kept the center fires ablaze. They honored their bodies as sanctums of Sophia.

Seers and sorceresses. Celestial oracles and scryers. Medicine women, soul midwives, and mystics. Reformers and rebels.

Under the moon, they gathered to spell, chant, sing, and speak truths.

Heretics, witches, wild women, and shrews—they held each other's hands when it was not safe to be seen.

Together, they bled, birthed, and blessed the earth.

They erected the red tents.

Wore the red veil.

Passed down the wisdom.

Way-showed The Way.

They were keepers of the sacred wells.

Pythia, sacred prostitutes, Serpentessas, and sages.

Women woven through time by the red thread.

They paved the way for where we are today.

And now, we stand.

I know I am one of these women.

If you are reading this, trust that you are, too.

To answer the call is no small thing.

It is a call of radical authenticity.

It requires facing ancestral wounds, the fear of rejection, the terror of persecution, the shadows of self-doubt, and imposter syndrome.

It demands we release righteous hurt, melt the armor around our hearts, and heal the scars upon our wombs.

This work is immense.

But we were born for it.

After Magdalene awoke in me, I felt a renewed relationship with my own radiance. I knew that beneath the layers of the human cloak, there was a holiness in me, untouched, waiting to be reclaimed.

Call it truth, essence, flame, innocence.

I call it Christ.

Magdalene is many things to many people. But for me, she is the Sophia-Christos—the Feminine Christ.

At one point in my journey, she stopped me from asking: "Who *was* Mary Magdalene?"

Instead, she whispered, "Who *is* Mary Magdalene?"

And suddenly, it didn't matter if she was a priestess, an apostle, a prostitute, or a lost voice in the Gospel.

When I began asking, "Who *is* Mary Magdalene?" I saw that she was my portal to the eternal, infinite, omniscient energy of Oneness.

As humans, we cannot hold such immense energy alone. We need bridges—higher aspects of light to span the divide.

And when I asked, "Who *is* Mary Magdalene?" she unveiled herself as an aspect of me.

This is when our real work together began.

"It is time to abide in the Feminine Christ," she whispered.

Christ. Christos. Crystal. Crystalline.

The pure, incandescent light of our original design.

The soul blueprint. Fully Human. Fully Divine.

So I sat in stillness, the rose-gold flame burning between our hearts.

And I began to speak the words:

"I am the frequency of the Feminine Christ.
I am the light of Christ.
My cells vibrate to the octave of Christ light.
I AM the Feminine Christ."

Over and over.

At first, I recoiled. Who am I to say this?

My inner voice raged: *How dare you call yourself Christ.*

But I knew I was not claiming Christ as my own.

I was simply reconnecting with the untouched aspect of my being—the part that is pure, powerful, and ever-present within my heart.

Still, the fear remained.

What if people found out?

Even now, as I write this, I feel the echoes of judgment, rejection, and projection rising in my chest.

But then I remember:

> *"Our deepest fear is not that we are inadequate.*
> *Our deepest fear is that we are powerful beyond measure."*
> —**Marianne Williamson**

One evening, as I engaged with the Feminine Christ frequency, something happened.

My entire being began to hum.

Light radiated from every pore.

Unlike my first encounter, when Magdalene's presence overwhelmed me, this time, I held the frequency with her.

The separation collapsed.

Her hologram stepped into me, overlaying my human self like a Russian doll.

We became the portal together.

Light flowed from me like warm liquid nectar, spilling into the great web of life, touching every point of light in creation.

I had thought I was answering the call to be a priestess, start a mystery school, initiate women, and build a new earth temple.

But this.

THIS.

This was the real ministry Magdalene was guiding me to.

The Ministry of Beingness—the I AM.

To BE the most luminous, unhindered, love-filled version of myself.

A generator of Love.

An open chalice.

A holy grail.

A hollow bone for God.

Ultimately, this third initiation was the rite of passage through paradigms.

I had to completely release the notion of what my lower self insisted was a purposeful life. This included influence, impact, abundance, and visibility. Instead, I had to authentically embrace that the greatest service is not about what we *do*. It is about who we *become*.

> *"If you endeavor to raise the Christ within you, you help to raise all humankind. You cannot make one effort toward heaven without the whole world being better for it."*
>
> —*White Eagle*

Once I yielded, I understood the depth and breadth of this ministry. Magdalene was guiding me to be ever-present with myself and not go unconscious. The core of my ministry is the devoted commitment to stay aligned with the Christ within—my "I AM" Presence.

To have taken up the mantle of this ministry has changed everything.

I stopped living life, and life started living me.

The miracles that have unfolded continue to surprise me.

Yet sometimes, when I forget, I hear Magdalene and the rose council sing my name. It is their way of calling me back through the chaos of the world into the wonder of my own holiness.

They remind me that to walk as a holy woman is my ultimate leadership. They remind me that to BE the "Church of Love" is erecting the consciousness of a new world.

One day. Some day. I, too, will sing the names of those who come after me.

For now, my prayer for us all is simply this:

May we remember: The Way of Love is to offer the highest, truest essence of ourselves to others. In this, we become the Living Grail—the Sacred Chalice, a holy vessel bridging heaven and earth. For there is no greater fulfillment for the human soul than to give of the holiness we are. And as we give, so do we receive.

Marin Bach-Antonson

Marin Bach-Antonson is a devotee of the "I AM" Feminine Christ path, a Magdalene Rose Priestess, and a mystic deeply woven into the living transmission of the Divine Mother. She is a carrier of the Magdalene Rose Temple Codes, guiding women to awaken their soul's remembrance, embody the sacred feminine, and anchor the Sophia-Christ light on Earth.

As a temple keeper and initiator, Marin creates sacred spaces, both seen and unseen, where deep activations take place. Through mystery school programs, private mentorship, multi-dimensional ceremony, and Magdalene Rose retreats worldwide, she facilitates feminine soul initiations that awaken the inner priestess and activate the holy woman within.

She walks as a way-shower of embodied wisdom, living the path of devotion and anchoring a new paradigm of feminine ministry leadership—one rooted in love, remembrance, and divine sovereignty.

Marin is currently writing *The Magdalene Rose Temple Codes,* a book that restores and transmits the sacred teachings of the Rose Lineage, offering keys to the resurrection of the Divine Feminine and the return of the Golden Age. Her full-length book will be published soon.

Learn more:
www.priestessrising.com
Instagram: @marin_priestess_rising

The Magdalene Golden Chalice Activation—Becoming the Holy Vessel

If your soul stirs at the call of Magdalene...
If you are ready to take up the mantle and step into your sacred VESSELHOOD...
Then I invite you to join me for this holy activation.

Magdalene beckons.
She is the sacred mirror, reflecting the truth your soul has always known.
Her rising presence on Earth is no accident
She comes to awaken you.
To remind you that you are a Magdalena:
A watchtower of light,
A way-shower of the Rose
An awakened one,
Here to walk the path of love
Rooted in the world yet no longer bound by it.

This free gift includes:

- **2-hour ceremonial temple activation** with Marin in the Magdalene Rose Temple.
- **Golden Rose Chalice Vibra-key**—a vibrational key code image for your altar.
- **22-page Magdalene Rose Priestess ebook** that includes invocations, "I AM" priestess decrees, additional video links, and a powerful ceremony template for embodying your holy grail codes.

Access here:
https://priestessrising.com/magdalene-chalice-activation

CHAPTER 6

RECLAIMING MY SACRED BLOOD

by Elizabeth Brett

The ocean roared around us, a symphony of rising walls and crashing collapse. My daughter clung to me, her small fingers digging into my skin. Her weight, the pull of the sea—everything felt heavier by the second.

We went under again, then again, and I kept pulling us up. My body was burning. My mind was counting the seconds between waves, tracking my breath, gauging her weight, my strength, the distance. I knew, with terrifying clarity: I was running out of time.

The ocean was changing, as she likes to, shifting around us. I noticed Grace growing more tired, her arms tightening around me. Then, after another set of waves, Grace lost her strength. Her fingers gripped harder, but her legs stopped kicking. She couldn't keep herself up anymore.

I saw more waves coming, unyielding. We dove under again, and when we came up, I knew I was down to seconds. Treading water, unable to touch the bottom, I kept calculating: How much longer can I hold her? How much longer can I fight?

The sea has always been my sanctuary. I could sit with my toes in the sand for hours, letting her rhythm sing to me like a lullaby. Since I was a kid, I would tell Mama Ocean the dreams I didn't dare speak aloud anywhere else. I would let her carry my heartbreak, my disappointment, my longing away, one wave at a time. And this specific stretch of coastline—with her velvet-soft sand, the smell of salt mixed with fresh-cut grass and her unpredictable temper—was the first place I had ever truly felt held.

I stood on this very shore the morning I found out I was pregnant with Grace, my salty tears of disbelief and deep joy mingling with her fierce, hungry ebb and flow. We've come every summer since, and by now at seven years old, this place has become part of Grace, too. A shared altar between us.

But on this day, it wasn't a simple swim. It wasn't a quick exit.

The next wave hit, and instinct took over. A primal force roared inside me. I was no longer thinking. I was only surviving. I had no choice but to push beyond exhaustion, beyond reason. I screamed for help, my voice raw and desperate. My cousin, standing on the shore, heard me. By some miracle, he made it in time. I pushed my daughter toward him, every muscle in my body trembling with effort. And then, I let go.

A sound tore from my throat: something ancient, something raw. It was the release of everything I had been holding, the final act of a mother who had given everything to get her child to safety. I knew she would be okay. And in that moment, I had nothing left to give. I surrendered to the ocean. I felt my body go limp, the salt water envelop me like a lover, the currents pull me into their embrace.

Instead of fear, I felt something entirely unexpected: peace. Not just peace like a blanket, soft and warm. It was exquisite, pulsing, blissful. I wasn't afraid. I wasn't fighting. Whether I made it back to shore or not, I knew it didn't matter. Everything was as it was meant to be.

Somewhere, deep in my bones, I felt a presence, a deep remembering. I wasn't alone. I was held. In that moment of total surrender, I knew I had come home not only to the ocean but also to myself, and that I was held here by a force greater than me. I didn't have the language for it yet, but it felt like golden liquid light and smelled like roses. The Magdalene was asking me to surrender fully into the unknown, into the mystery.

In the next few minutes, I don't even remember what happened. I have no idea how I made it back to shore. I just remember crawling out of the water and turning around to look at this magnificent ocean.

It took me days, weeks, and even months to fully process this experience. But in that moment, as I looked back at the water, I knew—*the woman who entered the ocean with her daughter that day did not return.* Somewhere between the struggle and the surrender, she was released into the waves. The woman who crawled back onto the shore was a whole new version of me.

One who knew that there was no more hiding. One who knew from that moment forward that I wanted to feel deeply and fully alive every day, in everything I do. I knew exactly who I was and what I wanted, and I had to stop pretending to be anything other than that.

My plans to attend grad school to become a therapist shattered instantly. Although I was signed up to start in just two weeks, I knew it wasn't my path. I no longer had anything to prove to anyone. Instead, it was time for me to rise and step fully into my sovereignty as a modern-day priestess.

I wonder if this is how Mary Magdalene must have felt, devoting her life to a lineage that most people wouldn't understand. I believe she is the mirror for so many of us as women in the modern world. Sometimes, I can't help but wonder how people treated her when she was alive, if they revered her as a high priestess and understood she was the feminine Christ in her lifetime, or if she was already doubted, misunderstood, and made the scapegoat of people's fears.

When I first discovered what had been done to Mary Magdalene in the retelling of her story, I was fire-hot with rage. Heat started in my womb and surged outward through every cell in my body. My skin sizzled with disgust. I felt like vomiting. Men who were threatened by the sacred power of women had turned a priestess into a prostitute. They had stolen her divinity and erased her sovereignty.

A part of me that had been long buried suddenly and furiously came alive. I started to remember. I sat, hot with astonishment. How could I have been so deeply conditioned? How could *we* have forgotten so much?

Of course women were wisdom keepers.

Of course we were storytellers.

Of course we were powerful, magnetic, and spiritual leaders in our own right.

Of course we carried the codes of creation in our blood.

Was I the only woman in my family to remember this?

My mother's lips become a tight line as I excitedly share about this other Mary Magdalene—the one who was Yeshua's partner, the feminine Christ, the holy spirit. For her, my words aren't just uncomfortable; they are incomprehensible. They can't penetrate the belief system she's so invested in, where God and all his leaders are men, and she is so accustomed to playing the role of the subservient female who longs to be taken care of. I see my words ricochet off her devotion and know there's no point in sharing my truth with someone unable to hear it.

For years afterward, we politely avoid conversations about religion or spirituality, and she doesn't ask questions about my relationship with Mary Magdalene at all. Until it spills onto these pages, I decide it's better to keep my truth safe within a very tight circle of trusted priestess sisters to protect the sacredness and avoid being influenced by anyone else's judgment. But sometimes, my mom does ask me to pray for her if she's sick or has a specific request.

I want to share with her how I pray with my whole body, how I feel the desire in my bones, and allow my body to *become* the altar. I want to share how my prayers transform into colors and take the most beautiful shapes as I move with them. How sometimes, they smell like roses or peonies and feel like sunlight when it first touches your skin. But I don't. I know my words have no place to go.

Instead, I tell her all that I've been discovering about our ancestors by testing my blood through one of those websites. I ask my mother what she knows of our heritage, of the Viking blood in our veins or the Visigoth, and how both ended up in Great Britain. She says she's never looked into our ancestry and only knows her great-grandfather was an elaborate woodworker in Denmark. I tell her I'm going to dig deeper, to try to discover how the women in our lineage used to live, used to pray. And again, we go silent.

How are we, as women, so good at avoiding and denial and omission? We have been so perfectly trained to do whatever it takes in order to keep the peace.

My journey of reclamation really started in earnest five years ago when I went to a sacred feminine ceremony for the first time. The instant I entered the temple space with my mentor and other women, I felt a deep remembrance like a bolt of lightning coursing through my veins: I knew I had been here before. It was the first time I was aware of my claircognizance (although I didn't even know that word existed then, let alone what it meant). It didn't make sense, but I "knew" I had been studying the sacred arts as a priestess for lifetimes. It was in my DNA.

Even though I wouldn't dare call myself a priestess (and I would keep my spiritual gifts neatly tucked away for years), I knew: I was home. It was oxygen to a part of me I hadn't known was suffocating. This experience of knowing with my body instead of my mind shook my entire sense of reality. How could I feel so disconnected from my immediate relatives and yet feel so connected to my ancestors?

Deep in meditation with my mentor not long after that first temple, I felt the leaves crinkling beneath my bare feet as I walked on a path in the woods. I came to a clearing where I saw a line of women, all with their backs turned to me, that didn't seem to have an end. As I got closer, I could see they were passing something down the line, and at one point, it seemed to completely stop.

One of the women turned to me. She was a fierce and radiant Viking warrior with blonde hair braided like a crown trailing down to her waist, a sword resting between her shoulder blades, and eyes like ice-blue fire. She was the embodiment of devotion and strength. When her gaze met mine, I felt completely seen. Not just in that moment, but across lifetimes.

I knew instantly she was my ancestor, as were all the women in the line, generation after generation. She held my gaze, then spoke: "We have been waiting for you." In her hands was a large, weathered stone. As she passed it to me, it pulsed with something ancient. Heavy, yes, but also alive. As though it had been humming my name for centuries.

I understood, without words, that this was a keystone from an ancient temple I was meant to rebuild. Not of brick or stone, but of memory, of devotion, of truth. She didn't tell me what it would require. I didn't ask. I had no idea what this stone would come to mean in my life. And still, I received it fully. My hands trembled. I was both terrified and exhilarated.

In that moment, my journey felt like it locked into place within me. I knew my path would never be the same. I vowed to honor the wisdom encoded in my DNA. To listen to my inner knowing. To walk with reverence into the mystery. To rebuild what had been forgotten.

The first time I tried anointing myself with holy oils blended by a beloved scent priestess mentor, I broke down in tears. How could I, someone who had avoided my reflection in the mirror for years, who hated being in photos, who had completely disconnected from my body, perform such an intimate, loving act of devotion toward myself? It felt almost unbearable, too sacred. And yet, I thought of Mary Magdalene, who was a scent priestess herself, and how she anointed with reverence, not as performance, but as prayer.

So I began with the one place I had come to trust the most and despise the most—the part of me that carried life, that had stretched and softened and opened again and again: my womb. If I could love myself there, maybe I could learn to love the rest of me, too. Maybe I could move outward, one breath, one drop at a time.

Anointing brought me back to my body in a literal sense. I made it a daily devotion, speaking to my body as my most intimate ally. It allowed me to soften toward myself, using a dozen different blends to love and open different parts of myself. It started as an experiment, a curiosity. Something so foreign and yet so natural. I took time to get to know each oil, to feel it on my skin and receive its medicine. Within one year, my relationship with my body was revolutionized— totally unrecognizable. It became a holy practice. My body became sacred. I could once again look at myself in the mirror and now—maybe for the first time—really see who was looking back at me.

Each drop became a portal. Rose opened my heart and reminded me of my softness. Myrrh reconnected me to my grief and the ancient women who came before me. Frankincense brought clarity and connection to my inner knowing I didn't realize I could access without words. As I anointed, I remembered. Not in a mental way, but in my bones. The kind of remembering that doesn't require proof—only presence.

It was another way home to myself. Another layer of conditioning to be shed, another reclamation not just for myself but for all of the women before me who had forgotten the holiness of their bodies, too. I no longer treated my body as something to be managed or fixed. She became my temple. My oracle. My most trusted compass.

Then, deep in meditation with a shamanka, my claircognizance opened a doorway. A memory surged forward. One I hadn't lived in this lifetime but felt as real as breath. My own words… twisted. Used against one of my dearest friends. It was during the burning times. I saw her trial. I watched the flames take her. And I stood frozen, powerless to stop it.

I never forgave myself.

From that moment forward, my throat carried the weight of it: constricted, bound, unable to fully open. I knew this wasn't just mine. This was an inherited wound. A grief carved into my bloodline. The shamanka looked at me gently and asked, "Are you ready to release this?"

Something primal tore loose. I howled. I cried. I shook. Sounds I didn't know I could make erupted from my throat. Then came the scream: raw, guttural, ancient.

"YES," I screamed. Again and again, louder and freer.

For as long as I could remember, rage had been locked in my body. I'd tried to scream, but the sound never came. The rage and powerlessness was trapped. Held in my blood, waiting to be released. Until now. The spell was broken.

When it was over, she told me the final release would come through my moonblood that month. "Offer it to the land," she said. "Create an altar. Let the Earth hold it for you."

I had never even considered saving blood from my "moontime" as I'd affectionately started calling it, trying to rub off the negative energy I'd poured into this part of being female for so many years. Growing up, my period was something to hide, shrouded with shame. It was treated as something messy, embarrassing, even dirty.

But somewhere along the way, I had read *The Red Tent* and other sacred texts that told a different story: that before patriarchy, menstruating women were revered. That to bleed without dying was seen not as a burden but as a monthly miracle. That a woman's womb—her ability to create life, to shed and renew—was holy. A sign of her closeness to the divine.

Could I see mine this way?

I was stunned to discover that collecting my blood didn't disgust me. It *moved* me. The act felt like a ceremony. I was filled with awe, reverence. I had remembered so much about my blood in how it connected me to my lineage and my sacred wisdom, but how had I forgotten to see my blood itself as sacred? This ancient, cyclical release that was mine?

Even the word *blood* comes from a root that means to *bloom*. My Visigoth ancestors likely used a version closer to the French—*sang*—meaning vitality and essence. For thousands of years, blood has been a symbol of life force. Even the Bible says blood is sacred, and in Leviticus claims blood is "the place where the soul resides."

Of course it is. Blood is the literal thread that connects us to our ancestors. It holds memory. Mystery. Power. And still, I had overlooked this part of my womanhood for so long. Or worse, I purposely avoided it. Denied it. Felt ashamed by it.

But this time, I didn't turn away. I turned toward it. I honored it. I *received* it.

It was a heavy bleed. I collected the blood slowly, reverently. I knew part of me was asking to be recohered. When it came time to create the altar, I happened to walk past a mirror on my way outside to begin. And I saw it. *I was the altar.* Of course I was. I had always been. I stood there facing the mirror, frozen in wonder.

I dipped my fingers into the bowl of blood and looked into my own eyes. I marked my cheeks with crimson stripes. I drew a lemniscate across my forehead as a symbol of the infinite, the eternal, the unbroken lineage of women who came before and the ones still to come. And I offered the rest to the land. This reclamation was not mine alone. It was for every woman who had been ashamed of her body and its cycle. Every woman who had swallowed her scream.

I reclaimed our blood. Our power. Our sovereignty. For my ancestors. For myself. This was my final initiation in reclaiming my blood as sacred in all the ways. It was done.

And suddenly, I knew that no matter what they tried to take away from Mary Magdalene, they could never take her sacred blood. Just like mine, it pulsed with memory. With truth.

My journey hasn't been about becoming someone new. It's been a long, aching return. A path of unbecoming, of unwinding everything I was taught to be, so I could finally learn the truth:

That my blood is holy.

That my body is the altar.

That I get to rewrite the rules and bring the ancient ways forward.

The ocean knew before I did. She pulled me under, not to drown me but to baptize me back into my body. Magdalene met me in the depths. She did not offer answers. She offered remembrance. Not through words, not in theory, but in the salt. In the blood. In the smell of roses. In the roar of the waves and the silence between them.

And I remembered with my cells that our blood carries the stories of our lineage. It is a map. A song. A vow.

We are the pulse of every priestess who ever dared to claim her spiritual gifts.

We are sovereign. We are sacred. With ancient wisdom coursing through our veins.

May my journey be a wave that wakes us up fully. A call to the women silently weeping in their kitchens. A call to the mothers packing lunches while their souls beg to be fed. A call to every woman who has felt the stirrings of something more but hasn't known where to begin.

Begin here. Begin with the blood.

Reclaim your unique rhythm. Reclaim your sacred rage. Reclaim your untamed rituals.

It's time to stop turning outward. To stop disconnecting from your body, from your ancestry, from the wisdom only you hold. You are not lost. You are being asked to surrender and rise into the fullness of who you are.

Elizabeth Brett

Elizabeth Brett is a former NBC reporter turned modern-day priestess, soul alchemist and guide. She's been featured on The Today Show, The New York Times, The Wall Street Journal, Shape magazine, and hosts her raved-about podcast, Sacred & Sovereign.

Known for her unshakable presence and energetic precision, she works with high-capacity women to reclaim their inner fire, feminine fullness, and sacred sovereignty. Through 1:1 mentoring and group experiences, she takes women on journeys of soul-level transformation, helping them remember who they were before the world told them who to be.

Elizabeth lives in Austin, TX, with her husband and two kids. She is allergic to surface-level conversation and loves belly laughs, adventures, and wiggling her toes in the sand.

Learn more:
https://www.elizabethbrett.com

SACRED GIFT

Soul Code Quiz

Discover who you were before the world told you who to be.

Reconnect with the part of you that was never meant to be tamed—the part that knows, trusts, dreams, and leads from within. Your Soul Code isn't about becoming someone new. It's about remembering the power, the magic, and the truth that has always lived inside you. Take the two-minute quiz and begin your journey home.

Access here:
https://www.elizabethbrett.com/quiz

CHAPTER 7

Chief Magdalene Officer

by Beth Cavagnolo

Within three years, I was fired from two cherished senior executive roles. I was angry, frustrated, and exhausted. Yet, at the same time, this shift in my employment allowed me to be open, receptive, and curious about my future. This is my story of stepping out of the corporate rat race, returning, leaving again, and ultimately finding a way to do fulfilling work—this time through the archetype of Mary Magdalene guided by healthy boundaries, heart-centered leadership, and the courageous vulnerability I now embody. Through it all, I came to understand this truth: You are not less of a Priestess for working within capitalism or engaging with those who seek to etch patriarchy into the fabric of humanity. Rather, the Priestess walks where she is needed, bringing light and transformation into even the most entrenched systems.

I return to 2018, where high above Midtown Manhattan, inside the walls of a major international law firm, my otherwise sunlit office felt stifling and dark. My face flushed, and my stomach lurched. My vision narrowed, and I worked hard to control my breathing. Thirty minutes earlier, my boss and I had met to discuss my departure from the job I had dreamed about for years. It was a role that I worked so hard to "get," and now I was being fired.

Firing is something that happens to other people, not to senior executives like me. Firing people is what *I* did in my role, but now the tables were turned. Firing happens to people who just can't hack it, you know, poor performers… Oh, wait. Was I a poor performer? Why couldn't I turn these two senior executive roles into a lifetime of brilliant success?

Let's go back to the beginning of this journey. We'll start with law school, where, although I exhibited talent in public speaking and moot court, I was an average student. My mother's sudden death during my third year had thrust me into an untethered world of survival and competition. Without her as my emotional, physical, and financial safety net, I felt fearful and worried, so I applied myself to my work as a talent management executive in law firms. I stood strong in my leadership, applying myself to tough projects and conducting difficult conversations. I became known as the team player who'd take on the most challenging tasks and get them done with effortless grace. My commitment to education and the corresponding certifications made for an ever-increasing list of initials following my name. In addition to my law degree, I pursued and earned a master's degree in organizational psychology from an Ivy League university. I authored articles that others would cite, presented at industry conferences, and was a trusted advisor amongst firm leadership. From the outside, I believed all could admire me and think, "She's got it all!"

I now know I was disconnected from my heart, my light, and my divine feminine. I lived very much from a place of rejecting intuition and anything "soft" or "mushy." My masculine energy was apparent in my appearance, enveloping my voice and my behavior. This masculine energy entirely displaced my femininity, which likely (and sadly) contributed to the appearance of my success as measured by the capitalist patriarchy. In fact, I was so disconnected from my own heart magic that when a mentor suggested that I take time each morning to surround myself with a golden light of protection, I scoffed at the useless suggestion. First, who needs energetic protection? Not this tough leader! And second, what a load of weird shit. With my logical mind insisting that this kind of energetic protection wasn't real, I continued to push through, struggling with a mismatch of energy and purpose.

At this point, it was clear to me that things weren't going so well at the office, but I didn't know how to turn it around. I was outside my energetic limits; I'd canceled more vacations that I'd taken because I wanted to assert that I was reliable and willing to sacrifice anything "personal" for the job and firm. In fact, I wore a hairshirt every day that looked a lot like a designer suit, replete with matching shoes and handbag. Yet deep inside, I didn't have confidence in myself, which undermined all attempts at relationships with my colleagues and direct reports. I was far too afraid of losing my status and identity to speak truth to power, which meant not adequately advocating for my team or department. Furthermore, my vision for any future became blurry—I always felt tired. I was burned out, and everyone around me knew it. It was time for me to know it, too.

Consequently, my boss gratefully offered a generous severance agreement. She asked me to stay through one project that I was keen to complete, and I agreed. The winddown of my position in this job took about two months. In my heart, I was grieving, but on the outside, I was again playing the role of compliant and complicit department leader.

My projects wrapped up, and the team threw me a lovely going-away party. The very next day, I boarded a plane to Oaxaca, Mexico, where I spent the next 10 days in a writing retreat, enjoying the city with my boyfriend and his wonderful mother and relaxing into a rediscovered space of life. It seemed the perfect start to a sabbatical year that was forced, not chosen. Newly refreshed and ready to go, I returned to New York City. However, the universe would unveil other plans.

Living in New York City isn't cheap, and despite my hefty savings and contributions from my hard-working boyfriend, I decided to find a job to cover daily expenses. I was still too tired from nearly 20 years of executive life, so I took up cat-sitting in Queens and Brooklyn instead of pursuing another senior role. No joke, it was the ideal situation for me at that time. Not only did I acquire clients all over the city, but I also had the chance to visit newly adopted kittens every day. Some shy kittens needed some confidence-building work, and others simply wanted to play hard for an hour in the middle of the day. This work may seem mindless to some, but it was an important beginning to my relationship with Mary Magdalene.

Working with cats demanded that I not only modulate my internal and external energies but also understand the entire spectrum from which they emerged. I had to be calm and completely present with my "clients." My energy could not be scattered or stressed because cats withdraw from discordant feelings. If my body language was not harmonious with my heart language, the cats sensed the discordance and became aloof, fearful, or even aggressive. I had to fully represent my heart in every moment.

In my ongoing state of chaos, caring for these small beings taught me to co-regulate my energy. The lessons I shared with those furry clients—play freely, sleep peacefully, love wantonly—returned to me and within me tenfold. Little did I know that in being quiet and still, I was cultivating a long-dismissed feminine energy—shifting from the active and directional energy of my masculine self into the softer, more receptive, and magnetic energy of my feminine. In these quiet moments of presence, I began to reclaim my soul's calling as a Priestess, as a bridge between heaven and earth, here and there, now and tomorrow.

Luckily enough, since I wasn't working full-time, I found more hours in the day than I knew what to do with. I used that free time to rediscover the metaphysical interests of my younger self. I returned to tarot and oracle card reading, astrology, crystal work, and meditation. My lifelong interest in astrology grew, and I enjoyed taking classes and reading books. I began doing witchcraft again and felt my internal sovereignty growing. I connected more deeply with goddess energy through the archetypes of Danu, Hecate, and Kali. And yet, for many reasons, Mary Magdalene was still hovering on the periphery of my consciousness, outside the focused lens of my heart. I found it difficult to connect with Magdalene as a true feminine spiritual leader when I'd been told my whole life that women can't be spiritual leaders or even leaders at all. I was especially averse to her traditional Christian framing as a mere prostitute, and the stories told about her through modern literature and film felt overly fictionalized. However, she was there, always in her red veil, watching and waiting. It would be another year before I felt her consciously in my heart, and I see now how she was gently bringing me closer to her throughout my studies and practices.

During this sabbatical year, I barely and partially recovered from the burnout. Despite my best efforts, my ego wasn't yet ready to shed my hard-won career character, and it was shockingly easy to repeat the same pattern of over-identifying with work and productivity. So, when an opportunity came to be a C-Suite leader in a technology company, I jumped at the chance to build a company from the ground up. My partner and I moved cities, uprooting our lives for what we thought might be a long-term career with this growing startup. Unfortunately, after two years and numerous frustrations between myself and my employer, my employment was again terminated.

At this point, I can see how you might want the sordid details to know exactly what went wrong. Honestly, it doesn't matter. It's not about the employers or what went "right" or "wrong." In hindsight, all of it was "right." The continuous line is that my internal stories and ego attachments caused me to over-identify with professional roles and their titles as the sources of my identity and self-esteem. Like many of us, I was socialized to believe that I must look outside myself for validation and worthiness. For me, that validation arrived by way of my career. Yet it was like eating piles of sugar every day; sure, I was plugged into energy, but nutrition was nowhere to be found.

After I was fired from this second executive role, a crisis of consciousness began to unfold. "What is WRONG with me?!" my heart cried out. Why couldn't I find success in these roles that I worked so hard to achieve? I gave two decades of my life to corporate America. I sobbed. I raged. I felt victimized by capitalism, my employers, my successful family, and society at large. I turned against myself, convinced that if I could be stronger, faster, and smarter, I could change course and discover a new empire of work worthy of my devotion and talents. However, in my heart, I knew this attachment to the fleeting identity of "employee" wasn't sustainable. I couldn't keep jumping from job to job without figuring out what was going on inside me that refused to let me reside in my power. It was at this point of mental exhaustion that Mary Magdalene's energy began to ripple throughout my life. Not in a blast of trumpets or all at once, of course—she moves with unparalleled grace, taking her time to prepare you for her lessons.

First, I restored my feminine sovereignty and reacquainted myself with my small, quiet inner voice. I also spent more time outdoors, which was easy in my new town. I sought out women's spaces and spiritual mentorship. Then, I revisited the books from my teenage and college years, written by feminist theologians who offered a more intellectual foundation for all of this. I started to remember my childhood experiences with the Goddess.

During this time, I joined a growing legal consultancy where I still happily work today. In this role, I collaborate with people who want to collaborate with me. There is space and a receptiveness here for me to skillfully weave heart-centered energy with strategy. As I speak the language of the capitalist patriarchy *and* the Goddess with those around me, I hold in my mantra to be totally honest and totally kind.

As I became more receptive to the work of the Goddess, she appeared to me as Mary Magdalene, the Apostle of the Apostles. I sought out and read her Gospel and then every book written about her—I learned quite a bit about the early Christian movement, as well as Isis cults and the role of the sacred priestess throughout history and across the cultures of humankind. My relationship with Mary Magdalene catalyzed my unraveling, unfolding, and ultimately, my opening. She had always been there, waiting for a time when I'd be quiet, still, and receptive to her loving energy.

She came through at this point in my life because I actively sought the example of feminine spiritual leadership and was no longer seeking merely logical answers or direction but rather a deeper knowing of what it means to be human, to be a living woman. She showed me, slowly and with great divinity that everything I felt to be true in my body about women and women's spirituality was true and real. She came to me first as a leader, which was the easiest way for me to meet her and to open to her lessons on breathing feminine leadership into a patriarchal system.

Mary Magdalene offers this template of fully integrated leadership within and throughout her archetype. She bravely stood with Yeshua throughout his trial and crucifixion. She was the first to see and speak with the resurrected Christ. She stood and spoke to the lamentations of her fellow disciples regarding how they would be received by the same community that crucified Yeshua. She fearlessly testified before the court of Caesar Tiberius and, unwavering in her faith, performed the miracle of the Red Egg. When her life was threatened, she crossed the Mediterranean and formed a new community in Southern France. She led when and where no one else would. Her life is an example of a woman walking in faith and leading through crisis, even within the ruthless and misogynistic culture of the region and era. She was a woman of authority, heart, courage, and a willingness to step into leadership.

Mary Magdalene spoke plainly in her gospel, and I am sure she was clear and direct with Caesar Tiberius. There was no room for double talk or hidden meanings, especially since Roman society in the early Christ movement sought opportunities to misinterpret and thereby malign the words of Yeshua and his apostles.

She inspired me to find my own unique leadership style and voice. Using Mary as an example, I learned to be logical and transparent while also encouraging emotional expression in the workplace, especially joy and laughter. I became adept at guiding leaders to consider meetings as a time of focused, energetic intention where teams can be creative and responsive to the needs of the organization. My actions became more courageous, and I found myself speaking up and advocating not only for what was right but also for what the leaders could do to create more love in their organizations. Is there LOVE in corporate America? Of course. There's LOVE everywhere.

From time to time, I slip back into victimhood, thinking my life has been wasted on my work/career, but I know intimately how broader systems work and sustain themselves. I've done plenty as a white woman, intentionally and unintentionally, to reinforce the capitalist patriarchy. I take responsibility for what I've built and what I've deconstructed. It's been a bumpy road of honesty, humility, and reconciliation to see how I was a tool of corporate America despite thinking I was a rebel. However, this time of reflection also allowed me to see that I'm well-positioned as a torchbearer within these dark halls.

You, like me, may be called to serve the Divine Feminine. Please know she wants you exactly as you are right now. There is nothing you must change to heed her call. Eventually, you may go through the process of realigning your work with your values, but there is no expectation that you become a professional priestess. I dare suggest that we are most needed in the places we already inhabit: those aforementioned dark halls of capitalist patriarchy. We know these patterns and behaviors. We understand those values and beliefs. We also know these stories no longer have any hold over us or within us; we see past the funhouse mirrors set before us and to the truth of all processes. We are deconstructing and reconstructing our society, even if it's just one meeting at a time. And let's keep being honest: it's not always desirable or realistic to create and build your own business. That's why it's important to know you can serve Her through any and every corporate role. There is no obligation for you to leave your day job to become more of a Priestess.

It can feel disheartening to realize you're meant to keep challenging the status quo, to stay in the ring and go a few more rounds. You may love your hard-won career as much as I did; perhaps it's financially lucrative, mentally stimulating, and deeply creative, or maybe you are simply supported by your organization and team, and you're able to make your work your own. You are not less of a Priestess for working in and engaging with capitalism and with those who seek to etch the patriarchy into the lives of all of humanity.

But it feels so different when you know you're approaching your work from this place of divine centeredness. When you do get caught in bureaucracy, it's a chance to heal the shadows of the company. Every time you speak up, speak out, and hold space, you change their pattern to more lovingly reflect that which is sacred. Every time you laugh or allow tears, you change the pattern. Every time you listen to your intuition rather than the data, you change the pattern. You are a storyteller, and your colleagues and clients are listening. Every interaction is a chance to be love—to share the good and help overcome the powers of the ego and worse. We need women to do the work of the Priestess as a Secretary, Doctor, Lawyer, and Executive.

Please know that my journey is far from over. These plugs into the 3D world are hard to fully remove. My work experiences provided me with a lot of energetic reinforcement. Even writing this essay required me to reckon with how I was seduced by the siren's song of power and authority that comes from intense corporate work.

Gradual change can feel frustrating for those of us who are transformational leaders. Yet, when we look to the Earth, we see that slow shifts can lead to monumental transformation—or sometimes just a subtle but meaningful variation. Just as Mary Magdalene's wisdom has rippled through generations of women, shaping the collective consciousness over time, we, too, can trust the pace of our own unfolding. But never abandon your dream of being a Priestess within the corporate world—your own Chief Magdalene Officer.

Beth Cavagnolo

Beth Cavagnolo is a lawyer, organizational psychologist, astrologer, and Priestess of the Divine Feminine. With over 20 years as a corporate executive, she has designed and implemented programs that redefined human resources and enriched organizational culture. Beth is known for her hands-on leadership style and improves internal systems, processes, and communication so they align with the organization's overall strategy.

Beth lives with her husband and two cats on a small farm north of Nashville, Tennessee.

Learn more:
https://www.instagram.com/the_kitten_witch/

Facebook astrology page:
https://www.facebook.com/winterwitch1221

CHAPTER 8

Bridging the New Paradigm

Resurrecting the Sacred Temple of Unconditional Love

by Dianne Chalifour

"Do not fear darkness; the darkness will lead you where the eyes cannot."

And so it was, the message that came through six years ago, as I wrote my chapter for the book *Sacred Body Wisdom, Igniting the Flame of Our Divine Humanity*.

Eight years ago, Divine Mother guided me to relocate my sacred business with clear instructions to "help ground the divine feminine consciousness" and "lead with a retail shoppe" filled with crystals, incense, candles, statues, sound bowls, and an Infrared Sauna, like the warmth of the womb. All things to support rebalancing and awakening feminine consciousness from the erasure that began long ago.

The Temple was erected on the second level above the retail area, a space dedicated to the remembrance of the Goddess. "Avalon" was clearly received when I asked for the temple name. I would later come to remember that Avalon was not only once a sacred land where Priestesses trained in the sacred arts, but a template imprinted within the collective consciousness. The Priestesses of the lineage of the Rose are awakening en masse. This is the lineage that called me, and my soul responded to the clarion call to awaken and remember the power of LOVE. As Priestesses of Avalon, we came to experience separation, knowing that we also had the template of the Divine Mother within us. It's a vow we once made to be here, now, in this timeline of intense separation, to shine the Light of Love. To remember the art of surrender into the Mother frequency, allowing Her light to lead us through any apparent darkness. To heal the separation from Mother that was ripped from us eons ago.

It's as if the mystery has been sprinkling rose petals upon my path so that I would find my way back. Nearly twenty years ago, as we pulled out of the hospital with our second born—our first daughter—a powerful knowing dropped into my awareness as if out of nowhere… "ROSE!" I shouted to my husband. "Her middle name is not Rachael, it's Rose!" When our third child was born—our second daughter—it was my husband who had a strong knowing and insistence that her middle name be Alexandra. Though he could not say why, I trusted his conviction and later sensed a connection to the Goddess temples. I feel a deep knowing we have served the Goddess temples in other lifetimes. I fondly recall my maternal grandmother tending her garden of many rose bushes and how much they meant to her. For many years, they lined the trellis at her front door in the terrace where she lived. Until one day, the powers that be ruled that they must be taken down as they weren't uniform with the other residences. There it was: dominance, control, decimation. My grandmother's beloved roses—and her heart—disregarded.

My temple resided in the background while the shoppe became a place of connection, healing, and refuge for many. I often felt frustrated that it wasn't unfolding quickly enough, but it was in those moments that I realized that the healing *was* happening! Right there in the shoppe, where tears flowed, people opened their hearts, and new friendships formed. She was always right there, yet so easy to miss when we're attached to an outcome we think is supposed to look a certain way.

That same year I opened the shoppe, I felt drawn to attend an anointing retreat in Glastonbury, England, believed to be the ancient site of Avalon. Diving deeply into healing collective trauma inflicted over thousands of years upon the feminine at the hands of patriarchal conditioning. Women sobbed and held one another in sisterhood as I clearly heard, "This is what the women need. Your mother didn't have this. Bring Avalon home." I flashed back to several years prior. In meditation, I lay across the lap of a Priestess dressed in a white cotton gown. She gently stroked my hair, saying, "This is what the women need now." I retracted at this notion, thinking, *I can't do that… I don't know how… women aren't ready…* surprised when I realized this being was Isis. I had experienced Her fierceness as an ally in energy clearings, but this was an entirely new side of her. This intimate mother-like nurturing was unfamiliar to me, but in that moment, I felt something deep down, an ache that I hadn't realized was missing from my life. My relationship with my own mother and two stepmothers after her was deeply strained growing up.

"Isis?" I asked.

"That's right. This is another form of power. This is what the women need," she responded in a soft, elegant voice.

I felt fear. As a spirit guide, she had shown me the power of fierceness, breaking through, and commanding energetic space. "But I can't hold that kind of power, that level of tenderness, of intimacy!" She was initiating me to remember another side of power—the power of love. Like the unconditional love of a mother, stroking the brow of a child with complete devotion.

Isis's words resonated deeply, and I knew with every fiber of my being that this was a path I was meant to walk. And so began my deeper journey over the next eight years...

As Priestess walking the way of love, there is a way in which we are both in the story of our life and viewing the story of our life. There would be many initiations in my business that challenged me to hold a higher frequency of love, no matter what arose. There were several floods requiring flooring and sheetrock replacement and painting. There were building construction disruptions, a loud and unpredictable window replacement project requiring my shoppe sign to be taken down, and brick refacing work on the exterior wall, creating a disastrous mess two days before a collaborative business event. I felt so angry after being told there would be no mess or business disruption. I felt so angry about the number of hours I would spend cleaning it up. I felt so angry about my session room, which was still awaiting repairs nearly two years after the last flood. I felt so angry the landlord refused to compensate me for an unusable, damaged space caused by no fault of my own. I felt so angry for being given multiple excuses as to why my sign replacement was continuously delayed.

It was the brick-refacing project that activated something deep within me. The words, *This is a reckless disregard for my business* came flowing through me as I expressed my utter frustration to management. Management... aka the patriarchal, hierarchical powers in charge! I felt like suddenly a powerful channel opened up, and I was being initiated into saying "NO MORE!"

As these disruptions continued, an inner knowing grew, and a bigger metaphor became clear to me: *We have been here before!* The ancient Goddess temples, once sacred and revered, were defaced and dismantled by patriarchal forces seeking control. Those who wanted to dominate were threatened by the ways of the divine feminine that held high spiritual principles in the nature of alchemy and awakening to the Godself within. It was an attempt to destroy the power of our divine connection so they could exert power *over*. The temples in ancient Egypt were defaced by the Romans. For thousands upon thousands of years, temples—and women's bodies as sacred temples—have been violated, defaced, shut down, and boarded up. The reckless disregard for the temple, for my business, my livelihood, *my* sacred space, felt like a living reflection of *Herstory*—a mythic pattern repeating itself once more. I felt Kali Ma once again, the fierce mother wielding her sword of justice within me. My body, my temple—the sanctuary where healing happens—where we remember who we are—must be reclaimed! The inner and outer sanctuary both exist as a hologram for the awakening of Divine Feminine consciousness. Justice and fierceness are essential aspects of love, just as vital as the soft, pure, open heart. It is the choice to uphold boundaries while remaining open and rooted in love, and to continue forth as an unwavering vessel of feminine consciousness.

For too long, women in particular have been caught in a victim consciousness loop from being perpetrated against. Each time, we have fallen deeper into separation because it activates old beliefs around all the times we have felt unsupported, unsafe, silenced, and unloved. We have developed a mistrust deep within after being violated and have become shut down. It's this consciousness that creates an illusion of separation from the Mother and initiates us to awaken into a new paradigm.

In a sea of chaos, there's only one true way through the confusion. It's resting in the internal knowing that always guides the way forth through to the truth in each moment. The middle way, where all that would separate, dissolves into oneness. By following the whispers of the soul, we are transported to our purest essence. Walking the way of love is a deeply alchemical process of continual transmutation. It's choosing to welcome all our experiences as necessary to illuminate the way forth while not judging ourselves for being caught in any kind of victim consciousness. Because when we judge ourselves, we are in separation. When we fully allow ourselves to feel a traumatic response—sinking all the way into it—we create the possibility of breaking through to the other side, into its ecstatic counterpart of creational life force energy. I have had to love the victim part of myself that has felt so angry, hurt, disconnected, and fearful in order to come through to the other side.

During the many hours spent cleaning all the sacred items in the shoppe after the masonry mess, I felt resentful that I wasn't spending time with my beloved Aunt Donna, my mother's sister, who had entered hospice just days before. We had been estranged for several years, but I loved her dearly. I had visited her in hospice the first night she arrived and thought surely she had more time. Upon my arrival, my cousin, whom I had not been in contact with for many years, decided to leave—she could not seem to face my presence there. When the nurse indicated concern for Aunt Donna because of her daughter's abrupt departure, my aunt excused the behavior, saying she was just hurting because she was losing her mom. "She loves me," my aunt said in a desperate tone.

In those words, I heard the deeper truth beneath them. It was a story carried through my entire maternal lineage: "I don't believe I am lovable." Though I treasured my aunt deeply, and we once were very close, she would inevitably push away anyone who got too close to her. She didn't trust love after a lifetime of trauma and pain. She closed off her heart in an effort to protect herself. I could see it in my bitter cousin choosing to stay stuck in a victim-perpetrator loop. I could clearly see it because I, too, have spent years healing this lineage wound. I saw it play out with my own parents, who, after twenty years of marriage, went through a bitter, ugly divorce when I was five years old. For over thirty-five years of my life, I believed my parents hated each other. But in the final days, when my mom was in hospice, my parents gifted me with their expression of love for one another. During my last visit with my aunt, she held up a metaphorical mirror, revealing once again the depth of this deeply ingrained belief within my lineage—the pattern of choosing to remain stuck in victim consciousness, shutting down, and closing ourselves off to love simply because we didn't believe it was possible.

And in understanding my aunt's struggle, I began to more deeply understand the work that needed to be done—the work of healing the wound of separation.

To heal this wound of separation, we must see clearly where we have turned away from true intimacy and resisted love. The disconnected feminine holds powerful keys for reconnecting to the true power of unconditional love, unfurling the rose-petaled heart, and resurrecting the noble masculine—

opening the way of the Rosa Mystica. Eons ago, Priestesses, Shamans, seers, and oracles prophesied these times to come and took vows to return. The Priestesses were well-trained in the art of alchemical union, marrying shadow and light into wholeness. Remembering that separation is an illusion that requires particular training to be able to choose love over hate, trust over fear, and compassion over judgment. Remembering that love is ever-present but requires us to consciously choose it for ourselves by enfolding any victimhood in love. We choose love again and again as an embodied frequency that is capable of dissolving the illusion of separation.

Humanity has been stuck in a paradigm of victim consciousness and toxic love because it has been deeply imprinted in our collective consciousness. However, just like Avalon consciousness, the opposite of this wounded story also holds true. We reimprint the template of love when we wake up and see that life is happening *for* us, not *to* us. Everything is offered to us as an opportunity to grow—to choose a new paradigm where we once again remember the power of love.

Unconditional love is the embodied expression of Divine Feminine consciousness. After thousands of years of oppression and the desecration of Her temples, we are being called to remember and rise—to resist the urge to shut out this sacred love in a world that so desperately needs love as a unifying force. So many of us are afraid to open to the power of love because unconsciously, we fear it will be taken from us again, or we'll be hurt, just like the decimation of Her temples thousands of years ago. We have been born into these collective and ancestral stories with little to no true imprinting of the Mother's unconditional loving presence. Our own mothers didn't experience it, yet they were imprinted with the wounding. Our relationship with them serves as a mirror for our ability to bond, shaping how we give and receive love. It influences whether we turn away or commit, whether we allow ourselves to depend on others, and ultimately, whether we can surrender into trusting the power and presence of love.

We must heal the collective rupture of trust in the sacredness of the temple—both within and without—after it has been violated, decimated, and shut down by those who have forgotten, those who have never known the depth of love we are now being called to remember. The true way of love lies in the unshakable trust that it can never be taken from us. We are never truly separate from love; as fractals of the Divine, we are initiated to remember that we are love, and to choose LOVE—even in the face of victimization, desecration, or defilement. When we allow ourselves to surrender to the embodied frequency of unconditional love—the frequency of the Mother—we will be shown the way.

Just as Isis's temple of Philae was reconstructed in a new location, we, too, must choose to reclaim and rebuild our own sacred temples again. It's messy and uncomfortable. We will encounter forces of the old paradigm that only know domination, control, greed, and deception. But we must break through the old paradigm and resurrect the Divine Feminine to experience the empowerment that comes with what we've learned. The reconstruction of our sacred temples—our bodies, our places of devotion—must take place within a new paradigm of consciousness whose foundation is built upon the way of love. We can no longer create from the wounded story that has been playing out for eons, where victim consciousness has us mistakenly believing that it isn't safe to trust our hearts and that our attempts at connection are unworthy and futile. It's time we step in and create a new timeline of consciousness, facing into the collective, karmic, and ancestral patterning that has created barriers to the unconditional love of the Mother. This is an alchemical initiation into the heart, requiring we feel and face all the ways we have projected our pain upon, judged, or withheld love and forgiveness from each other.

It's courageous and gratifying to choose the soul-seeking journey. We die to who we have been, that we may be resurrected into new life, awakening the soul self. "Do not fear darkness; the darkness will lead you where the eyes cannot." We must descend into the darkness, where we are initiated through multilayered versions of reality. We discover deep meaning and integrate lessons as we ascend with deeper wisdom. We are resurrected into a higher awareness, reconsecrated as we die to old beliefs. Sometimes, as with Aunt Donna and my mother, we die to be reborn into the everlasting nature of unconditional love. The death portal, be that physical or alchemical, brings us into rebirth. Aunt Donna had to die to the belief she was unlovable. I, too, have had to die to that belief over and over again, and choose to reconsecrate, to build that temple over and over again, no matter how many times it has been defaced, over and over again throughout history—*herstory*.

As a Priestess of Avalon, of the lineage of the Rose, I remember my vow to help ground this consciousness for this time of collective awakening. And so I choose to erect the temple in a new location after having been initiated through these experiences. I may continue to experience defacing and being shut down in various ways. But rather than seeing it as happening *to* me, I choose to see these initiating experiences as happening *for* me in order that I may rise above and transcend the old story of victim consciousness. From this embodied experience, I am taking everything I have learned into the consecration of the sacred—for my inner temple and for the physical temple space.

There is grief and pain in letting go of the current structure of my business, of this beautiful co-creation. But more so, through my willingness to feel it all, there is a deeper trust present. The wide range of experiences has served my soul's evolution, and I am being brought to another level of my sacred work. The temple is now front and center. This is a full-circle moment, showing me WHY I was brought here to help ground the divine feminine consciousness. It's a huge act of trusting in the unknown, and I feel excitement in what's to come!

Magdalene is a consciousness—an immense power forged through the frequency of unconditional love. To truly experience the full lattice of love, we must accept everything that appears upon our path as teachers. This requires we face our judgments, fears, resistances, and feelings of inadequacy and instead choose to transcend the stories that keep us locked in pain.

To move beyond it all, we must soften the layers of our shielded hearts, uncovering the eternal truth of love that has always lived within us. As we choose to let go, the consciousness of past experiences begins to dissolve—freeing us to embody love once more.

I choose the template of Sophia/Christ consciousness—the unconditional love of the Divine Mother and Father. The time for our sacred union has arrived. *Forgive them, for they know not what they do.* The old paradigm remains blind to the deep afflictions placed upon the feminine, unable to recognize the suffering caused by the invasive choices of patriarchal ways. I choose love while still holding firm boundaries. I choose to honor what has been lost by reconstructing the temple elsewhere—just as we did long, long ago.

I remember the vow of Love—and the resurrection of our sacred temples.

Dianne Chalifour

Dianne Chalifour is a transformational leader and ordained Priestess with over 30 years in the healing arts. Her down-to-earth nature creates a warm feeling of welcoming embrace to her presence. Her passionate support of the awakening feminine consciousness was born through Dianne's own healing journey and experiences of remembering the unconditionally loving presence of the Mother as a pathway to embodied wholeness. She holds this healing as essential to healing the split within our own relationships, particularly between mothers, daughters, and the Divine Mother.

Dianne holds deep, soulful temple experiences that support the awakening of inner wisdom and the embodiment of our true essence. Her guidance allows one to feel safe and seen while building a deeply rooted sense of authenticity and self-empowerment. Through 1:1 journeys, retreats, and group experiences, Dianne's devotion pours into all she puts her focus on.

As a metaphysical shoppe owner for over 8 years, Dianne shared her passion for incorporating sacred tools and practices to support humanity in shifting states of consciousness and awakening the sacred in our everyday lives. This passion pours forth as a faculty member of Priestess Presence Quintessia Mystery School, where Dianne guides women in awakening and remembering their medicine in a second-year curriculum called Apothecarium.

Dianne joyfully incorporates her love and deep connection to the magic of crystals, sacred anointing oils, and sound healing tools into all areas of her life, including her devotion as a certified anointing Priestess through the Rosa Mystica Mystery School. When she is not serving through her devotional work, Dianne enjoys quiet reflective time, connection with the natural world, and family time with her three young adult children, husband, and four cat familiars.

Learn more:
Email: dchalifour@earthharmonywellness.com
https://www.earthharmonywellness.com
https://www.facebook.com/earthharmonywellness
https://www.instagram.com/earth.harmony.wellness

Meditation ~ Sacred Temple of Unconditional Love
A journey of remembrance and inner marriage ritual

This 24-minute guided meditation and energetic transmission by Dianne is spoken with reverence and softness.

You will be guided to reconnect with your inner heart temple, meet the wisdom of the Mother, the nobility of the Father, and heal the separation within—gently, sacredly, and in your own time. You will be invited to write your own sacred vows as a remembrance of walking the way of love.

Accompanied by a beautifully crafted reflection guide featuring writing prompts, a rose anointing ritual, sacred imagery, and gentle practices inspired by the chapter.

Access here:
https://www.earthharmonywellness.com/sacred-free-gift

CHAPTER 9

WHAT WOULD LOVE DO?

by Sandra Corcoran

Over the past decade, there appears to have been a resurrection of interest in Mary Magdalene. Conversely, she has always been there, quiet, sometimes hidden, but nonetheless there to find. Perhaps Pope Francis's 2016 repentant liturgical speech elevating Magdalene's memory from sinner to "the Apostle of the Apostles" legitimized her religious position. Though for many, she has always represented a transcendent power of grace.

Mary Magdalene was not the only female apostle; others, like Joanna and Junia, are named in the New Testament. However, Magdalene always was avatar, priestess wife, and teacher of the "Christed" word. She never needed an outside orthodox authority to confirm the powerful role historically stolen from her. Mary Magdalene, in her nondenominational messages, encouraged inner exploration for spiritual transformation.

One of Magdalene's missions was to evangelize the teachings of Yeshua. The word "evangelize" comes from the Greek word *euangelizesthai,* which means to "share the news." Mary was not only the first one to see Yeshua in his Christed form, but also the first one to bring that news to the other apostles—although this news is at the heart of the Christian gospel, it is also what made the others envious of her.

The Gospel of Mary was a papyrus codex discovered in 1868 in Egypt and purchased by a German diplomat from Berlin. In Mary's words, she shared that Yeshua's teachings focused on the soul's spiritual journey—that we are whole unto ourselves and need no outside authority to find the Divine within. That becoming conscious of the Divine's deep love and embracing the realization of our own light starts with our descent into the heart, as a means toward enlightenment. Mary's teachings were to share what she and Yeshua had learned together—liberation of the soul does not need to come through death but is attainable in life.

Harvard-trained theologian Meggan Watterson has pointed out in her work that "Three copies of the Gospel of Mary have been recovered—two in Greek and one in Coptic. All three versions of her gospel are missing the beginning six pages, and then also, four pages in the middle." What was so incendiary that the political-religious leadership at that time, till today, do not want us to know? Was this why she was vilified for being a prostitute by powerful clergy over time? Was this why Pope Gregory the Great claimed that Yeshua removed 7 deadly sins from her? Was this why the apostles accused her of arrogance when she washed Yeshua's feet with spikenard? The truth is, Mary Magdalene was not a prostitute; that was Mary of Egypt who approached the hem of Yeshua's robe. Mary Magdalene did not carry 7 deadly sins—Yeshua was aligning her chakras for the divine work they would complete together. And the spikenard she carried was because she was a Myrraphore Priestess. She would apply Spikenard 3x's. Once to his feet at the wedding in Bethany; once when she threw her jar into the secret meeting when he met with Nicodemus, Joseph of Arimathea and some of the Sanhedrin before his death; and finally on Golgotha at the last supper when she anointed his crown for what was to come.

Despite centuries of spiritual and patriarchal bondage—starting with Magdalene's rejection by apostles Paul, Andrew, and especially Peter in the institution they organized; the Albigensian Crusade massacres; the Inquisition, even the unholy punishments executed on women by women in the Magdalene Laundries—Mary's teachings of love have been remembered, followed, and held holy by groups of both women and men throughout history. Her story has never faded because she lives in the hearts of the people.

Magdalene shared the "codes of love" after witnessing the death of her beloved. Death, as an alchemical process, forces us to enter the abyss and work our way back to the light. It is the dark womb where the soul must surrender to descent in order to transcend the mysteries held between life and death. Descent pulls us towards the soul's becoming. It is a part of the shamanic path, esoteric traditions, and often part of the priestesses' path. This was Mary Magdalene's path, in part because of her deep loss—to carry the mission of Love and Light, sharing Christ's teachings for humanity's spiritual transfiguration.

Death stepped onto my path as an unwanted teacher when, as a young mom, I lost my first daughter at sixteen months old, shortly after her openheart surgery. Death of "a beloved" is an excruciating initiation. It forces you to question everything, to exile the outer world, and enter the darkness alone. Death transforms you in unexplainable ways. It takes everything you thought you knew away from you, and in that deep loss, that woman, that "me" died, too.

My first daughter passed during a September Equinox, a time when the natural world is said to be in balance. Her loss forced me into one of the most unbalanced times in my life. I had been brought up Catholic but had rejected that rhetoric years before. However, I questioned if this was not a punishment for that rejection. Guilt programs and my early home life, along with those religious teachings, promoted punishment for not obeying the rules.

In the weeks that followed her death, I simply did not want to be here. I could not even comprehend where "here" was. It was in that place of pain that my first Indigenous mentor found me. In what I still believe was a miraculous gift offered through the Divine Mother's grace and love, a woman appeared in my life and told me, "It is time."

She Who Makes the Song of the Earth shared that I had promised to learn from a handful of Indigenous women, and she was to be my first teacher. Resistance was my first response. She insisted I had made Spirit this promise. I argued I had no memory of that promise. I was annoyed with her presumption; did she not sense I was deep in grief? It was then that she confided that she, too, had lost her first daughter. I had never said anything about my loss. I certainly had no context for any of this. After a few weepy standoffs, I figured I had nothing to lose; I had already lost it all, and so I agreed to work with her.

After several years learning to work with the elements, the elementals, the art of divination, and energy healing, I found myself entrenched in and enriched by these efforts. I also maintained my profession as a Special Needs Educator, although I did not disclose to many in my outer circle what I was doing. My initial desire to share was often met with their lack of appreciation, if not ridicule, for my excitement.

Over the years, one of her main teachings was to "work the energies" for what she simply called Moon Ceremony. Eventually, this led to my initiation in my late thirties into a sisterhood called the Sisters of the Violet Flame. These teachings had come out of Egypt, through France, and were bestowed upon *She Who Makes the Song of the Earth* in her late thirties by her Mohawk grandmother and a group of European priestesses.

This energetic transmission brought two things into my world for which I have profound gratitude: a deep healing from my grief resulting in the conception of my second daughter, who is a constant beacon of joy with her deep wisdom and wit. And one evening during Moon ceremony, as I "opened the gates," a voice from whom I perceived was the Dark Celestial Mother whispered a new name, *Starwalker Woman*.

Shortly after receiving my name, my next Native elder came into my world in yet another unexpected way. She would be my primary teacher and most cherished mentor for fourteen years. Grandmother Twylah Hurd Nitsch of the

Seneca People, *She Whose Voice Rides the Wind* and Keeper of the Traditions of the Wolf Clan, had also lost a child. Death and life are such fragile teachers.

Gram Twylah taught me a philosophical system called the Wisdom Wheels, which I still use in my therapeutic practice today. Her teachings centered on the power of the spoken word, teachings from the Star Nations, dreamtime decoding, and navigating the cycles we all encounter through the challenges and choices we make in life.

In the cosmo-vision of most ancient Indigenous cultures, the entire universe is alive and conscious. Stars, planets, moons, and galaxies continuously are birthed, expand, and dissolve in the great void, seen as a dark womb of light. They teach that the personification of Mother Earth is a central figure to be honored and respected, for she brings forth life within everything as her gifts to us. She receives her knowledge from the First Mother, the Dark Celestial Mother, for Earth, too, is within that "greater womb."

The original Black Madonna is an aspect of the First Mother. Ancient cultures saw her as a divine feminine principle, embodied in both the night sky and the dirt we walk on. As the Earth holds seeds in its black soil for germination, the Black Madonna holds space for us to seed consciousness. Her deep love and guidance lead to the awareness that there is always a wider reality than what we are experiencing—be that a mother's grief or a lover's grief.

Pre-Christian myths hold the Black Madonna as a spiritual force who creates and protects. She holds the twelve hermetic universal laws. She welcomes the dead home. She teaches the interconnectedness of all things and resides in our collective unconscious.

Post-Christianity would connect her to the Virgin Mary and concretize her form initially into black statues, called Black Virgins, which can be seen throughout Europe, especially in Italy and the south of France. The Holy Family was from Palestine and fled Herod from Alexandria, Egypt; they were dark-skinned. It wasn't until the Renaissance, when the Vatican commissioned great painters, that their countenance shifted to white, appeasing the ruling class.

Those devoted to the ancient Black Mother—both then and now—understand that whether she appears as Mother Mary, the Magdalene, or Saint Sarah Kali, the beloved servant honored by the Romani people in Saintes-Maries-de-la-Mer, France, she carries the same essence. Sarah Kali, said to have arrived in a rudderless boat alongside Mary Magdalene, her siblings Lazarus and Martha, Mary Jacobe, Mary Salome, Mary of Cleophas, Joseph of Arimathea, and Maximin, is part of a shared lineage. They are united in origin and purpose:

to teach the Way of Love to all beings. I believe Sarah Kali was not a servant but a midwife, traveling with Mary Magdalene to help her give birth to the child she was carrying (a daughter who would receive the name Sara and carry on the Holy bloodline, Sangreal).

The Black Madonna became my inner teacher. She knew the way through "my dark." Just as the Myrrhophore priestess Mary Magdalene anointed Yeshua three times with her unguent for his soul's liberation, the Black Madonna applied her liminal balm, encouraging me to rise again. Grief slowly released its dark grip, the teachings lit my path forward, and her love guided me back to a renewed sense of self.

My Native teachers saw the quality of black as the infinite mysteries held in the void of the All that Is; that is why they call it the Great Mystery. The night's darkness is a time of introspection, a time to listen to the ancestors, and the quiet time needed to shift perspectives. One of Gram's teaching places was out at night under the Milky Way. She felt the ancestors came from star systems, and "when we drop our robes," it was where we would return.

We talked about origin myths, the cycles of planetary times—Lemuria, Atlantis, the coming timeline called the 5th World or 6th Sun—all manner of topics. On this night as we sat with our tea, she asked me to find the Pleiades. She commented that ancient cultures across most continents share comparable stories about the Pleiades, known as the "Seven Sisters." That they are important female archetypes in many creation stories, heralded as star teachers, forces of nature, or divine beings. For generations, Indigenous cultures passed their oral stories down to immortalize ancestral knowledge and traditions for seven generations forward.

Gram Twylah instructed that the Pleiades are visible from nearly every part of the globe, which is why so many myths and stories surround this star cluster. Some Native American stories referred to the Pleiades as orphans who fled to the stars because they were not cared for by their families. In this interpretation, they symbolize coping with grief. I figured because my sorrow cropped up when I least expected it, that she was gently prodding me to evaluate how I continued to hold "my story." As usual, though, she was leading me to a more ancient myth to help connect myself with the infinite.

Without going into detail, expanding a bit on the role of the Seven Sisters is important to Mary Magdalene's story. The information comes from wisdom shared by my mentors and personal downloads in sacred sites from the Americas to Egypt and especially throughout France. These are not the Greek or Roman identifications with the Pleiades as goddesses, although they, too, offer one perspective; these were far older cosmic stories.

The Seven Sisters each had an aspect that they brought to the Earth plane to source into DNA during the Lemurian timelines. Ancient cultures did not consider Lemuria or Atlantis as mythological places; Lemuria predated Atlantis. This more ethereal continent was "seeded" to be the first enlightened, aware civilization of this evolving planet. The planet and those souls who volunteered for this grand experiment would take many incarnations to evolve. Other cosmic teachers and avatars would descend into physicality during certain epochs to encourage, remind, and "light" the way.

Also called the seven Star Mothers, they each held a "wisdom root" to be shared. Their gnosis, or spiritual truths, were seen as "the mysteries." Though each sister had a unique role, their unified purpose was to shift consciousness to advance Earth's and humanity's future incarnations. The goal, to remind us to resonate with the vibrations of Light and Love as cornerstones of our divinity. Introducing a few of the Seven Sisters will help to appreciate Mary Magdalene's role.

Alcyone was the sister who never experienced being earthbound. She held the space of constant light, infinite possibilities, and potentiality within the dark cosmic ocean. She is the Cosmic Dark Mother, Pachamama, Ma'at—the feminine force that serves as the foundational underpinning of universes.

Sterope was akin to Mother Mary, Isis, or the Hindu goddess Anjana in their conception abilities—the virgin concept of birthing new worlds from the void. In eons past, "virgin" did not mean "untouched." It referred to a woman who was autonomous in her sovereignty. Their mystery training was to bring forth something out of nothingness. The transformative power of inner alchemy as the concept of immaculate birth, or parthenogenesis, to bring the Light of the Sun/ the Love of the Son, to Earth.

Tarygeta could redirect evil, destroying that which was not vibrating in right relationship with the Laws of the Universe, to heal, restore order, and protect. Deconstruction to heal seems nuanced, but exercised with balance, it is still a divine calling toward evolution. Her lineage includes Sekhmet, Kali-ma, and White Buffalo Calf Woman.

Electra's initiatory power was to anchor energy like Hathor, Mary Magdalene, and Kaya Kwan Yin, using tantric vibrations to open and heal the heart. Tantra was (and is) spirituality combined with sexuality, not as sex but as directed life force energy. This lineage was to heal wounded warriors before they returned to their families, as well as to assist male avatars wishing to ascend into the full capacity of their divine lightbody construct. Their energetic role offered men a way to receive the imprint of pure light source energy, opening the eye of the heart to unconditional love, healing their inner separation, bringing them whole into their divine essence. These teachings embraced the purity of orgasmic divine union as a means of spiritual evolution.

Mary Magdalene's training came down through this lineage. It is important to consider that her job was to activate high-frequency energy—love and light—as a necessary pathway through the union of the physical body to open and actualize the lightbody. As avatars, Mary Magdalene and Yeshua both mastered divine union. As Christed souls, she served to assist Yeshua to be initiated into his ascension versus his actual physical death.

In his book *The Gospel of Mary Magdalene,* Jean-Yves Leloup suggests that "part of being in their human incarnation, these two avatars were in physical bodies; they were sexual beings." Each was tasked with elevating the other to hold the energy of their Light bodies within their physical bodies, to connect to Divine Consciousness.

By dissolving the boundaries of separation inherent in duality, and equally harmonizing to the divine within themselves, they succeeded in elevating consciousness within the other. The soul's yearning to be in union with the beloved, the Divine, is sparked by the holy fire within each of us, and made whole by the realization that we are not separate from the Divine. They offered a blueprint for humanity's ascension, though the physical self might encounter death, our divine Self does not.

These female lineages descending through the Pleiadian activation were also called the Seven Doves, Sophia, or the Mari's. The Sophia mysteries, the female aspect of the Godhead, is the energy from which all priestesses, goddesses, and feminine divinities evolved. Caves, temples, crypts, waterways, even sacred medicine rites, were hallowed spaces where initiates traveled to the stars or connected to other dimensions, for spiritual rebirth as well as consciously linking to the underlying awareness of the multi-verses.

In Aramaic, Mary comes from Miriam or "enlightened one." In ancient Egyptian, the root *mry* means "beloved." In their seminal work *Womb Awakening,* Azra and Seren Bertrand found in early Semitic cultures, the word for cave, or *marh,* also contains the root *mar*—the name of the Mari/Maria priestesses of "the old ways." They also share that in ancient Sumerian texts, "the word *mar* meant both 'sea' and 'womb.'" It is my belief that in the "ancient of days," Mary was a title, not a name.

As the female aspect of God, the Goddess—Holy Spirit, the Dove, or Sophia—brings forth all life through the sacred marriage of opposing energies. She is represented as a universal womb, seen from our perspective on Earth as the cleft of stars, the vaginal opening we perceive as the Milky Way, where all life comes through a universal portal, not ruled by time or space, infinite, and everlasting.

The Goddess represents the other half of duality—heaven and earth, spirit and matter, intellect and intuition, light and dark, fire and water, life and death, male and female. Yet, they all emerge from a singularity. Singularity ignited the spark of the primordial creation that birthed universes, just as the sperm and egg come together to spark our existence. Each relies on the other to exist; the Divine has two faces within its sole essence.

Life is not a linear path. Even pain is an invitation to evolve in our human journey. That is why the ascent begins with descent; to embody the inner work makes the unconscious, conscious. Mary Magdalene and Christ both knew this. Their spiritual gift was that the wisdom of this Divine plan is achieved through descent into human form, to "re-member" that we are not separate within ourselves nor from the All That Is. The soul's journey back to the Divine is an intimate one of recognizing the *I* in the *I AM*.

The Divine Feminine, whether as a symbol, philosophy, personification or even Her energetic imprint still palpable at sacred sites, is a beacon to bring us "home to ourselves." Sadly, history has continued to limit and marginalize Her importance across societal roles and laws. It is not only the patriarchy of religions or governments—unfortunately, females have also denigrated other women in the name of ownership. No one has ownership over Her teachings, and all have access to Her voice.

Understanding that this wisdom is not gender-specific can open pathways for any of us. A more harmonious route for humanity during these changing timelines demands an obligation from both women and men to restore psychological and societal beliefs and structures—through the reclamation and respect of the Divine Feminine, which by the very definition of creation is present in everything.

We will each face many types of deaths in our lives, some limiting, some overwhelming, each meant to redirect our life's course. Great or small, grief cannot be bypassed. To neglect loss removes one spoke in the "Great Wheel of Life." Grief reveals our faith, and as Gram often counseled, "You can't teach faith. You either have it, or you don't."

Death, whether one's personal loss or the death of a societal system to better serve humankind, is exactly what Mary Magdalene and the Christ were teaching: humankind's evolution depends on faith, despite life's harshness in finding a spark of love to expand connectedness. Which brings me back to, "What would love do?"

In the same way Mary Magdalene lived her life to share the codes of love despite her great loss... In the same way women across generations, whether through their bodies or as agents, created something new energetically... In the same way the Black Madonna and my mentors guided me to honor my daughter's short life as a precious gift of love...

My answer to this question is an echo of Gram Twylah's words: "Love is a choice, a commitment to something greater than the challenge."

Sandra Corcoran

Sandra Corcoran, M.ED., is an integrative coach in private practice whose work bridges the mundane with the cosmic. She is a trained shamanic practitioner, Akashic Record teacher, and internationally renowned intuitive Thoth Tarot Consultant for both businesses and personal clients.

Sandy worked as a Special Needs Educator and for three years as the Liaison Director of Education for her then-community homeless shelters. She is certified in a variety of modalities: Cranial-sacral therapy, PSYCH-K, TAG trauma method, and Kusick's Biofield Tuning. She developed a soul retrieval method called ART: Alchemical Reintegration Therapy.™

With a background in psychology, biology, and metaphysics, she was also mentored by Indigenous cultures throughout the Americas to navigate within the liminal spaces to recognize our innate connection to the world of living energies. Sandy uses a combination of systems to guide clients to make the unconscious, conscious.

Her cosmic initiation came from years as a contactee, and work with the late Harvard University professor, Dr. John Mack, in his Program of Extraordinary Experiences Research. She was one of only three cases of shared contact brought before the Human Subjects Committee at Harvard Medical School.

For 25 years, Sandy's insatiable curiosity has inspired her to lead sacred journeys throughout Mexico, Peru, the UK, and Türkiye. Her passions are initiating seekers in the ancient temples throughout Egypt and in France, guiding women to connect to the Divine Feminine archetypes of the Black Madonna, Mary Magdalene, and Mother Mary.

Author of *Shamanic Awakening*, she is an initiated Priestess in the Sisters of the Violet Flame. Her ultimate joy is time spent with her daughter, an Esoteric Astrologer who lives in CA, and acknowledging the joy participants exhibit during her pilgrimages when uncovering the mystery and magic within themselves.

Learn more:
www.starwalkervisions.com
www.StarwalkerVisions-SacredTravel.com

Thoth Akashic Record Reading

Receive $25 off a half-hour Thoth Akashic Record Reading with Sandy (normally $175).

I have offered readings internationally for 35 years as a supportive transformational tool for individuals in their personal evolution to make the unconscious, conscious. Your higher self is always trying to communicate concerning current life choices or challenges, but ofttimes we perceive the string of underlying issues as separate situations when there is always a link. A reading can bring both clarity and comfort during these changing timelines.

To claim your discount, simply email **sandy@starwalkervisions.com** with proof of your book purchase to arrange your session. I look forward to connecting with you!

CHAPTER 10

THE UNWRITTEN PATH—
NEITHER MARTHA, NOR MARY

by Sarah Devereux

When I was four, I wanted to fly—not so much with wings, but I was really interested in moving really fast and not touching the ground. Speed flying??? I rigged up the furniture in my bedroom—which was really the living room of our Victorian house—and worked out that if I jumped from the bed to the sewing box to the chair to my sister's bed and back to my bed, I could get around the room without ever touching the ground. I could do this faster and faster—and very early in the morning. Strangely enough, my mother objected to this use of her precious furniture. Particularly as it had been rescued after we lost our house in my dad's redundancy. It was a house filled with precious furniture and so many opportunities not to touch the ground.

Eventually, I broke the leg of the sewing box, and my flying career came to an end. My mother just bitterly said, "I knew that would happen if you kept jumping on the furniture." I looked at her in disbelief; I was not jumping. I was flying.

I did not want to sit—I did not want to sit at anyone's feet. The story circle in nursery was a case in point. I sat away and outside of the circle. I loved stories but I did not want to sit cross-legged and tight-lipped. One day, I drifted off, sitting on the outside of the circle and wondered what would happen if you put your fingers right inside you… I know I was bored, so I stuck my fingers down my throat to see what would happen. Can you tickle yourself from the inside out? Of course, I threw up and then had the guilt of being taken care of because I was poorly.

I hated sitting at the teacher's feet—I liked lying down or rolling or never being still. I rolled down hills a lot—Richmond Hill was favourite.

I liked being with my dad—he did interesting things, and I learnt quite quickly if I went with him, I did interesting things. I went in the car and I went places. Almost as good as flying. I did not like staying in. I did not want to stay in *ever*.

Mothers, aunts, and cousins stayed in and cooked things and cleaned things. They cooked and cleaned, and they hated it. My mother hated it. I hated it.

Women washed, scrubbed, cleaned, and cooked in my world, circa 1973. Men ate and drank, smoked, and talked. They went out and did things. I know what I was going to do, so I did. I was not going to be a woman and stay still.

At Christmas, men went to the pub and women stayed in and cooked. At Easter, men went to the pub and women cooked. At _____ (fill in the blank space for any or every high day and holiday or Sunday or Friday), fuck that, I was not going to stay at home and cook. Nobody in my house liked when cooking happened—my mother felt the food was out to get her and did not bend to her will, so why would I want to cook? If everything interesting was going on in the pub, why would I not want to be there? I used to stand outside the closed doors of pubs and smell the beer and smoke, knowing that by hook or by crook, I was going to enter the sacred ground. Or at least, on my 18th birthday.

I discovered pretty early—about 9—the delights of takeout and deli counters! Nothing could appease my mother more than me saying I would nip to the burger place for food—not the chip shop that was only for Fridays and fish. Her fingers whipped her purse out faster than greased lightning. Fortunately for me, in about 1979, a very fancy—to our eyes—American burger joint opened around the corner in not very cosmopolitan Fulham. It was allowed—it was foreign and posh!

I heard the story of Mary and Martha—I did not want to be either of them. According to the Catholic church, Mary sat quietly at Jesus's feet and listened. Martha stays in the kitchen and works. Why would I want to be a version of these Roman Catholic, late sixties, early seventies, post-Vatican council saints? I wanted to move—I wanted to fly and run and dance. I liked my body when it was in motion.

Luke 10:38-42, *New International Version*

[38] As Jesus and his disciples were on their way, he came to a village where a woman named Martha opened her home to him. [39] She had a sister called Mary, who sat at the Lord's feet listening to what he said. [40] But Martha was distracted by all the preparations that had to be made. She came to him and asked, "Lord, don't you care that my sister has left me to do the work by myself? Tell her to help me!" [41] "Martha, Martha," the Lord answered, "you are worried and upset about many things, [42] but few things are needed—or indeed only one.[a] Mary has chosen what is better, and it will not be taken away from her."

As I did not want what Mary wanted and as I certainly did not want what Martha wanted, I spent my childhood running away from kitchens and cross-legged circles. Once, as a "treat," I was taken to help a childhood friend's mum with her cleaning job. You can imagine my 9-year-old chagrin at this "treat"—no amount of hamburger and chips at the Wimpy was going to make up for the loss of my precious Saturday afternoon… cleaning?! To add insult to injury, it also necessitated the removal of highly coloured sticky sweets from a white velvet rug.

I hated staying in and I hated cleaning—was I odd? I did not fit either saint mould, and therefore, I did not fit in the culture of my family or environment! "Sit still" and "Be quiet" were the mantras that followed me always.

As I grew older, I developed a reputation for disappearing as much as possible—a fiver in my back pocket could mean at least a day and a half's absence from the house.

I was 13 when the disbelief grew into rage—I was standing in the church hall kitchen, assisting as was my lot on one of the interminable church do's when a priest came in. An able-bodied man with two arms and legs just dropped by. The whole kitchen, full of women of all ages, some elderly and infirm, up to their eyes in providing food for the church community, all immediately stopped and began preparing food—something completely different and infinitely superior from what was on offer—for this man. I felt the rage rise in me. He caught my eyes and made what seemed a somewhat feeble excuse whilst chomping on his ill-gotten gains. They were stopping work to talk to him—he had fuck all to say, as I had witnessed on numerous other occasions! This man, who demanded my time and energy by virtue of his gender and his dog collar. I did not want to be Luke's version of Martha and Mary again!

Time passed, and I observed how much I could not bear domestic tasks and how my mother could not bear domestic tasks. I learned to bake, but this was on my grandmother's terms—we baked for ourselves, in her kitchen, whatever we wanted, and we ate it whenever we fancied. We also drew, painted, and read. She taught me to work but for myself, to read, to learn, and to fly.

I was pregnant and *still* not still—I went, and my son came with me. We travelled all over London and then Europe exploring. We ate Deli and take away. Every weekend took us on an adventure. I kept moving.

Over the course of time, as grief and loss have confronted me, I have kept moving. It has been in the movement of the railway carriage, the sway of a coach, and the thrum of a plane that my soul has been quieted and my body soothed. At one point, I only had to hear the engine or a coach or train start, and my tears would flow. I never inhabited a kitchen or sat at the feet of anyone. I sat on floors rather than chairs—faster exits. I never locked a door or stayed in a kitchen longer than the time a pot of water boiled.

I baked less and moved more.

Not Martha or Mary.

And then.

What happened was miraculous—I did not learn to cook or clean, but I began the journey of returning and remembering. I began a journey of return—not listening without question at the feet of or serving in exhaustion but living in community and devotion.

I found the temple of the priestess. I found a sanctuary I did not know I needed. I found a place that I initially dismissed and until someone told me not to be a p----- and come in.

The first year I was anointed, I coughed and cried until my throat was raw and aching and my sides burned as I released into loving arms all of the pain. That year I learnt that I could be held in stillness—that I could sit *with*. Not at the feet of, but by the side of and in the arms of.

The second year, I learnt trust and respect on the anointing table—the trust of a woman to ask specifically for what she wanted and implicit trust that I would be able to give her this and that she would be able to respond in kind.

The third year, I moved from anointing table to anointing table holding space for, assisting, laying hands on, moving in the dance, music of body, the ethereal scent and contact of the oils, and understanding this was the gift—the dance of the sublime—in sweat, oils, tears, freed voices, and bodies.

The fourth year was to understand in lockdown that very little could lock my soul down if I chose to fly in temple.

And what of Martha and Mary? It has been this journey that has shown me the shackles of the interpretation of Martha and Mary—no more representative of the Magdalene or Martha.

The False Binary is just that—false. There is no "Mary vs. Martha" dichotomy. It took many years for me to rid my system of the traditional interpretation. My life was characterised by pitting Mary and Martha against each other, reinforcing a false binary. Service or silent stillness?

Neither woman chose between service and stillness—this was merely the utilitarian approach adopted by a male gaze for thousands of years. Neither Martha nor Mary was Martha or Mary. No woman or man is wholly contemplative or active. They are, as we are, both. We and they exist in multiple spaces.

The fifth year, I held a sword of initiation and reclaimed agency for myself and my lineage—for the grandmother, who died in childbirth and the grandmother, forced to give up work and independence, the women denied the value in their service or their stillness. They were neither Mary nor Martha.

The sixth year, I experienced the return of prayer as devotion—the remembrance of the rosary as prayer and a walking prayer, at that. I walked and prayed and remembered that prayer is the channel.

I remembered my father and the rare moments of stillness with him. My dad said the rosary, and he spent patient hours trying (and sometimes succeeding) in getting me to sit still enough to listen to the stories of the mysteries. He never required me to cook or clean.

Modern Christian feminism builds on the story of Mary and Martha to challenge patriarchal norms, reclaim women's roles in faith communities, and advocate for gender equity. Contemporary sources say their story serves as a powerful symbol of women's agency in both domestic and spiritual spheres.

From a secular feminist perspective, sources say Mary and Martha's story is not about competition but about women navigating gender roles and claiming space in a patriarchal society. Both women are important, and Jesus' response challenges the limitations placed on women, affirming their agency in choosing how they engage in the world.

For me, the binary position of either Martha or Mary denies the complexity and depth of the marriage of the human and divine, which both women embodied—there was no Martha or Mary, created by Luke and utilised to create one-dimensional versions of multidimensional spiritual leaders. Yeshua did not choose either one but demonstrated respect and reverence to equals in the spiritual path.

The seventh year, I was initiated into the community of touch.

Luke 7:38, *New International Version*

[38] As she stood behind him at his feet weeping, she began to wet his feet with her tears. Then she wiped them with her hair, kissed them and poured perfume on them.

    I lay on the table believing in my arrogance that I was there to instruct, help, assist, and excuse. I lay on the table, four women assembled, and the tears flowed. As I surrendered to the touch, I became aware that there was no beginning or end, no ego or personality—there was simply devotion and adoration. The kiss of the divine on the body, the sacred practice of four divine beings. No stillness or service but deep and committed practice in love and remembrance.

    My tears flowed into my hair—their tears and hair tangled and mingled with mine and truly, healing flowed between us all.

    The Magdalene's gift to Yeshua was the anointing of the priest by the priestess, the healing and haling by the wise woman, the anaesthetic before the challenge of initiation, and the love of a woman for her soul partner. There is no binary here, only the multidimensional gift of the priestess to the anointed one.

    My gratitude for this remembrance and work in the world is immeasurable. I never wanted to be Martha or Mary—neither did they.

    I do not sit still. But I do hold space, and I have come to know the sacred within me.

    Not in a kitchen, not in a church, but a temple built in motion, in memory, in the fierce devotion of women who refused to sit still or be still unless by choice in communion. The path was never between stillness and service—it was the dance between them, the sacred choreography of spirit in form, of devotion, of fierce reverence.

    The work—this remembering—is not a retreat into silence or servitude. It is a rising, a return, a reclaiming.

    I do not cook. But I do feed.

    I do not clean. But I do clear.

    I do not kneel. But I pray in devotion.

    I was born of the desire for the temple, the table, the open road, the anointing. I was born to remember that devotion is not submission—it is presence.

    And I still don't cook.

Acknowledgments

In gratitude for the journey: Elayne Kalila Doughty for the invitation and endless love, Jacquie Shenton for the "push," Clodagh O'Connor for her devotion, Susan Usman for her strength and care, Carmen Angelique for her belief and Jackie Kamlet for her courage.

SARAH DEVEREUX

Sarah Devereux is a psychotherapist and apprentice focaliser on the 13 Moon Mystery School path. She is passionate about the process of change through the reclamation of our story and in the validation, its ability to support everyone in living the life that they wish to live. Sarah worked in mental health services in the public sector for twenty-five years and delights in supporting people to find the space and strength to gain clarity around patterns of relating and ways of behaving that may no longer serve them. Sarah has been known to throw everything in the air from time to time and 6 years ago moved from London, her home and comfort zone, to Hereford, 1/2 mile down a single-track lane. She is meditating on, enquiring in, and now writing about the new iteration of the witch at the end of the lane or, more likely, the priestess at the end of the path. Sarah is as ever supported by the love of the Priestess Presence temple and initiation and sisterhood in Enter the Mystery circle. To the one heart.

Learn more:
https://sarahdevereux.uk

SACRED GIFT

Audio Version of Sarah's Chapter

My words are on my website—an audio of this chapter—my words in my words—please come along, have a listen to this chapter and other writing, and then let me know your thoughts!

Access here:
https://sarahdevereux.uk

CHAPTER 11

The Magdalene Apocalypse

by Elayne Kalila Sophia Doughty

I am the Death Maiden.

I am the Illuminatrix.

I am the threshold between the worlds of form and formlessness.

I am she who holds you as you slip between the veils of the worlds—
the visible and the invisible.

I am the beginning and the ending:
life, death, and rebirth.
I am the promise of immortality and resurrection.

I stand at the gateway, holding the lamp of illumination
that comes from the distillation of your soul essence.

I am the silence and still power.

I am she who signals that there is a great transition underway.

I bring you to the still point, and whisper in your ear
that it is time to take a journey into the underworld to shed your skin
and reveal the greater truth of who is here now.

Deep in the night, I sit in candlelight. I call Her forward as I so often do in this way. I simply open my computer and begin to let the words flow.

As I empty, an image of the veiled Magdalene arises. Her veil touches my skin and caresses me. I am drawn between the worlds with her twirling and whirling like a Sufi dancer...

I am taken.

In this timeless space, over and over again, she reveals herself, the ethereal mist of her veil lifting and falling away. I make out the contours of her face, the shape of her presence. I feel intoxicated.

And I remember...

The veils are falling... the time is now... *apocalypse* is rooted in the Greek word apokálypsis, which means "uncovering, disclosure, revelation."

The UNVEILING.

Breathing heavily as if I have been dancing for a long time, I resurface...

What if this unveiling, this apocalypse, was one that reveals all that has been hidden? Not just shadowy, horrifying deceits and abuse but also incredible beauty and potential. All the light and shadow that has hidden behind the veil of this insanely imbalanced patriarchal nightmare we have been living through in the last few thousand years...

Magdalene Speaks...

I love veils. There is allure, mystery, and drama in my veil.
All the classic movie stars knew the power of the veil fluttering before your eyes.

To be veiled is powerful when it is by choice. And to enter between the veils is to be able to navigate between worlds of form and formlessness.

The veil has afforded me a way to make my entrance from the realms of the hidden, to enter in without being fully seen, from the opaque and the oblique.
I am at home living here.

I have been veiled for a very long time—I am one who walks between the veils.

I am she whose face has been hidden in plain sight within every woman—
and yet veiled.

Do you see me?

The veils are like a soft mist rolling off the dewy grass as the sun rises, when all is silent and quiet. I am clothed in dark and light, and I shapeshift, bringing you with me between the worlds. I am liminal by nature. And you will never fully see me, for I am not of this world, and yet I am within you.

There are layers and layers of tulle-like veils that I walk with. Some of them are there by design, and some have been placed to hide and silence me. There is discernment in being veiled. Some things need the diffusion of the veil for us to come to them.

Brides wear veils, and so do those who are grief-stricken and mourning. And then those of us who feel the shiver at the mention of the Magdalenas who walked as the Red Veiled Sisters…

Hail the white veil that holds the secret of the untainted, fresh innocence of the bride at oneness with Goddess—the original virgin. For those who have been taken back into the essence of who they are. We cannot look the innocence in the eye, or we might taint it.

Hail the red veil that holds the secrets of our blood mysteries—the most taboo and maligned of our wisdom. It is for those who hold the power of our feminine flow, for those who know the magic and mystery of birth.

Hail the black veil that holds the tears and keening wails of the grief-stricken ones. For those who are moving between the realms, grief walking, death walking. We cannot look death straight in the eye—we might be petrified by it… we must first see it through veiled eyes.

To be veiled is powerful when it is by choice. To enter between the veils is to be able to navigate between the worlds of form and formlessness.

The Black Veil

I am lying in the ER hospital bed. My heart is racing, flying out of my chest like a rabid jazz band is playing inside of me. I am sweating, my head feels like it is going to explode, and my stomach is cramping and burning so much that I can't breathe. Somewhere deep inside, I wonder, *Am I dying?* I am covered in monitors and IV tubes.

I am scared.

I feel myself slipping between the veils.

At some point, they say, "Your heart is asynchronous, and we must admit you." I am wheeled onto the cardiac ward. I slip still further into the dark. I am in some bad movie.

A doctor comes in and says to me that I have an acute case of diverticulitis and arrhythmia.

Right there and then, I feel the black veil being placed over my head. And I am taken.

I am squirming—I want out of here. I don't want a bloody black veil over my head, and I certainly don't want to be in this pain. And I don't want to see what is here.

I am plunged into a state of panic.

I am swirling and twirling, resisting and fighting.

Yet somewhere right at the very back edges of my veiled consciousness, I know this place. I have been here before. This is not the first time I have been taken to the underworld.

I am tussling in the dark, demons in every corner. I am in more pain than I have ever been in my life. Pain that is searing through every cell of my being, not just physically; my mind is being tormented... somewhere deep in the dark, I hear myself wailing.

It's the drugs. The Dilaudid is making me hallucinate. I am seeing ghoulish figures, decaying bodies. I feel like I am in a horror movie.

Am I losing my mind? Will I ever find my way out of here?

I am in the dark. And as I descend deeper...

I can sense Her. The Death Maiden. The Myrrohphore. The Magdalene.

She is sitting very still in the centre of the blackness, a black veil covering her entire body. A bright white pearlescent light pulsating from her heart.

She begins to speak, her voice a quiet hum that vibrates in my bones, uttering words that I know to be true but still do not want to hear:

> *Beloved, the black veil does not conceal—it reveals. What you fear in the shadows is only the mirror of what you have yet to love within yourself. The black veil of death is but a passage, a chrysalis from which the soul emerges renewed. Do not look away from the darkness, for it is where I dwell, holding the lamp aloft to guide your steps. I am here to illuminate the way.*

This is the apocalypse of your being. This is the revelation of all that has been hidden in plain sight. The unveiling is not to destroy but to transform. It is not to punish but to heal.

Let this be your initiation, your awakening. Take the black veil with you into the depths, and there, shed what no longer serves.

She swoops around me, and I feel her veils pulling me deeper still. I am too tired to tussle.

I land in a dark cave. *Not here again,* I wail. The last time I was here ten years ago, it was a miscarriage that had thrust me between the veils into the underworld.

As I lay there, too weak to fight, the air around me shifts. The veil sharpens my perception, allowing me to peer into spaces hidden from ordinary sight. Sitting in the corner is a veiled woman sobbing, then wailing, then keening. She is wracked with grief, shuddering and swaying. I go to her and embrace her. Her tears become my tears, her keening mine. I dissolve into her... swaying, rocking, crying, wailing, keening...

The keening grows louder—a symphony of anguish that fills the cavern. It is primal and raw, and it terrifies me with its depth. Yet, as I dissolve further into the embrace of the veiled woman, I realize it is not just hers, not just mine—it is the collective grief of generations of women who have suffered in silence, their voices muffled by veils *not* of their choosing. It is the pain of the earth herself, crying out through us.

The Magdalene's voice hums softly again, like a thread weaving through the cacophony.

Beloved, this is the alchemy of grief. The wailing rends the veil, splitting it open to reveal what lies beyond. Let it tear you apart. Let it make you whole. Come deeper into that which you are terrified of, lean in, move closer...

I turn in the darkness and stare straight into my Mother's face. Her eyes are watery. I resist the urge to turn away—I hold myself there. I have spent my life turning away from her. And as I stay, I feel a powerful shuddering in the core of my body.

My Mother, Maggie, suffered from diverticulitis along with many other illnesses, including four rounds of cancer. She had medical and psychological issues her whole life. She lost so much. And we lost each other.

Memories begin to shudder free from my blood, breath, and bones. I see images unveiling themselves from the past.

Me at 5 years old, seeing her not able to walk or speak properly after six weeks of being in a coma from meningitis.

Me at 6 years old, seeing her skeletal and bald after her chemotherapy.

Me at 8 years old, saying goodbye to her, her arms wrapped around me as she convulsed in tears of longing and grief.

Me at 9 years old, telling my Father that I didn't want to go and visit her anymore through my own convulsive tears.

Me at 51 years old, at the funeral home, anointing her body and laying rose petals all around her.

The memories of heartbreak and unrequited love sear through me—a deluge of inconceivable grief and tangled loss.

I couldn't save her, I didn't know how to help her, I couldn't help her suffering, I was scared of her and scared of becoming like her…

I ran from her.

I put 6,000 miles between us.

I was terrified of being her.

But more than that, I was also terrified of admitting that I had hated myself for leaving her.

I feel a crack in my heart. The palpitations are racing so fast. I feel like my heart has shattered into a thousand pieces. I feel all of the ways that I shut out my mum's pain, all the ways that I avoided feeling her suffering. All the ways that I judged her and kept myself separate for fear that if I felt it all, I would die.

I feel her suffering, her fear, her pain—all the sickness that she endured in her life. And all the ways in which I avoided her. I am broken into pieces. I am being pulverised by the waves of grief.

In the suffocating darkness—when I can no longer fight—I surrender.

And I finally feel the love that I had withheld from her all of my life begin to melt in the darkness, the feverish moans, the nowhere to hide and nowhere to run. The apocalypse of my own well-tended strategies for avoidance being revealed.

I am ready now.

The veiled woman before me shifts, her sobs quieting as she lifts her head. Her face is a mirror of my own, streaked with tears, her eyes hollow yet filled with a profound knowing. She reaches up and begins to unravel the black veil, thread by thread, until it floats away into the shadows. Beneath it, she is luminous, her face radiant with a light that seems to pour from within.

I hear her whisper, "This is your inheritance: to carry the grief, to feel it fully, and to transmute it into love. You are stronger than you know."

And then she is gone.

I sit alone in the cave, the silence like a balm. The darkness no longer frightens me; it is soft and comforting, a womb holding me as I begin to rise. My body feels different, lighter, as though I have shed more than just tears. I am still weak, still trembling, but there is a clarity now—a sense that I have touched something eternal within me.

I feel something very ancient arising, as if the very fabric of my being is unraveling, not into destruction but into liberation. The veils I have worn—the stories, the identities, the fears—falling away, and in their place, a new garment of light begins to weave itself around me. It is not something I am to wear; it is something I am becoming. A robe of illumination spun from the essence of my soul.

As I emerge from the cave, I see the Magdalene waiting, her veils shimmering like gossamer in the twilight. She extends her hand, and I take it.

She speaks again, her voice a gentle murmur against the backdrop of birdsong.

> *The dance of the seven veils is ancient and much misunderstood. It is the dance of being veiled and unveiled. To be veiled is to wield power through mystery. It is to protect what is sacred, to draw others into the depth of their curiosity and reverence. The veil is the guardian of truth, offering a space where transformation can occur unseen, like the seed germinating in the dark soil. The veil shelters what is tender, what is not yet ready to be exposed to the harsh light of the world.*

> *To be unveiled is an act of courage and revelation. It is to stand in the fullness of your truth, bare and radiant, offering yourself as a mirror to the world. The unveiling is not a loss of mystery but a sharing of it, an invitation for others to see the infinite facets of your being. To unveil is to claim your place as both human and divine, the seen and the unseen united in one.*

> *Both states are sacred. To veil is to hold the power of the hidden. To unveil is to share the light of the revealed. You must learn to move between them as I do, as the tides ebb and flow. The veils are not boundaries; they are bridges. They are the weave of life itself, connecting the worlds of form and formlessness.*

Feel the wisdom of the veils within you now. Know when to cover and when to uncover, when to hold close, and when to let go. You are the keeper of this mystery, and in your hands lies the power to weave a new world. The veils are not gone; they are yours to don and discard as you walk the eternal dance of the unveiled and the veiled. And so the unveiling continues.

Beloved, you are no longer bound by the veils placed upon you by fear, by shame, by the past. You are the one who chooses now. Carry the black veil when you need it; let it guide you through the shadows. But remember, you are more than the veils you wear. You are the light that shines beyond them.

I am the ouroboros eating her tail.

I am the place of rest and regeneration.

I am the resurrection that awaits you in the darkness.

I am the great fertile void to which everything is composted.

I am here to take the old garments that kept you clothed in a form that's no longer alive…

Set Sail, Set Sail, One thing becomes another in the realms of the Mother.

Receive me, for I am here to anoint you with a garment of illumination— a robe of light.

I am the wick of the candle that is lit and

I hold the door open, so you may let go.

Release.

Step over the threshold.

Elayne Kalila Sophia Doughty

Elayne Kalila Sophia Doughty is a visionary spiritual leader, ordained priestess, transformational guide, and author devoted to the rise of the Divine Feminine. She is the founder of the Priestess Presence Temple—a global sanctuary where women reclaim their sacred power, embody their truth, and lead with fierce grace.

An ordained priestess and focalizer of both the 13 Moon Mystery School and the Rosa Mystica Mystery School, Elayne Kalila brings decades of depth, devotion, and embodied wisdom to her work. Through ritual, spiritual mentorship, and priestess arts, she initiates women into a life of purpose, presence, and soul-rooted leadership.

She is the author of multiple sacred works, including *The Sacred Call of the Ancient Priestess: Birthing of a New Divine Feminine Archetype, Voices of the Avalonian Priestesses: Hearing the Call of Essence, The Path of the Priestess: Discover Your Divine Purpose, The New Feminine Evolutionary,* and the beloved *Magdalene Rose Oracle.* Each creation is a living transmission of the feminine mysteries, designed to awaken and empower the modern-day priestess.

Elayne Kalila is also a devoted teacher of Mary Magdalene's mysteries and has taught highly acclaimed programs with The Shift Network, where she has cultivated a powerful body of work that brings the Magdalene consciousness alive through deeply experiential, embodied, and transformational temple teachings.

She is the host of The Red Podcast—a bold, unfiltered space for RED women leading from the edge, birthing new worlds through their bodies, hearts, and minds.

With deep reverence for beauty, shadow, and transformation, Elayne Kalila offers retreats, summits, mentorship, and ceremonial spaces that empower women to rise as conscious, heart-centered leaders. Her presence is a sacred invitation—to remember who you are, root into your essence, and walk the path of embodied devotion.

Learn more:
https://pp.priestesspresence.com
https://elaynekalila.com

SACRED GIFT

Awaken Your Inner Magdalene
Explore Your Unique Expression of the Divine Feminine with the Magdalene Rose Oracle Quiz & The Red Podcast Council

The Magdalene Rose Oracle Quiz
Which of the 6 Faces of the Magdalene is Most Alive in You? This is your invitation to step deeper onto the hidden path within, guided by the living presence of the Magdalene. The quiz lifts the veil on your inner oracle, revealing which Rose archetype is walking with you now. It offers you a symbolic map to remember your innate wisdom, your gifts of love and consciousness, and how to embody them in your daily life as a living flame of the Magdalene.

The Red Podcast Council
The Return of the Notorious Red Women

Raw. Revealing. Reverent.
Join spiritual rebels, temple keepers, and wild women leaders in intimate conversations about power, longing, and sovereign embodiment. This is a sacred audio circle, a living council where the voice of the Magdalene rides the breath, weaving stories, sharing transmissions, and calling you to act from your deepest truth. Each episode brings you closer to the heartbeat of the Sisterhood of the Rose—reminding you that your voice, your truth, and your presence are part of a global web of inspiration that dissolves old bindings and frees the wild fulfillment already alive within you.

What fire did you come here to burn?

Access here:
https://discover.priestesspresence.com/magdalene-unveiled-opt-in-page-2025

CHAPTER 12

INITIATION—THE HIGH PRIESTESS PATH

by Molly Douglas

"The wound is the place where the light enters you."

—Rumi

I release and surrender to the flow of love that will heal me.
I release the wounds that end with me.
I release the conditions, beliefs, and behaviors that no longer serve me.

I am here to heal a legacy and embody a frequency of safety, peace, and tranquility. Within the body, mind, spirit, and soul,
I create a new sanctuary inside and out of me.

To all those lifetimes when it has not been safe to be an embodied, sexual, sensual, mystical, confident, independent, authentic, empowered feminine being…
this is our time.

We have a right to be free.
And so it is!

Mary Magdalene has been a guiding light at every pivotal moment of my soul's journey. She has helped me remember and reclaim the archetypes and parts of myself that align with my true essence and purpose here on Earth. Through her guidance, I've come to understand that Mary and the Magdalenes are the role models for the modern-day priestess, guiding me and so many others to fully embrace the high priestess path and Divine Feminine awakening happening on the planet at this time, to restore harmony and balance. It's a path of liberation from shame, fear, and isolation—a return to Love without conditions.

As a feminine leader in this transformative era of *her-story*, I've realized that my wounds are the very places where I've discovered my gifts and soul purpose—gifts I am called to share in service to others. To be a truth-teller for the illusions of how women have been programmed not to feel worthy or divine. Gathering tools to transcend generational sexual shame and trauma and reclaim divine power and pleasure by embodying the feminine and empowering the soul, knowing the truest, most authentic version of myself. A Divine Alchemist and self-healer, a Creatrix and conscious co-creator with the universe. A Holy Rebel and spiritual leader who is a keeper of ancient wisdom and a voice to speak truth. An oracular channel and guide for others. This path is to go against the grain of societal and patriarchal systems and deeply ingrained misogyny. It is a journey of reclaiming our true value and worth while planting the seeds of this divine birthright for others to nurture and expand upon. This is not just a *me* thing but a *we* thing. This profound insight surfaced during my first women's retreat in the UK, a journey that marked a significant turning point in my spiritual awakening.

A Remembrance of Something Sacred

On June 10th, 2019, I traveled 5,000 miles to Rise Sister Rise, a spiritual self-care retreat, where I gathered with 23 other women. After three planes, two trains, and a taxi ride, I arrived. The energy here was quite magical—so much familiarity among the women. Faces, eyes, stories, jobs… it all felt so familiar. *How do we know each other?* I asked myself. I knew deep in my soul I was supposed to be with these particular women.

"What does your soul want?" This was the first question our mentor and guide Rebecca Campbell asked that evening as we gathered in our first of many sacred circles.

To heal and be nourished by the Mother and so much more, I answered silently. I had no idea what was in store with this request I had just sent out to the Universe.

That next morning, Rebecca guided us through a meditation called "Gifts of the 3 Graces: The Maiden, The Mother, The Elder." This meditation prepared us for our outing to the sacred sites in Glastonbury, including the Tor, the Chalice Well, and the Red and White Springs. I had vivid and moving visions while in this meditation. My gifts came through as follows:

From the Maiden, I saw myself naked, dancing with my sisters, embraced and surrounded by sacred living waters. Rising without shame or fear. Just LOVE.

From the Mother, I saw Mary Magdalene place her hand over my heart and say, "The heart is enough. Here is where I wrap you in wings of love."

From the Elder, a flowing, wise, and luminescent being came over and swirled something up over my chest. I heard *trust the magic*. She then waved her hand over my third eye, opening it up, and laid a crown of wisdom on top of my head. I had body chills everywhere when I came out of the meditation, feeling the sacred energy so strong within and around me. I had also just learned that Glastonbury holds the frequency of the heart chakra of the planet and also the third eye! I would continue to have such strong visions while on this trip, including seeing auras and ancient symbols on people, as if I could see their true spiritual lightbody shining through their skin.

The Tor

Our first stop was visiting the ancient Grandmother Oak tree on our way to the Tor. Listening and sending love to the great Oak, we made our way forward. As I walked up the ancient Tor site with the rest of the women, I noticed on my phone that it was 11:11 am on the 11th of the month. I took a screenshot. I had my phone out, taking many pictures, including white petals scattered on the ground in the shape of hearts and other sacred symbols jumping out at me as we made our way along the path.

As we began our climb up the hill to the Tor, I had a strong sense I had done this before, but this time felt different. I wanted to circle it, moving up in a slow spiral, but we were walking up one side to walk down the other. It was so cold and windy at the top and, unfortunately, quite unpleasant. It was hard to connect, and the fierce winds kept throwing me off balance. I just wanted to go back down. This was not what I had imagined.

The Chalice Well

Our next stop was the Chalice Well. The weather seemed to shift once we came down, and we had an enjoyable lunch on the grass at the well gardens. Again, I noticed sacred numbers as we ate. It was 12:12 pm! I took another screenshot. I was in awe of the beauty around me with the flowers and the sacred symbols. As I ate my lunch, I listened to Craig—Rebecca's husband and one of our guides—share stories about the Red Spring and White Spring. He talked about the White Spring and how protected and sacred the community holds it. He told us that if we wanted to get in, we could and that even though the water is ice cold, straight out of the Earth, some choose to dip their feet in it or even get in naked. *Naked.* This idea felt powerful to me. Sacred. The words ritual and ceremony came to mind. Rebecca had told us earlier that the Red Spring was connected to the sacred feminine and the White to the sacred masculine. Although we had private access to the White Spring, the Guardians of the Spring—who were all males—would be there as they took their jobs very seriously. We could anoint sacred possessions, drink from either spring and bring our swimsuits if we felt called to get into the white spring, which would be our last stop for the day.

We were free to roam after lunch, and I found myself over by the Chalice Well. I sat for a few minutes with others in silence but was drawn to head over to a little cove next to the well where there was a statue of Mary holding a child and a small altar with a few lit candles. A couple of my sisters from the retreat were there, and I found a seat on a bench next to one of them. As I looked down, I saw a cute little porthole with an iron cover. It looked like it might have been another opening to the well. As I continued sitting there in silence, I began to hear music! I thought it might be coming from outside the garden somewhere, but as I listened in more closely, I realized it was coming from the opening in the ground! As I sat there immersed in the joy of the peaceful sound, I began to receive visions of a green dress. A ceremony. A sacred gathering. I could see a young woman coming of age.

The Initiation. I remember.

I remembered being a girl of 14, standing on the threshold of a sacred initiation into a sisterhood—a Druid Priestesshood, as my guides would later reveal. I felt a profound sense of sacredness and a vow to Mary Magdalene. So loved. So cherished. I was being given a job—a responsibility to be a keeper of sacred power and magic. I would be known as a Priestess, a Keeper of Sacred Knowledge, following in the footsteps of my sister. Her time was now. Mine would come later.

I saw myself back in an ancient time, walking down the spiral of the Tor, having just been marked by the feminine. So much emotion was flooding through me. I was sobbing on the bench, trying to write down in my journal what was coming through the visions I was seeing. A sister reached over and touched my leg to let me know I was being supported.

As I sat there remembering, I became overwhelmed with feelings of betrayal. Hurt and anger began to rise in my chest. *She did not keep me safe. She betrayed me. She did not protect me.* I struggled with a range of emotions as these ancient memories surfaced. Was this actually now? This story. It was a familiar one. A repeat of this lifetime. Familial wounds. Ancestral wounds. I paused in reflection and then brought myself back to the story being shown to me as clearly as a movie in my mind. *What happened? How did it end?* I asked my guides to show me more. They then revealed memories of being torched for casting her magic. She trusted her Divine. She spoke her spiritual truth. She owned her gifts of divine alchemy and oracular insight. Then she was ridiculed and her sisterhood persecuted before her. She was then burned alive. The deep, guttural fear of being fully *seen* and *heard*—a struggle I've carried so heavily in this lifetime—was finally beginning to make sense. This was the ROOT—the hot, hot root of it all.

The Mother(s) Wounds

I began to auto-write as the pieces of my mother wound were being illuminated for me to see through. I wrote:

> *It is safe for you to return now, Divine Child of the Stars.*
> *Your voice is needed. Your leadership is empowered,*
> *and your creative energies are gifted.*
> *Use them all now.*
> *Share them without restriction.*
> *Rise. It is time for you to lead again without fear or shame.*
> *It's time to unblock your voice, knowing that your power to lead is safe now.*
> *We will hold you over and over again.*

I took a breath and thanked my guides—especially Mary Magdalene and Mother Mary, who shared this message with me.

A Stranger Holds Me

As I gathered myself back up and out of the gardens, I found a clearing and some sunshine and heard the sound of water running. I saw the Red Spring opening—it looked like a beautiful tropical water fountain. I decided to walk through the sacred wading pool to soak up any gifts I could. As I sat down to take off my shoes and socks, I looked over and saw a man who appeared as though he could have come out of the Renaissance period. He had his back turned to me, talking to a woman next to him. He must have felt me looking over as I walked to the pool. I met his eyes and almost froze in my steps. As his gaze met mine with a gentle smile, I saw he had my brother's eyes. My oh-so-wounded brother! My brother, who struggled to find his way in this lifetime. My brother, who felt his own betrayal by his mother. My brother, who was my childhood abuser and who had chosen to commit suicide a few years earlier.

As I walked through the pool and back out, I knew he was here with me. Cleansing his wounds, too. His mother wounds. His soul wounds. As I put my socks and shoes back on, I walked toward the doorway and past the man. He was alone now, sitting peacefully on the bench. I can't explain why, but my body stopped right in front of him. Without a word, he stood up. I started to say something to him to explain why I was staring over at him so much, but I couldn't speak. Instead, I started crying, and he reached out his arms and just held me. I found out his name was Tor. He was a guide at the well. Once I was able to get out the words and share with him that he had my brother's eyes, he said to me, "He is here with you. Healing his wounds, too. You shared something here. The wounded masculine needs to feel safe to step into their sacred roles as well." I thanked him for the hug and the insight. I had so much to process. I had to find my way out of the garden because I knew we were getting ready to go to the White Spring next.

White Spring. Re-initiation.

As I found my way toward the exit, I saw some of the other women gathered around the bathroom, getting their swimsuits on. I had brought mine, but as I was walking out of the garden, I did not want to put it on. I had the urge to keep it tucked in my bag. I quickly thought of myself being the only one naked, with 23 other women in suits staring at me, mouths open in disbelief. After all, I had just experienced at the well, I was feeling very vulnerable, yet also clear that I didn't want any restriction on my body as I entered into these sacred waters. The desire to join the holy waters fully nude was overpowering. I needed to be fully cleansed, and it just felt so unnatural to be in a swimsuit. I didn't want to hide my body in shame or modesty like there was something wrong with me. As I dipped into the unknown, into this sacred, freezing pool, I wanted to be free and feel liberated in my soul's renewal.

Thoughts raced through my mind, like, *She's just doing it for attention*—I felt a deep fear of being judged or rejected by the women I had just met and genuinely liked. Overwhelmed by the flood of insecurity, I immediately headed into the bathroom to change.

Even as I stood there, waiting for a stall to open, I didn't want to do it. Deep down, I wanted to trust my intuition. Even getting my swimsuit on was a struggle—it felt like it was fighting me! Still, I begrudgingly convinced myself that putting it on would spare me the pain, shame, and humiliation I was so afraid of. I slipped my clothes over the swimsuit and headed back out to join the group.

We gathered and made our way to the entrance of the White Spring. As I walked up the hill, I fell into an easy conversation with a couple of women. We talked about the spring and shared our desire to cleanse and clear after such a big day. One of the women mentioned not bringing a swimsuit and was just planning to go in her bra and underwear or possibly naked. *Naked.* "Yes!" I said out loud. "Yes! I will do that with you." I confessed my need to do this naked, and then another woman walking with us said she had the same desire, too. We introduced ourselves to each other and giggled with excitement at taking the plunge. The three of us: Cat, Bec, and Molly. Together. Nude. Relief and fear struck me at the same time.

As we made our way up the hill and to the entrance of the White Spring, we were told of the history by the head Guardian of the spring, who just happened to be there that day. He told us of the reconstruction going on with the altars in each corner. One to Goddess Bridget, one to the Black Madonna, one to the Green Man, and one that was currently "a work in progress" that would integrate the masculine and feminine for the first time in the Spring! We made our way behind the green gate with sacred symbols running down it into a cave-like entrance. It was dark and wet and lit only by candlelight and a smaller opening in the ceiling above the integrated altar. I could see an open area with a large stone wading pool in a crescent moon shape right in front with pillars on each side of a stone arch. Even though I had never seen this space, it felt so familiar. Looking around, I could see four separate pools, two of which were smaller and tiered up to the left. There was a nest-like homemade teepee/cave in the left corner behind me for the Goddess Bridget, and I could see another structure to the right with the Green Man toward the back wall. The altar to the Black Madonna was in the upper left corner by one of the small pools, and the "work in progress" altar was to our right. We were instructed not to talk. As we all huddled in front of the biggest pool, all I could think about was getting naked and the fear or freedom that was going to come of it. I had a hard time focusing on what Rebecca was saying until we started singing/ chanting "unbound, unbound, forever unbound." We all made our way around to the different altars, paying our respects. After 5-10 minutes, some women started stripping down in the freezing cave to their swimsuits and wading around in the water. I looked around, trying to see where my plunge buddies were. I found Cat first as we gave each other the silent signal that we were still in. We started over towards where others were undressing and saw Bec. We all three gave the nod. *Let's do this.*

Still singing, we began to strip down in just the warm glow of the candlelight. Taking off our final pieces of clothing, I left my mala beads around my neck and grabbed onto each of the women's hands. The three of us. Cat to my right and Bec to my left. Naked. Stripped of all our shame and fear. Some women were in front of us waiting to enter the pool; some were behind, still at the altars. I couldn't see them but knew their presence was there. The three of us held on to the other with our eyes and hands with love and bravery. As Cat led the way, we made our way into each pool. As if we stepped into an ancient sacred priestess water ceremony, a remembering was happening between us. It was ice cold and came up around my shins. I continued to sing as we walked in a circle into the first pool, in total synchronization, as if remembering a sacred dance together. We continued on, stepping out of the first pool and making our way into the one tucked in the far back. Still holding hands, we walked up and over a stone ledge and down into the next pool, not knowing how deep it was. Water came up to our waists this time, and without missing a beat, we started our sacred circle dance again. Stepping out onto the next ledge when finished, Cat led us into the next pool where the statue of the Black Madonna stood. This pool could not have been bigger than three feet across, and somehow, all three of us easily got in.

Continuing to keep a hold of each other, we sang and looked into each other's eyes as we sank into the water up to our chest, still holding tightly to each other's hands. Giving a gentle nod, we moved out and into the last pool. This one was not as small but deeper. As we stepped in, we helped each other find our footing. Up to our shoulders, we gathered in our circle, nodded our heads, and dunked ourselves under the sacred water. 1... 2... 3... Down we went and back up together as if we had just practiced this the day before. Three times. Each time, going under to cleanse and heal all the pain in the mother wound. Heart. Mind. Soul. After the third time, we just stared in awe at each other, bathed in the warmth of each other's glow. We made our way back up to the ledge between the pools and stood hand in hand, singing, illuminated like glitter and gold. I saw myself naked with my sisters. Embracing. Rising without shame or fear. Just LOVE. Surrounded by the Living Waters of remembrance. Glowing like the Triple Goddesses we were. Initiated. Sacred. Empowered. The Maidan, The Mother, and the Elder. Stripped of all the fears and shame carried through the generations.

Magical. Healing. Sacred Power. A reenactment of the past. Lived before. *Way before.* In the Druid Priesshood. A Sacred Sisterhood of the following of Mary Magdalene. This was our initiation into the mystery school of Goddess Isis. This was part of our sacred ritual—being cleansed in the holy waters before being dressed and led up the Tor's spiral path by our sister and High Priestess, where we were ceremonially welcomed into the sacred priesshood of the divine feminine and divine masculine. This was a re-membering.

I looked around and saw we were being witnessed by She. I could see the Goddess looking back at us through the eyes of my sisters. *I see you,* a voice said. So powerful. The Spark was ignited. I was standing and could feel us as illuminated sacred women of the divine. Glowing like embodied Goddesses of the Light, warmed by love and held by all. I was truly being SEEN. Witnessed and held in unconditional LOVE. I could feel this resonance echoing deep into my soul.

Later that night, when we all gathered to share our experiences of the day, I discovered that it wasn't just the three of us who remembered the water ceremony and ritual initiation at the white spring. Several—if not most—of the women experienced a similar sense of remembering a sacred ceremony and ritual they had once enacted during our time in the Spring. It was a group remembering and activation! This activation was one of the most powerful experiences I have had in my life. All because I allowed my intuition to lead me to my soul's truth and desire to remember and reclaim The High Priestess Path.

As we closed the night together, this poem came through from Her:

We are being called to stand in our power, magic, and light. Together.

We are being called to empower our voices again. Together.

We are being called to heal our wounds by stepping out of the spiritual closet and speaking our authentic truth. Together.

We are being called to unlock our divine gifts and reclaim who we truly are. Together.

We are being called to honor our sacred feminine gifts of creativity, intuition, alchemy, and divine wisdom. Together.

We are being called to reawaken and shed old layers of what no longer serves as we transform thousands of years of personal and collective shame and fear. Together.

It's time to stop living through the lens of self-doubt, fear, shame, and not-enoughness and embody a life of love, freedom, and spiritual abundance. Together.

It is safe to shine our light out into the world once again. Together.

Together WE Rise.

Forever Unbound, Forever Free.

By trusting what I was being shown in Glastonbury and saying yes to each soul-led initiation into releasing, healing, and integrating through shadow work, I was shining a light on the darkest, most hidden aspects of myself that held the most pain, shame, trauma, and fear.

Walking through the fires of initiation on the divine feminine path is probably one of the hardest things I will do and the most liberating as I continue to shed the person I was taught to be and stand in the light of the Soul I came here to be.

Before stepping onto this path, I had pushed Christianity and even the Marys away for a while from the pain of the patriarchal lens. I only heard about the Kingdom of Christ growing up. But now, I have found my relationship and clarity back to the truth of what has been missing from *her-story* for so long. As we are birthing a new Earth, Mary Magdalene is the way-shower to the feminine "Queendom of Christ." Together, the Kingdom and the Queendom create the whole and holy inner Divine union. It's time we are no longer held back by our fears and align with our most authentic truth. The messages of Mary Magdalene teach us that light comes from within and that nothing outside of ourselves is greater than that light. She reminds us of the divine that loves and lives within us all. Living through her truly means being human and bringing the sacred embodiment of the light back into form.

Magdalene is a symbol, a call to remember to return to spirit and embody the soul—to love without condition or dependency, to return to sacredness to self, our relationships, and this planet. She has been our missing link, hidden in plain sight. No more will I hide. She is calling me out, calling us out into the light. Our call is to be brave, strong, courageous, and aligned with her heart, so we can bring the new Age of Light into being.

As the echoes of the Glastonbury initiations reverberate through my being, I am forever changed. The veils have been lifted, the wounds acknowledged, and the power reclaimed. No longer will I—or any of us—shrink into the shadows. The call to be brave, to be seen, and to shine our authentic light is not just a whisper but a resounding roar. Let us step out of the spiritual closet, speak our truth, and embody the divine beings we were always meant to become.

Together, we rise.

Forever unbound, forever free.

Molly Douglas

Molly Douglas is an art therapist, visionary artist, and writer who channels the Divine Feminine Frequency to guide others on transformative journeys of self-discovery and soul alignment. As a mentor and therapist for sacred leaders, she empowers women to reclaim their gifts and step into their fullest power.

As the founder of *Lit from Within*™, a mystery school for the Sacred Feminine Healing and Sensual Arts, Molly combines nearly two decades of psycho-spiritual expertise with ancient teachings fostering personal transformation and collective evolution. Her work bridges the realms of deep shadow work, somatic and quantum healing, creativity, tantra, and the sacred sensual arts, helping souls embody their divine gifts and align with their higher purpose.

As a modern-day priestess and multidimensional healer, Molly assists others through spiritual awakenings, guiding them to embrace their truth, wisdom, and liberation. Her mystery school *Lit from Within*™ offers a path of soul embodiment, self-expression, inner spiritual authority, and sacred leadership.

Her influence extends beyond her teachings, as she embodies the principles of the Divine Feminine in her own life, serving as a beacon of empowerment and inspiration for others. Molly's work continues to shape the movement, encouraging a deeper connection to the sacred within ourselves and the world around us. Her work harmonizes the Sacred Feminine and Masculine energies, inspiring balance and spiritual alignment within individuals and communities. By leading workshops, retreats, and sacred site journeys, Molly has brought the Divine Feminine movement to a global stage, helping others embody their highest selves and live in alignment with their soul's purpose.

Molly is a visionary artist devoted to cocreating with the universe and like-minded souls. She is the creator of "The Art of the Sacred Feminine Oracle Deck," featuring powerful visual portal images, and has a collaborated crystal jewelry collection tailored for the Starseed's spiritual awakening journey.

Learn more:
http://www.iamlitfromwithin.com
https://www.instagram.com/iamlitfromwithin_
https://insighttimer.com/litfromwithin
https://www.facebook.com/iamlitfromwithin

A Healing Arts Method

A creative, expressive quantum healing tool to guide you through any challenges or obstacles and move you out of fear and into love.

Access here:
https://lit-from-within.teachable.com/p/a-healing-arts-method

CHAPTER 13

The Passion of the Magdalene

by Kathy Forest

This chapter is written for the woman who is seeking something real. She longs for an authentic connection with the Divine—one that doesn't separate her from it but reminds her that she is it. She's grown tired of the mundane and cliché, the overly polished or sparkly paths that offer little depth. Instead, she craves truth—real life, real wisdom, real Soul. She's beginning to remember that the sacred lives within her, that her highest truth has always been quietly waiting beneath the surface. She is ready now. Ready to live it, speak it, and walk it. She dares to dream her boldest dreams and has the courage to step into the unknown to make them real. *Do you relate?*

If something in you stirred as you read this… then this is for you. Chances are you have had your own experiences with the Archetypal Energy I know as "Maggie" or Mary Magdalene. My experiences with her have been the most precious of my life. I have discovered that She has always been there for me, always held me, and always guarded my steps in those pivotal moments in life when I was not quite sure what direction to take. Her wisdom and guidance have always been spot-on and have given me the clarity to make tough choices. And I have found that her words were never just for me—they were always meant to be shared with others.

When my co-authors and I agreed to write this book together, we had no idea what would be ahead in the very near future. We did not dream we would be witnessing the massive shifts and earth calamities that we are witnessing now. But She did. She pinged all of us at just the right moment. My goal in writing this is to give her voice a platform, another place from which to speak. And I want to remind you that she reaches out and is here for ALL of us, even if we consider ourselves somewhat broken… maybe even especially if we consider ourselves broken. As she reminds all of my priestesses, She wants all of our "broken" parts. This is where the Goddess does her best work. I also want to show you that this isn't some fanciful projection of a woman's mind. It is real. It happens to real women every day. She speaks to all of us. She has answers for us, hiding in plain sight. As I began to outline my journey with her, She began speaking more about what She wants us to know and how She can help us. So, as I share my journey, I hope you will hear what you need to hear in Her words.

Life with "Maggie"

When I was 13, I fell in love. Not with a boy... with Yeshua. I grew up in the 60s and 70s and was a part of the great Jesus Movement that took place back then. I spent every summer at church camp. My experience of growing up in church was anything but casual. It was literally ALL my family did, and ALL my extended family did. It was "our thing." I have several uncles and cousins who are ministers. My father was on the "Board of Elders" in the church. It permeated our existence. I still consider this the most valuable foundation I could have ever had, and I am deeply grateful for it—and I also realize now that this is not really the norm for most people. However, growing up in the 70s in a small Missouri town, I really thought it was (or from the perspective of my upbringing, "IT SHOULD HAVE BEEN!"). But make no mistake, I was not your ordinary church girl. I was not brainwashed by the church fathers with all their doctrine and dogma. Rather, the intense focus and influence from my family caused this awkwardly shy and quiet girl to go inward and get lost in books, many of them delving into alternative Christian doctrine. So, I spent my high school years questioning (arguing with?) ministers just like Yeshua argued with the Pharisees.

I have always been drawn to all studies of spirituality, finding the mystical traditions most enriching. My love of Yeshua led me down many paths, delighting in all their similarities. So, it was no surprise for me when the anointing of the Divine Feminine hit this planet, and I learned that Mary Magdalene had a much more significant role in His life than just a "prostitute turned follower." She had been coming to me in visions long before that news made it to the press.

My parents sent me to Bible College to marry a minister. But after two years, I dropped out and ran off with an alcoholic wife abuser. Most would say that was a bad call. I say it saved my life! It kept me out of the clutches of a dogmatic institution that would surely have choked the goddess lifeblood right out of me.

Twenty years and three marriages later, I found myself married to a shamanic healer, offering earth ceremonies (sweat lodges and fire walks) to hungry seekers of truth. It was then that "Maggie" made another appearance. Like many she appears to, I had the experience of seeing through her eyes, feeling through her heart. I knew exactly what she was feeling, seeing, thinking, and doing when she anointed His feet. I never once thought it was me. I always knew She was showing me Her experiences. She popped up later many times throughout my career as a healer and teacher of women's mysteries.

She showed up during a frankincense womb cleanse right before we went to see the movie, "The Passion of Christ." I found myself bent double on the bathroom floor, weeping for all of humanity.

She showed up years later when I was considering canceling my Moon Lodge Mystery School because of a lack of attendance. She reminded me of the absolute importance of the woman's divine body and womb health. She said, "The womb is the storehouse of all knowledge, a library of—all history—all knowing—for all time as you know it. When a pure seed enters a pure womb, it has access to the highest knowledge, the largest amounts, so to speak. Within this library, there is a vast storehouse of information. The purity of the womb determines the availability of this information. The information—the tools—necessary to make this radical shift in a very short period of time are housed within the wombs of women of this age. You have the ability to heal your planet and save your world." So of course, I didn't stop teaching this information and continue to teach it today. Or rather, She teaches through me.

She also shows up in my healings. When I do psychic surgery, I can watch Her hands work through mine. This has never been a surprise to me. It always just seemed normal, like, "Well, of course." When I found the book *The Expected One* by Kathleen McGowen, I fell even deeper in love with both the Magdalene and Yeshua.

Magdalene now oversees every Priestess Circle I run. It just seems normal to me.

But what doesn't seem normal, what I will forever stand in awe and wonder of, is her courage, strength, and ability to do the seemingly impossible… to create a movement of love that has spanned the globe in the face of such tragedy and trauma. I am no stranger to the "Passion of the Christ," but what about the "Passion of the Magdalene?"

How do you watch the love of your life, the father of your unborn child, your teacher, your confidant, your best friend, be brutally murdered by a cold and spiteful, blood-hungry pack of politicians and then manage to go on living? And not only that, but how do you go on to do what He taught you, to STAY IN LOVE, to share that love, to live forgiveness, to see the mission through to completion amidst so many obstacles? Men wanting to kill you, snuff you out, keep you quiet... We know so little of Her, yet She did so much to establish the true teachings of Yeshua on this planet.

And now, She comes to me again, telling me: "You are coming to a time on this planet where *this* medicine—the teachings of the open heart and unconditional love—are critical. You have reached critical mass—it is time to open your hearts and shine your soul's light like you never have before. NOW! Now is when the teachings are necessary. Heal the sick, feed the hungry, and care for the poor. Cultivate the rich soil of your Soul. Do the impossible, dream the unimaginable. Dream LOVE. Dream BIG! Deep in your soul is something so rare and so special, something that AI can never duplicate: THE FREQUENCY OF DIVINE LOVE! It is in you. It is in all of you. It is now time for this frequency to awaken and blanket the planet."

And later: "THIS is why I am here! This is why I am making myself so available right now! You are witnessing the transition of the ages. Many of you are right in the thick of it. *SO WAS I!* I am here to help walk you through it. Look at what is happening all around you. Governments are at war internally and externally, failing and harming their people in unimaginable ways. The planet is shifting, causing pain and suffering. It is happening all around you. I lived through this. I walked this. And yet, the seeds I planted two thousand years ago continue to grow. While the world rages around you, while everyone is busy fighting, grabbing, and warring with each other, find quiet places to plant your seeds! You are being given plenty of opportunity."

Her Teachings of Grace

"How?" you might ask. How did She do it, and how can we? With the magical elixir of Grace and Fierce Love—the Love you brought with you... the Love in your Soul. Magdalene's love was (and is) a fierce love, a love that produces some of the most powerful female forces: holy rage, sacred anger, sheer will and determination, and positive aggression. This deep feminine power is the power that ends wars, that brings home missing children, that seeks justice for the earth and those who can't defend themselves. William Blake said, "The voice of honest indignation is the voice of God." This kind of fierce love keeps us protected and reminds the world of the pure strength of feminine power. Sometimes horrendous atrocities can put us into direct contact with our true strength, our true power. This kind of power moves us out of pure emotion and into conscious action. It causes us to act from conviction and love. In his book, *The Gene Keys*, Richard Rudd tells us: "True Grace is difficult to describe in words. The reason for this is that you need to experience it in order to know what it is. Grace needs to be treated with the utmost respect. Grace has to be earned through Graciousness… to find graciousness in the face of suffering and perhaps find something more… holiness, itself, wearing a disguise. It teaches us not to turn our face away from the pain life offers us. We are all here to be tested until we show that faith in nature herself can never again be lost."

I believe this was the path that Magdalene chose, "The Path of Grace." In a world spinning out of control, we, too, need to begin to cultivate grace in our lives. This may be easier said than done. The division and derisiveness that have been cultivated and grown on this planet can sometimes make this proposition feel hopeless. I am reminded of something one of my spirit guides told me long ago. The reason we have had such difficulties in the last few hundred years is we have forgotten this fundamental truth: "Everything you plant here grows." It would appear that the whole world has forgotten to plant the seeds of Love and Grace that we need to bring our precious planet back to balance.

In order for us to find the grace we seek, we must begin to plant it. We have to *BE* it. We have to *BE* gracious in the face of suffering. Right now, the whole planet feels like it is suffering. There is injustice, pain, and fear everywhere you look. We are certainly not at a loss of opportunity to cultivate grace. It may help us to remember that the atrocities that cause us to want to turn away, to bury our heads in the proverbial sand, are *gifts from the Divine* to help us cultivate GRACE.

The Path to Grace—My Experience of the Soul

I believe that a path back to Grace is through a deep, abiding connection with our own Soul. I know that may sound vague and a bit hokey, especially if you have never experienced this kind of connection. My journey with my Soul began in October of 2023. I had been learning about Sacred Geometry and was experimenting with different body meditation techniques. I was chanting in front of my altar when I had a random experience that changed my life forever. Suddenly, I felt a zipline of energy shoot through the top of my head and down through my body and out both feet. This was not a physiological experience, although I could feel it in my body. I know because I had a similar experience during a Priestess Initiation years before this, but it was a planned and requested experience. This, at least consciously, was not. Both chakras on the bottoms of my feet were tingling, and I continued to experience the effects of this for a few moments. As this was happening, it was as if a feminine energy was moving through my body, looking at all the "structures" I had set up for myself and my business. She was kind and smiling but skeptical. I knew at that moment everything in my world was going to change. And it did.

In an effort to understand what had happened, I reached out to a colleague who gave me a soul retrieval. During this experience, I was reconnected with my Soul and had the experience of "feeling in my body," the kind of love Creator/Creatrix has for this planet. I knew at that moment that THAT was the kind of love I was here to bring to the planet. I also knew that I had literally brought that flavor of love with me—in my body. The only way to describe what I was feeling was what I felt when I was 13, at church camp, when I fell in love with the Divine. The only difference is that now I know where to find it. I don't have to seek out an experience somewhere. I can now drop my awareness down into a specific spot in my heart space and find it.

After that event, everything in my life changed. I was suddenly receiving huge downloads of guidance and information about what was happening on the planet—and why. I woke up at 3 am every morning, excited to go down and begin creating. In a short three-month window of time, I created three new online classes complete with workbooks, slide presentations, and two card decks. I was joyful all the time! My life had a zest to it I had not experienced in years. In the early days, it was like being a child, waking up on Christmas morning every day.

The excitement has since subsided, but not the joy, and definitely not the Soul connection and constant flow of Divine Guidance. I am still learning, and I am now leading others to utilize the tools I used to find their own soul connection. It is sometimes a very strange place to be, to feel so much joy in the face of so much suffering.

Then She reminds me,

"This is how I did it. The key to holding the frequency is within you. It is within all of you. It will show up differently for all of you. But it is within you, and the time to awaken it is now. It is not a construct of any of your religions, but it can happen there. It can happen anywhere: on the Subway, in a sweat lodge, on a busy highway, or out under a tree. It is not a concoction of the new age mind or a fleeting fantasy, but it can show up like that as well. It is physiologically, energetically, and spiritually keyed into every living being on the planet. It is what some would call Spiritual Ecstasy, and it is coded to awaken now with the incoming Galactic Light and the shift on the planet. And most importantly, it is not optional. Your body is designed (has always been designed) to do so many grand and wondrous things. It is yours to create the environment for this awakening to happen and grow."

And She shows up again this morning:

"The message is simple. JUST LOVE EACH OTHER! You all came here with a frequency you were meant to share. That specific LOVE/LIFE FORCE that comes through you is specific to you… YOUR FLAVOR. It is the only one of its kind. If the planet didn't need it, She wouldn't have invited you. The original is buried deep inside your heart. So, its frequency permeates your cells. You truly don't have to *do anything* to share it. Just showing up is enough. But the 3-D realm is such an active place. You are always *doing something*. If you have been connecting with your inner light, your SOUL's light, your SOUL's frequency will always dictate your actions. But if your heart is covered over, if your ego has taken over and gotten you overwhelmed, your heart light may be weak. You are out of balance. The only way back to balance is through the doorway of the heart. *He* told you. *He* showed you. *He* lived it. And *He* invites you to live it, too. And *SO DO I*. Not by following a doctrine or religion, but by the frequency you hold, the light you bring, the thoughts you think, the prayers you pray, and most importantly, by the *CHOICES YOU MAKE!* That is what will determine both your personal outcomes, your planetary, and yes, even your Universal outcomes. It is not about religion or a doctrine, but if you look hard enough, sometimes you can find it there. It is about the frequency that still lives in your heart, buried under the *should-a, could-a, would-a, the guilt*, the shame, the "what-ifs," and "I gotta get that done."

When you find that frequency, when you are still long enough to feel it, when you let it guide you, you will always get to where you were meant to go. You will always do what you were meant to do. It may not always show up the way you thought. Even though I knew the outcome ahead of time, it didn't hurt any less. But you get to a place where it is less about you and more about the frequency you are here to bring. When you get there, you realize that the more you live in your Soul's frequency, your Soul will make sure you are on purpose, no matter what they say about you or what situation you find yourself in. Let your Soul be your guide. Let your Soul drive the car."

So, what is Magdalene's Passion?

YOU! She is here to tend the garden of love she planted over two thousand years ago. You are a seed, a plant in that garden. The frequency you hold is important and necessary. As we move through this turbulent time of change and transformation, your specific frequency of love is necessary to usher us into a new age of Light. When the storms of life become seemingly too much to hold, that Light of Source within you is your anchor. You brought it with you. You will always have it. You can always find your way home.

So, dear sisters, I invite you to join me. Let us open our hearts wider than ever before. Let us cultivate that frequency of Divine Love within us and share it freely with the world. Plant those seeds of grace, even in the midst of chaos. Nurture the garden of love that Magdalene has tended for two millennia. Step into your power, speak your truth, and let your Soul's light shine. The time is now. The world needs your love, your light, your unique frequency. Love Loudly. Go forth and be the embodiment of Magdalene's passion in your own beautiful way.

Kathy Forest

Kathy Forest, MS, CHt, is a Master Energy Healer, psychotherapist, and transformational life coach with over 30 years of experience in guiding individuals through profound personal and spiritual transformation. A wild woman, high priestess at heart, Kathy has dedicated her life to assisting women—and the men who love them—to heal their souls and transform their lives at the deepest cellular level.

Throughout her journey, Kathy has cultivated a rich array of tools and wisdom, wearing many hats as a ceremony leader, Pipe Carrier, ordained minister, Past Life Regression Therapist, and Akashic Records reader. For over 15 years, she has served as a High Priestess, leading hundreds of women through the sacred Priestess Portal, empowering them to reconnect with their inner strength and wisdom.

Kathy's philosophy is rooted in a powerful truth: "The female body is the most powerful shamanic tool on the planet." She believes that as women come to realize and honor this profound truth, they can transform not only their own lives but also the world around them.

Based in Sedalia, Missouri, Kathy offers a variety of online classes, including the transformative Priestess Process and in-person Medicine Wheel Retreats. She is the founder and owner of the Celestial Forest Institute of Energy Healing and Shamanic Studies, where she trains aspiring healers and priestesses to live soul-led lives and build businesses that bring them true fulfillment. Kathy's current passion is helping individuals connect with their Soul on a deeper level in Source Light School.

Learn more:
www.celestialforestinstitute.com
www.KathyForest.com

Source Light School, Magdalene Journey

If you're ready to deepen your connection to your soul, check out Kathy's Source Light School, where you can begin your Magdalene journey with two full-length videos, guided meditations, and all the handouts you need to start your transformative journey.

Access here:
https://www.kathyforest.com/copy-of-the-library

CHAPTER 14

THE DESERT WITHIN

Grief, Grace, and the Magdalene Path of Rebirth

By Dionisia Hatzis

"You can't receive communion when you're bleeding," my mother said, zipping up her dress for Easter week service.

"But why?" I pestered, teenage hormones dancing on my brazen tongue.

"Because when you bleed, you're unable to keep the blood of Christ inside you…"

I didn't love that response. I knew there was more to it. At my newly nubile age, I had become aware of the paradoxical tropes within the Church, especially the ultra-traditional Greek Orthodox Church, but I didn't quite have the language to support my suspicions.

According to the Canons, a woman must not receive communion while menstruating, which is considered a time of "impurity." While this biological function is *not necessarily* seen as a "sin," it nods as a stark reminder that the Church deems our natural process of womb renewal as a symptom of humanity's, notably women's, "fallen state."

"Humph," I mumbled as I searched for my winged maxi pad in the dark cave of my purse. "Just another reason why this whole Church business isn't for me."

The Church's perception of women's bodies as "unclean vessels" while we release the blood of our womb—the same blood that would nourish life if fertilized—felt inconceivable. This archaic rule revealed traditional Christianity's inability to honor the sacredness of the feminine. And, as a burgeoning feminist, I wanted nothing to do with it.

I clearly remember staring at the stained-glass windows as I pondered, *Where are all the women?* I was irked by the fact that girls weren't permitted behind the dais, where the altar boys would be running amok, close to these mysterious rituals that I would never have access to. Whenever I questioned why I wasn't permitted to do such things, the answer was always riddled with a different version of the same infuriating answer, "Just… because."

In only a matter of time, I'd learn that the Church had a disregard—truly, a disdain—for the female body, which planted the initial seed of my eventual departure from it.

Around that same time, I had an experience that I kept a small secret for most of my life. It felt so wrong that I buried it deep in my mind, never to see the light of day. As a precocious pre-teen sitting in the pews, I experienced erotic visions of Jesus. These titillating apparitions filled me with such shame, I hissed to myself, *Stop! This is sinful! Go away, Satan*! The more I attempted to push these hallucinations out of my mind, the clearer and more obstinate they became. They refused to go away.

A fiery blush of embarrassment spread across my cheeks. I prayed none of the churchgoers, and definitely not the priest, could read minds. I vowed to never speak of it, and as fortune would have it, the visions parked themselves in the dark crevices of my consciousness, secreted away into oblivion. Then, almost four decades later, while meditating on the Magdalene, the memory resurfaced. It was vivid, undeniable, and it needed to be acknowledged.

"There is nothing wrong with your sexuality. This is what makes you anthropos. 100% divine. 100% human," she smiled. Mary Magdalene, the Grief Walker, the Apostle to the Apostles, the Wise Priestess. Who knew? (All these years, I wished I had…)

The Magdalene had been walking alongside me since childhood, cloaked in enigma. I imagine her standing at the sidelines, silently ushering me through this lifetime, initiation after initiation, until I was truly ready for Her.

As I prepared to write this chapter, I sat in tea ceremony to summon her presence. Rose incense permeated the air, harmonic music hummed in the background, and the swirl of pu erh in my bowl tantalized my taste buds. *Magdalene, what do you want to come through my vessel? What do you want people to know through my story*? I pleaded.

"Show them how to travel the desert of grief and suffering—their own and that of others," she whispered. Alas, grief was how I came to know Her. Of course this was her request.

During the most tumultuous period of my life—one that led to isolation, loneliness, and unrelenting pain—Mary Magdalene emerged in my field as a priestess of sorrow. In a cocoon of grief over losing my 'well' body and the end of my life as I had known it, She finally progressed from the sidelines and arose, front and center, to guide me on my path. It was because She came to me that I am still here today. Her presence shined a light to help me see in the suffocating darkness. A glimmer of my own Resurrection after Crucifixion.

Three years ago, the sanctity of my body was violated by the scalpel of a negligent doctor in a brutally unnecessary medical procedure, after which I spiraled into a deep depression. In unbearable physical, mental, and emotional pain, I fantasized about all the ways I could escape the hell I found myself in. This same physical temple I had protected, revered, and cherished all my life had become my prison, my own internal desert exile.

The desert has long been a sacred landscape—a place of emptiness, silence, and purification, a threshold between the earthly and the divine. Stripped of distractions and comforts, the desert becomes an alchemical space where suffering is transmuted into wisdom. But it is so much more than just an eerily quiet, barren wilderness. It is an initiatory passage, a crucible where the soul is bared and the ego is forced to surrender its attachments and identities.

Christ fasted and experienced temptation after temptation in the desert. Mary Magdalene retreated to live in contemplation in the desert after his death. My desert was metaphorical, within the withering temple of my body, what had become a prison of suffering and surrender. This was my dark night of the soul, where I waited, grieved, and emptied into kenosis—so I could be filled with the presence of the Divine.

This mythical death cracked me open and pulled me deep into the core of my being, revealing my strength, resilience, and capacity to transcend through my darkest moments. This was my chance to take the pain, fear, and rage that accompanied me on the receiving end of wrongdoing and alchemize it into wisdom, compassion, and evolution.

It was during this time that I walked the path of inner alchemy. As the feminine indwelling presence of the Shekhinah cradled me, my battered womb became the threshold, my body the altar, my emotional darkness the vessel through which pure light could emerge. And it was here that I came to understand that those with the courage to wander their own wilderness, through the unraveling of everything they have ever been—will rise, if they accept the rite of walking through the darkness, alone.

After a turbulent year of tears that bathed me in bone-aching grief—succulent drops of yet-to-be-revealed insight—I vowed to reclaim my life. I learned to decode the hieroglyphs of agony held within my body. Slowly, I clawed my way out of the underworld, coated in the placenta of rebirth. Like Persephone, I emerged transformed.

The Magdalene's presence guided me to reclaim my strength, sovereignty, dignity, and divinity. She reminded me that no one could take away my power. My womb, my body, my soul—all are holy and unconquerable by another.

During this chapter of despair, no one said, "You're allowed to be angry." And yet, it was the only thing I longed to hear. I was consumed by an ocean of grief and anger, fed by the scars no one could see. The thick clouds of purgatory that lingered over my head were inescapable.

I was utterly drowning in unbearably dark emotions. I reached out to dear friends, meekly admitting that I was plagued with hopelessness. And yet, nothing but dismissive platitudes, spiritual bypassing, and toxic positivity. Tropes like, "God only gives you what you can handle," and "What did you do to call this in?" pierced my dumbfounded ears. Soon after, things went from bad to worse, and I landed back in the hospital three months after the procedure. Crippled with post-traumatic shock, pain pulsing through my body, I called my dearest friend, barely able to speak through the desperation. Her response? "Oh, Dio, I'm not surprised…" My jaw dropped, incredulous. I was completely alone in this portal of relentless undoing. What had I done to deserve this?

I needed love and support from my community more than ever—but they could not hold me in my anguish. They refused to touch the depths I was drowning in. I had been there for them through so many of their ups and downs, but when I became engulfed in the liminal waters of the River Styx, they diverted their eyes and hearts. Reeling in a web of heartbreak, rage, and dizzying confusion, the questions came pouring in. Did my friendships mean anything at all?

At the time, I didn't understand why they couldn't meet me in my darkness, but I do now—bitter medicine that still lingers acrid on my tongue. They had been trained to avoid and sugarcoat the heart-wrenching aspect of being a human—the suffering that accompanies being embodied souls. One by one, I saw beloved friends and family, like ostriches, burying their heads into the sand, falling into the false illusion that if they don't acknowledge the suffering, it's not really happening. If we don't name the discomfort we feel when we witness the unraveling of another, we won't have to acknowledge that the same fate might one day seize us, too.

We have been conditioned to fear death in all its forms—loss of identities, the endings of relationships, the crumbling of societies. And so, when one of us is thrust into the underworld, we attempt to "love and light" it away. Because in order to truly bear witness, we need to acknowledge and befriend our own shadows.

In my darkest hour, when no one else could hold me, the Magdalene appeared. When I was stripped of all that I was, everything I thought I'd become, She did not flinch. Priestess of Death, Holy Anointrix at the threshold between Heaven and Earth, the ultimate witness to endings (…and beginnings). She knew what others refused to acknowledge, as I prayed each night that I wouldn't wake up the following morning. Death is not to be feared, and Grief is not to be avoided. Both are an initiation, an invitation to transform, for Death cannot exist without Life, and Grief cannot be felt in the absence of Love.

Mary Magdalene sat in the wreckage with me, in the solitary ache of my pain. She bore witness to my endless nights of weeping. She was, alas, familiar with the potency of tears, having anointed the feet of Yeshua with her own sacred elixir of saline sorrow.

Magdalene priestessed me through the grief portal, letting it pour through me like the balm of Spikenard from her alabaster jar. With Her by my side, in the wake of searing loneliness and dejection, I met the Divine within myself in a way I never had before. My heart, my tenacious spirit lifted me out of the dark. I had always longed for a divine love like this—all-encompassing, etheric, grounded, and feminine—and through Her, I found it. Though the absence of friendship and the sister wound it left behind still occasionally stings, I've learned the art of discernment and empathy. Most importantly, I now know how to be my own sanctuary.

Once I allowed suffering to become my teacher, patience stepped in and began weaving itself into the red thread of longing for life. This red thread, intricately connecting the womb red bloodlines of all Magdalenas across space and time, prepared me for my Resurrection. I came to understand that this was part of my initiation into becoming a Magdalena. Had this adversity not happened, perhaps I wouldn't have stepped onto this path at all.

It was through the spiral descent of death and rebirth that I found my way home. Through Her—and Her unwavering presence—I came to know what it truly means to hold space with unwavering empathy in the presence of another's grief and say, *I see you. I am not afraid. I will not walk away in your darkest hour.*

On the 40th day after my metaphorical death, I emerged from my first cocoon of grief. The number 40 carries immense symbolic weight. The Israelites wandered the desert for 40 years. Moses sat on Mount Sinai for 40 nights. Jesus fasted for 40 days immediately following his baptism. In the Greek tradition, we memorialize our dearly departed on the 40th day after their passing, in what is called the "Mnimosino"—a "calling to memory."

On a hauntingly sunny winter afternoon in Taos, New Mexico, in memoriam of the woman I had been, and to celebrate the more textured version I was becoming, I captured this moment of emergence from the chrysalis in tintype photography. In one image, I embodied the grieving woman, with rivers of sorrow carved into my pallid complexion. In another, I posed nude, gently covering my breasts, reclaiming myself as a divinely human priestess of rebirth—pure, sensual, wise—just like Mary Magdalene.

This ritual was an act of Re-MEM-brance. In Aramaic, the language spoken by Yeshua and Mary Magdalene in ancient biblical times, "Mem" symbolizes the divine wisdom flowing like water into earthly existence, holding the potential for transformation. Water absorbs emotions and carries our prayer songs. It connects us with the womb waters of our earthly mother and the ocean womb of Gaia. Tears are the sacred waters of the soul, and in their release, we realize freedom. And, as I re-MEM-bered my past and re-MEMBERED my parts back into wholeness, the tears of my grief transmuted my pain into purpose—and marked my vow of devotion to life as a Priestess.

Years after emerging from this crucible, while on pilgrimage in Avalon, the Magdalene showed me more visions during a sacred movement practice. This time, the visions were painful, gruesome, and ancient. As I danced, I felt the rage from primordial imprints on my tired soul. Past lifetimes, traumas, and memories came rushing at dizzyingly warp speed.

Visions of an ancient temple flashed behind the black curtains of my eyelids. I was the temple dancer of this sacred space—a very powerful one—and was feared and demonized by the soldiers of the land. From above, I saw my naked body pinned down on a large marble altar, being violently desecrated by the cowardly men who feared my strength. Timelines collapsed as I relived the trauma of violation in ancient contexts, reflecting the wounds of my present reality. Surrounded by my Avalon sister pilgrims, I found myself longing to scream "*FUCK YOU!*" in a long, drawn-out lamentation. My fingers, arched old witch bone daggers, carved into the floor. I became the embodiment of sacred fury. *This is not just mine—and it's not just from this lifetime.*

Just as this boiling volcano of rage was about to erupt, the warm, comforting hands of my beloved Magdalene sisters surrounded me, dripping with aromatic holy oils to soothe my shivering body. Retching on the floor, I choked deliriously, "I need to release something big." Here, too, even in this state of absolute surrender, I was caught in the trap of being "too big, too much, too loud"— overly concerned with how my emotions might affect those around me. I had been chastised by some of my most beloved relations for my intensity in the past. Why wouldn't the same happen again here and now?

"Beloved, let it out. This is why we are here," one of the women whispered as she brushed my hair away from my sniveling mouth. In the loving embrace of my dear Rosa Mystica sisters, with Her right by our side, the floodgates opened. Magdalene nodded with approval, "This ends with you, my love."

"NEVER... AGAIIIINNNNNNNNNNN," I shrieked as the orgasmic climax of words thundered from the inky abyss of my throat—the holiest of holy rage. The roomful of women erupted with me—a convulsion of screams, cries, ancient wailsong. The stone walls pulsated in resonance with our collective howls—they, too, could crumble. *I'm in good company. My sisters feel this, too.*

"NEVER... AGAIIINNNNNNNNNNN!"

"NEVER... AGAIIINNNNNNNNNNN!"

Time stood still. Chronos collapsed on itself. Logic and reasoning vanished. I continued to keen until no screams were left in my lungs. I heaved into the freeing emptiness of fully expressed emotion. In that room, surrounded by sister Magdalenas working through their own journeys of reclamation and redemption, I broke the cycle of desecration, disrespect and abuse of my female body. And I reclaimed my own power, across all timelines, places, and dimensions.

This was—*IS*—the pain of generations of millions of women. By breaking this cycle, I heal not only myself but also the collective wounds of the feminine, the disregard of our sacred bodies and our wisdom, held by the gentle hands of Mary Magdalene.

Today, I carry this wisdom that comes with traversing one's inner barren desert, deep in my bones. I no longer seek solace in those who have not yet faced the underworld. I surround myself with those who have made the descent, who have sat at the threshold of death and crawled out anew. Those who know how to truly bear witness.

I have walked barefoot on the coals of life, and with patience and compassion, my frequency has shifted. My ability to be with others in their suffering has expanded. We meet in the knowing, in the gnosis, in the stillness between worlds. And we know that when the next soul begins their descent—as we all inevitably will—they will not go unaccompanied.

This. This is Church for me. Where the female body, in all our beauty and all our messiness, *IS* the holy grail. Where our blood *IS* the sacrament. Where grief *IS* held as the succulent seedling of our alchemy. Where compassionate space-holding *IS* the greatest act of love there is.

Where we can call each other on the edge of breaking and never hear from the opposite end of the line, "Oh, I'm not surprised…"

Dionisia Hatzis

Dionisia Hatzis is a writer, dancer, somatic practitioner, and workshop facilitator devoted to the rhythms of Earth and Spirit. As a Magdalene Priestess, she weaves ancient wisdom into modern life, guiding others in the art of ritual and sacred remembrance. Her work honors the divine feminine and the transformational power of ceremony, movement, and creative expression.

A lifelong lover of words, Dionisia studied English Literature at Colgate University before deepening her studies in embodied healing. She completed her yoga teacher training at Kripalu Yoga Center, is a Reiki Master and Breathwork facilitator, and certified Somatic Mind-Body Coach. Her life journey has taken her across the globe, from the temples of India to the high deserts of New Mexico, always following the call of beauty, wisdom, and transformation.

Dionisia is the Founder of SOMA Writing™—an immersive fusion of somatic movement, expressive dance, and creative writing—and The Sacred Cave, a ceremonial gathering space for women. Through poetry, movement, ritual, and plant magic, she invites others to reconnect with their body's wisdom and the living world around them.

When Dionisia lived in NYC, she had such an unstoppable need to dance that she turned sidewalks and subway platforms into her personal dance floors—much to the confusion of strangers, who got nothing but a big, unapologetic smile in return. She now lives in the foothills of the Rockies in Northern Colorado, where you can find her hiking to alpine lakes, whispering to flowers and trees, or anointing herself in holy oils.

Learn more:
dionisiahatzis.com
Instagram @JourneysOfRebirth

Embodied Magdalene: A Sacred Somatic Activation
A free gift to awaken your body as temple and your words as prayer.

This free PDF ritual guide is an invitation into sacred remembrance—where your body becomes the altar, your breath becomes the invocation, and your words become the offering. Inside, you'll receive a curated sequence of somatic and creative practices designed to awaken your connection to the Magdalene lineage as a living presence moving through your own body. This guide includes:

- A guided movement ritual to awaken Magdalene's wisdom as a living current in your body and in the natural world
- A breath work and visualization practice to receive your invocation
- A Magdalene-inspired writing prompt to channel deeper truth from within
- A holy oil anointing ritual to consecrate yourself as a vessel of the divine
- Techniques to help you channel Her message by unlocking the words held in your body through SOMA Writing™

Whether you're Magdalene-curious or deep in priestess devotion, this guidebook will meet you where you are, with invitations for ritual, reflection, and self-discovery. Let it initiate you into a new way of listening: to your cells, your stories, and the sacred feminine pulsing through your bones.

Access here:
https://www.dionisiahatzis.com/magdalene-unveiled-freegift

CHAPTER 15

Reborn, Here I AM

A Woman's Homecoming Journey to the Mother Through the Very Guidance of the Magdalene

by AnuMa Jackie Heydemann

I am the Magdalene.
I am the one you have always felt and seen.
I have been sent by the MOTHER
To guide you home to where you belong,
That for which you so profoundly and wildly long,
Into the depths of Her Sacred Waters,
the very Source of Life,
Into Her Holy Yoni-Womb Caves and Magical Forest, deep inside,
Onto parts and pieces of land where your soul finally feels at home,
Where your heart dances and sings, loves and enjoys being alive,
Where your body is profoundly and utterly alive,
making love with all of life.
~The Magdalene

Coming Back: A Near-Death Experience, A Call Back to Life

Suddenly, I could see myself on the operating table, surrounded by doctors and nurses. I was surprised and confused, but I could tell that they wanted to save my life.

My kidneys had been severely compromised due to repeated bouts of tonsillitis, and I had fallen into a coma. My parents were told that my chances of coming back were very slim. It happened on the exact day of my brother's fifth birthday, 20th February.

I was ten years old.

I was dying.

In that very moment, I felt a presence. A presence that was telling me my time had not yet come, that I was to live on and honour my soul's journey here on Earth.

I could feel myself returning to my body.

And although the body was familiar, something had changed. My life was never the same. I did not know how to express the enormity of what had happened to those around me, and I somehow no longer fit in. I felt isolated—and could sense a different energy starting to inhabit me.

Reborn, here I am, again and again...

The same presence that had communicated to me that I was to live began to guide me, helping me become more independent and autonomous very quickly. Only much later did I realise that this guide was Her, the Goddess, the Mother Herself, and that I had returned to my body so that I could live and embody my feminine soul essence here in this lifetime.

Before I understood this, however, I experienced the beginning of my moon cycle that same year. By the time I was 12, I had a woman's body and looked older than my age. Boys and men started to look at me differently, and I felt like the odd one out with my girlfriends whose bodies were still those of young girls.

I needed more and more space for my thoughts and feelings. Religion had never really touched me or spoken to me. I was longing for a spiritual, embodied female figure to guide me, but there were none. I deeply felt that something was "missing" in my life for me to be fully alive. What was it? Who was it? Where was it? I was so hungry for "something," but the food and nourishment I truly longed for was nowhere to be found. There was an empty hole inside me needing to be filled, but I could not fathom how. I sensed it was huge. It was something beyond my wildest dreams.

I felt the absence of initiation and true valuable guidance by women, be it by my own mother or other females, and a lack of conscious connection to Mother Earth and the Eternal Divine Mother.

Over the years, as an adolescent, that pain became ever stronger, and I developed an eating disorder. It was the outside manifestation of my inner hunger and quest for true feminine and female identity without being aware of it while becoming a young woman. However, my body always knew and expressed it in "her" own way.

And then as a young woman, the deeper I went, the more I could feel that presence again that was there with my 10-year-old self. I started to realise that this presence was HER—that SHE was there, had always been, and always would be. That SHE was that feminine presence I had been longing for—the Goddess, the Mother.

I also sensed that my quest had always been HER, me returning HOME to HER. Bits and pieces of my near-death experience started to come back during that time and almost every decade after until I remembered everything. I was more than ready. So I tried to follow HER call, but where was I supposed to go, and what was I supposed to do? I needed some kind of a plan. However, nothing worked out as I had imagined until the Mother brought me here near the Sea, the Mediterranean Sea, the Mother's Primordial Waters not far from the Magdalene's Sacred Sites in the South of France.

The Magdalene's Enchanted Forest

More than twenty years ago, when I was a young mother myself, I felt the energy of the Magdalene literally surrounding me, infusing my whole being. It was so palpable, almost physical. It happened in Her magical forest in Sainte Baume, in the southeastern part of France, not far from my home, where I have lived most of my life now.

Before that encounter, I regularly went to Les Saintes-Maries-de-la-Mer, a former fishermen's village located on the shore of Camargue in the South of France. It was actually the place where Mary Magdalene landed, together with Mary Jacobé, Mary Salomé, and Sara after their flight from Palestine. The three Maries and Sara escaped from the Holy Land and were, therefore, forced into exile. It is said they were sent away on a boat that drifted across the Mediterranean. It eventually ran aground on the shore of Camargue at a place that was later called Les Saintes-Maries-de-la-Mer—"The Holy Maries of the Sea."

Mary Magdalene is believed to have left Les Saintes-Maries-de-la-Mer and travelled to different places in France, as well as to Great Britain and other places in Europe, to spread Her embodied love and wisdom teachings. It is said that she retired in two caves in the forest and mountains of Sainte Baume.

I have always felt Her energy in this wonderful village in Camargue, whether visiting alone or with my son over the years. One day, I heard the call to pause halfway from home and Les Saintes-Maries-de-la-Mer and stay in Sainte Baume before continuing to my planned destination. I followed that call and stayed overnight at *La Maison de Marie Madeleine—The House of Mary Magdalene*. It was yet another important step in Her direction…

The next morning, She invited me to come closer and closer into Her energy field in the magical forest of Sainte Baume—a huge and lush forest filled with trees and plants of every kind. The soft, warm forest floor beneath my feet seemed to welcome me, as I felt myself sinking into the Mother's ground. At the entrance, a beautiful ancient tree known as "Merlin" greeted me and asked me to pay respect, show reverence, and make an offering before being allowed to enter this forest known for hosting and sheltering the Magdalene. It was an honour and a blessing as well as an initiation to be invited into Her sanctuary, Her queendom. What a gift from the Mother! *SHE knew what SHE was doing*.

The Magdalene's Holy Caves

Since then, I have visited the Magdalene countless times in Her sacred forest, especially in Her Holy Caves—nature's shrines to Her. I have visited Her alone, accompanied by close friends, family, women, and a few men. I also organised pilgrimages into the Roots of the Mother, following the footsteps of the Magdalene wherever and whenever She asked me to.

The more I entered into one of Her caves, the official cave recognised by the Catholic Church known as "Saint Mary Magdalene's Cave," the more I felt that there was another cave, and I asked Her for guidance. Then I discovered the cave I had been looking for—a wonderful Yoni-Womb-shaped Earth cave in honour and celebration of the Goddess, the Mother Herself, who therein initiated, blessed, and anointed the Magdalene.

The Magdalene invited me into this huge, ancient Yoni-Womb cave to be initiated again as a soul-embodied woman in Her sanctuary and to REMEMBER.

A poem inspired by Her is a tribute to this intense experience, which I lived to the very core of my being and soul.

In the inward Depths,
in the Holiest of Holy,
in the Yoni,
is She guiding me, the Great Mother,
in all Her Magnificence,
to the Magdalene.

In these inward Depths,
in such Holy Place,
in the Yoni,
is She appearing right in front of me,
deep in the Womb of Gaia, our Mother,
in all Her Glory,
the Magdalene.

In the inward Depths
of our all Mother,
in Her Yoni,
is She calling me,
She, the Initiate, She, the Blessed One,
in the name of our Mother,
with all Her Devotion,
the Magdalene.

That is what the Magdalene wanted me to remember. She had been calling me for a long time to guide women back to their true roots, the very Roots of our Beloved Mother. Through the Magdalene's guidance, wisdom, and feminine embodiment, we are invited to be initiated and reborn once more as the Daughters of the Mother. She made it very clear to me that it is deeply and utterly needed for the Feminine to be fully, fiercely, freely, deeply, wisely, and wildly alive and embodied again in all Her wholeness and holiness, and profoundly rooted in the Mother Herself.

Embodying The Goddess

The Mother first guided me to my ancestral roots through Her Holy Waters—the origin of all life and my favourite element. From there, She led me to the Magdalene's enchanted forest in Sainte Baume, where I could feel my roots in the earth once more. It was within Her ancient Sacred Yoni-Womb-Earth caves, both along the shores of the Mediterranean Sea and in Sainte Baume, where I was called into initiation, blessing, anointing, and remembrance.

Life—the Living Goddess, the Eternal Divine Mother—shows us again and again that profound healing takes place through our own feminine embodiment, *puissance*, trust, and courage. In every difficult situation, whether in this or in another lifetime, we are given the opportunity to remember, through our body temple, that we are ALREADY WHOLE and HOLY.

Although there may be more layers to come and be peeled away... through this our path shall we remember... through our womb, heart, body, and soul, right here, right now.

In the presence of the Magdalene, I am rooted in the Mother, deeply connected to the feminine mysteries through Her in my own womb, heart, body, and soul.

The Magdalene invited me deeper into Her teachings, knowledge, and wisdom during different moments and stages of my life, making me ever more aware of the Goddess, Great Mother, Mother Earth, and the Feminine in all their wholeness and holiness, profoundly soul-embodied and firmly earth-rooted.

The Call of The Goddess

In astrology, I am a Pisces (water), and in the Chinese horoscope, I am a tiger (fire), with Libra (air) as my ascendant. In this lifetime, one of my main tasks is to balance water and fire through air, and the other one is to reconnect both with the EARTH, anchoring into my deep, ancestral roots in Europe to remember where I come from, who I am, and the vastness beyond—something I have not yet fully realised.

The Mother Goddess calls me again and again. And I listen to HER call. SHE who is the primordial, irrepressible, untamable, wild, and so vibrant feminine creative life force, breath, and energy. I am one unique part of Her, the embodiment of one part of Her, the expression of one part of Her, the vibration of one part of Her. And so are you!

I feel my roots in Mother Earth, SHE who brings forth all life, and in the Goddess, the Eternal Divine Mother, the Source of all Beings and all Life. In HER, I root myself through and across my ancestral line throughout Europe and way, way back into the pre-Christian era, where SHE had always been worshiped, honoured and blessed, respected and loved, back to the First Mother of Humanity—the Sacred Black Feminine. From Mother to Daughter, from Daughter to Woman, from Woman to Woman, from Body to Body, from Voice to Voice, from Heart to Heart, from Womb to Womb, from Yoni to Yoni, from Blood to Blood, all the way back to Her, the Sacred Black Feminine, thus deeply honouring where we all come from, where I come from. And further back to Mother Earth and to the MOTHER. I bow. Nothing else to be done! Bowing to HER, to this very life, to the sacred gift of life on Gaia Ma.

This is not only a profound immersion into the Goddess, into Mother Earth, into the Sacred Black Feminine, into the Lineage of the Rose, into my whole Mother-line, but also into my own female being, my soft animal body, into my womb, and into my cervix ("*Muttermund*," mouth of the mother in German). It is an immersion into this sacred place and being, kissing us onto Mother Earth after having bathed and been nourished in the Sacred Waters of the Womb, where SHE is calling in our soul, loving and birthing spirit into flesh, form, matter as a whole, where we incarnate here on our Beloved Mother Earth.

And it is a recurring descent to my dark sister, the Goddess of the Underworld. Being stripped naked from what no longer serves me and initiated. Being infused with Her wisdom, *puissance*, fierceness, and wildness suppressed within me, within women and most of the feminine, and with the blessings and treasures hidden within vast female depths and realms still to be remembered and discovered.

I have been reborn several times in various ways in this lifetime, as you can see. I owe it ALL to the Mother and the Magdalene—I owe them EVERYTHING!

May You Listen to Her Call

The Magdalene always reminds me how and why She has been calling me to NO OTHER than the MOTHER. So that, in this lifetime, no doubt so ever may exist and persist as to my journey back to the Roots of the Mother through Her Guidance, inviting and guiding me on this ongoing life-changing journey by deeply anchoring me in the Sea, la MER(E).

SHE, the Sea, the Mediterranean, right in front of me,
Is my Altar, the place I deeply honour
First thing in the morning on my balcony:
I greet You, Mother, I love You, Mother, I thank You, Mother.

SHE, the Sea, the Mediterranean, right in front of me,
Embodies HER, the very palpable Essence
Of HER, and in HER oh so ever luminous Presence
Am I feeling HER so close, inside and around me, SHE.

SHE, the Sea, the Mediterranean, right in front of me,
Has drawn me here, making HER my home,
Has invited me to stay, I have never gone.
Is all and everything there is, was, will ever be.
SHE means everything, SHE means the World to me.

SHE, the Sea, the Mediterranean, right in front of me,
Cleanses me, heals me, nourishes me.
Stirs me up, calms me down, opens me.
Awakens joy within and sets me free.
As free as I can ever be in my Wild Woman's Body.

SHE, the Sea, the Mediterranean, right in front of me,
La MER(E), The MOTHER, Life Herself, welcoming me
Ever closer, ever deeper, ever wilder into Thee,
Where the Magdalene, again and again, guided me
To dive into roots far more ancient and profound
Than the ones I could ever imagine and those I found.
I owe HER all and everything, I owe HER my life,
I owe HER each and every day while I am alive.
Devotion and Gratitude make me thrive.

Thank you, Beloved Mother of all Life.
Thank you, Beloved Magdalene, in service of life.

May The Magdalene bestow Her love and devotion, Her *puissance* and wisdom, Her sensuality and embodiment upon you.

May The Magdalene call you, in Her own way, towards Her and that which so profoundly nourishes, rejoices, and speaks to you, to your womb, heart, body, spirit, and soul, right now, here in this lifetime, and MAY YOU LISTEN.

May you be honoured and blessed, loved and cherished, deeply nourished, alive, thrive, embodied and rooted, with the innermost knowing that you, YES YOU, are part of and do belong to the Eternal Divine Mother of all Life.

And so it is! JAI JAI MA!

Que l'amour t'appelle, te rappelle, te guide… vers ELLE, **la Madeleine en Toi!**

SHE, the Sea, the Mediterranean, right in front of me,
La MER(E), The MOTHER, Life Herself…
In Devotion and Gratitude…

And Shall I Always Remember Who I Truly Am!
And So Shall You!
And So It Is! Jai Jai Ma!

Sacred Women's Photographer: Kimberley Eastman
Cap d'Ail, Les Pissarelles, South of France, Magdalene-Yoni-Pilgrimage, May 2023

AnuMa Jackie Heydemann

AnuMa Jackie Heydemann is a Woman, Mother, Daughter, Sister, Companion, and Initiate of the Magdalene, a Rose Priestess, a Women's Ritual Guide, and a Devotee of the Goddess, the Mother of all Life.

She guides Women back home to the Roots of the Mother, back to the Source of their own Being, their Womb, Heart, and Soul, back to their primordial Roots through the guidance of the Magdalene by organising pilgrimages near the Mediterranean, the Mother's uterine primordial Sacred Waters, Source and Yoni-Earth-Water Cave, and in the Magdalene's Magical Forest and ancient Yoni-Earth Cave.

AnuMa was trained as a practitioner in psycho-corporal therapy specialising in feminine healing. She is a Thérapeute Prêtresse de la Rose Tantrique.

AnuMa is a passionate translator of the Goddess and the Magdalene, to whom she has been offering her voice, especially through poems.

Swimming naked in the Mediterranean all year long makes her feel fully and wildly alive, fills her with overflowing joy, and nourishes her whole and holy sensual female body and her divine feminine soul.

Learn more:
www.the-roots-of-the-mother.com

Acknowledgments

I am grateful beyond words for the initiations, guidance, instructions, and encouragement from women pioneers and embodied wisdom and peacekeepers.

I am very honoured to have attended life-changing trainings with trustworthy women teachers and guides such as Elodie Mas, Maleda Gebremedhin, Chameli Ardagh, Elayne Kalila Doughty, Lisa Schrader, Mayonah Bliss, Aletheia Sophia, Nhanga Christiane Grunow, Notburga Schaubmair and Margot Anand. I owe these women my deepest gratitude, my unwavering devotion, my profound love, and my total commitment.

I am beyond grateful for the Mother guiding me back into Her Sacred Waters and Her very Roots in this lifetime and for opening the initiation path of the Rose of the Magdalene.

I wish to give my deepest thanks to the women on my path, each teaching, showing, and offering so much for my growth and faith in the feminine.

I also wish to thank all the men I encountered on my path and those who are still in my life, with a huge blessing of love towards my son.

I honour my beloved mama and my whole Mother-line through all realms, timelines, and dimensions back to the very first Mother of Humanity, the Sacred Black Feminine. I also honour my beloved papa and my whole Father-line. I am an embodied prayer of these two ancestral lines.

My deepest bow to YOU, oh beloved Mother of all Life, for being alive.

SACRED GIFT

Rebirthing the Rite of the Yoni

This is a Sacred Ritual for the Worshipping of the Yoni in honour of and devotion for the Feminine, the creative life force energy. I reinitiated the Rite of the Yoni with rituals, prayers, blessings, poems arising from deep within, inspired by the Magdalene. I deeply wish to share it with all of you, because it is so dear and vital to my Yoni, Womb, Heart, Body, Spirit, and Divine Feminine Soul.

> *The Rite of the Yoni is reborn.*
> *The Rite of the Yoni is reinitiated.*
> *The Rite of the Yoni is ready to*
> *be transmitted and fully shared.*
> *Oh YONI MA,*
> *I bow to Your Greatness, to the Miracle of Life, to YOU.*

Access here:
www.the-roots-of-the-mother.com/resources/rebirthing-the-rite-of-the-yoni

CHAPTER 16

The Magdalene Path— Re-Birthing the Priestess

by Hallie Lifson

I've never "heard voices," and honestly, I was just fine keeping it that way. At fifty, I had successfully avoided that particular rabbit hole of human experience, and I wasn't exactly itching to dive in. So, imagine my surprise when I woke up on a perfectly peaceful vacation morning in Greece to not just a voice, but a COMMAND. And not a polite, "Excuse me, if you have a moment" kind of voice. No, this one came in hot, direct, and straight through my left ear.

There I was, the sun rising over ancient hills, blissfully swaying in slumber on our yacht, dreaming of who-knows-what. Suddenly, BAM. I was jolted upright like a startled cat, heart pounding, and there it was: "Reclaim your spiritual sovereignty." This wasn't a gentle nudge from the universe; it was a spiritual bullhorn. Strangely enough, I wasn't worried about my sanity—no time for that. My first priority? Finding my phone to jot this down, because this voice? It wasn't playing around.

So, there I sat, floating in the waters of Piraeus Harbor, staring out at the Acropolis where Mary Magdalene herself might've walked two thousand years ago while this celestial TED Talk continued. "Reclaim your spiritual sovereignty." I had questions—lots of them. What does this mean? Who's speaking? And why, of all things, did they pick my left ear?

It's not like I was new to answering calls. I've had whole-body "knowings" before—you know, those moments when you just know something is right. No booming voices needed. Like the time I knew I was supposed to become a doula and childbirth educator and bring people on adventures to the world's most beautiful places. Or how I just know when someone or something is for me—or very much not. Apparently, this is called clairsentience or "spirit whispers." But this was a whole new level of drama.

Being in Greece, surrounded by ancient ruins, timeless myths, and whispers of history and herstory, felt like stepping into a living museum—one where the exhibits insist on speaking directly to your soul. Everywhere I turned, the land seemed to hum with stories—the Acropolis towering above like a knowing grandmother, the Aegean shimmering below like it was hiding secrets, and the wild herbs practically shouting, "Remember who you are!" It was impossible not to feel everything that had come before: philosophers, priestesses, healers, poets—all those overachievers who, through whatever means necessary, built the foundation of civilization. But it wasn't just an intellectual awakening; it was visceral. Something ancient stirred within me, as if the very ground beneath my feet was reminding me of a lineage I'd forgotten. In that charged landscape, myth became personal, and I felt called to claim my place in it—not just as a spectator of history, but as an active participant in weaving *herstory*. Greece didn't just show me its past; it activated mine. I had been an amnesiac for too long. It was past time to remember, and I was ready.

For centuries, we were forced to forget. We were told to forget the priestess, the sacred feminine, the power of Mary Magdalene—a spiritual leader, not a footnote. We were told to forget the plant medicine that healed us, the rites that awakened us, and the wisdom that connected us to the divine. But if forgetting was something we did together, then remembering can be, too. Together, we can reclaim what was erased. Together, we can re-birth the priestess, the healer, the mystic, and the sacred power that lives within us all. The memory is not lost—it waits, like a seed, ready to birth into full bloom when we tend it with intention and love.

The Fear

Even having this visceral knowledge, I was afraid. Why was I afraid? Why did I care so much how my revelation would be received? I realize now that this is one of our deepest collective wounds—the wound of being cast out, rejected, and deemed "too much." I had spent years learning how to take up "just enough space." Not too much. Not too little. Don't be too mystical. Don't be too loud. Don't be too soft. This was a wound that went deep—not just in me, but in all of us who carry the memory of the priestess lineages, the mystics, the healers, the women who once held sacred power. I had the added terror of having family members who suffered from mental illness, and I definitely did not want to be seen as falling into that camp. The fear of stepping in fully was personal and collective. It was ancestral. And yet, Magdalene was calling me back.

Magdalene, the Midwife of Remembering

The Magdalene never left me. She simply waited, like all good midwives do, knowing that I would return. In hindsight, my soul longed for this remembrance, and Magdalene has been leaving breadcrumbs for me my entire lifetime. Greece was my rupture. My water breaking. My call back into the birth canal of awakening. The month before I left to guide this trip, my book club had chosen *Mary Magdalene Revealed* by Meagan Watterson. I was so fascinated that I insisted we follow it up with Cynthia Bourgeault's *The Meaning of Mary Magdalene*. I devoured the first book and listened to the second on Audible, soaking in every word. Maybe that deep listening "primed the pathway," as they say. Or maybe water really does hold memory—and in Greece, perhaps the waters still hum with the whispers of ancient priestesses. I like to think it was their collective voice calling me home. Home to myself. Home to all of us.

When I got back to the States from Greece jet-lagged but fired up, I wasted no time because I had my orders. Within days, I gathered a group of women to study Mary Magdalene's lost gospel, mapping out seven months of gatherings—one for each aspect of the ego that are described in her gospel. We began meeting, a gathering of seekers drawn to her story, her wisdom. Shortly after, as if the universe had been waiting for me, I opened my email and found an invitation for a Magdalene Path journey. It felt like a divine breadcrumb, so I didn't hesitate—I signed up immediately and roped a friend into joining me. I knew that if I was going to guide this group with the depth and reverence it deserved, I needed to learn everything I could. This wasn't just a project anymore; it was a calling, and I wanted to honor it fully. It was as if Magdalene herself was midwifing me into the next phase of my journey—guiding me as I was going to guide others.

Birth portal. Death Portal. Rebirth.

Again and again.

Reading about Mary Magdalene had lit a fire in me—a sacred bonfire with just a hint of rebellious smoke. Our group met once a month to discuss her lost gospel, because nothing says spiritual awakening like snacks and scripture. Growing up Episcopalian, I was already primed for a good ritual. I adored the "bells and smells" of high church: the frankincense, the candles, the music—basically, the Episcopalian starter pack. And let's be honest, Episcopalians are a welcoming bunch. We had centering prayer, yoga classes, Mary Oliver dropping by to talk poetry, and a farmers' market where communion wine probably wasn't the only thing people were sipping. We welcomed everyone to the communion table and let women preach, which felt refreshingly modern compared to other churches. And while we didn't take the Bible literally (thank God), something BIG was still missing. I couldn't name it then, but by the time I was 12, I could feel it in my bones—a deep ache, a whisper of more.

I approached this new journey with a deep sense of confidence, not just from my professional training as an occupational therapist skilled in guiding groups, but from something far older, something innate. My priestess skills had been quietly revealing themselves since I was nineteen, living on the beach in Pensacola, Florida. One day, I stumbled across a book on celtic ceremonies, and the moment I opened it, I knew. This was my path. With Celtic and Nordic roots coursing through me, the nature-based practice of co-creating with the universe felt like coming home. I began holding moon circles on the beach with my friends, instinctively weaving in ritual. We called in the directions, communed with the wind and water, danced around the fire, and spoke our desires aloud to be witnessed. What I didn't realize then was that I was stepping into the ancient lineage of the priestess—learning to create sacred space, to honor the elements, and to guide others in connecting with their own sacred truths. That knowing, born of fire and ocean, still lives in me today, even after forgetting it for years as I had been distracted by the pressures of raising my family and building a career. I was trying so hard to be "perfect" that I believed that I had little time for other pursuits.

Sure, I had yoga classes and book clubs—your standard suburban mother pursuits—but dancing around fires? That felt like it belonged to the wild, carefree maiden version of me, not the mom lugging around snacks and carpool schedules. I was deep in the forgetting, that phase where the spark of who you once were gets buried under PTA meetings and Costco runs. And let's be real, the other moms in my orbit didn't exactly seem like the type to jump at the chance to howl at the moon and dance around a fire—though, in fairness, I never actually asked. Maybe they would have surprised me, or maybe I was just too afraid of the sideways glances and polite excuses to risk finding out. This fear I now know can be encapsulated as "the witch wound." This is one of our biggest wounds... being cast out... rejected. The only way to heal it is to continue to step in despite this illogical fear, and I had a few things going for me in this department.

I was fortunate and started my formal education at a Montessori school, where the line between the ordinary and the extraordinary was gloriously blurred. It was a place where creativity and curiosity reigned, and formative experiences unfolded like myths in the making. I'll never forget the day a belly dancer came to our class, draped in shimmering silks, undulating with hypnotic grace, and, as if that weren't enough, carrying a live snake. To my four-year-old self, she wasn't just a dancer; she was an enchantress, a living embodiment of some ancient, magical archetype. "More, please," was the message to my little four-year-old self. I keep listening to her.

At this time, my father was working on his PhD at the University of Virginia, and we lived in married student housing, which was very multicultural for the 1970s. Around the same time, I started Montessori School. One day, to my mother's horror, I followed an Indian woman in a flowing red sari—she seemed to glide rather than walk—all the way to her home. There, she served me tea in delicate cups, the spices of chai swirling in the air like a blessing. I didn't have the language then to articulate it, but these moments awakened something in me—a connection to the archetypal frequency of the priestess, weaving mystery, beauty, and reverence into everyday life.

Years later, that connection blossomed fully during the most primal, transformative moment of my life: giving birth. It was a natural, orgasmic experience—a word I wouldn't have dared associate with childbirth until it happened to me. In that portal between worlds, I felt ancient wisdom flow through me, as if generations of women stood behind me, holding me in their strength. This wasn't just birth; it was initiation. Empowered by that experience, I felt called to be a guide at this sacred threshold for other women. I became a childbirth educator and doula, holding space for women as they, too, navigated this primal and powerful rite of passage.

But life has a way of pulling you away from your center, especially when survival mode kicks in. Caring for my severely and chronically ill father, divorce, graduate school, and the daily demands of providing for my two children thrust me right back into forgetting. The priestess, that wild and intuitive part of me, receded into the background as I balanced work, parenting, and the sheer grind of making it through. Those were years of resilience but also of disconnection—from my body, my deeper knowing, and the sacred rhythms of life. This time was brutal, yet it formed my character. Like all archetypes, the priestess didn't leave me. She simply waited, knowing I'd find my way back.

I see now that every great transition in my life has been a Magdalene initiation. She was there when I was nineteen, remembering Celtic ceremonies. She was there, within me, when I held moon circles on the beach, calling in the directions, speaking desires into the wind. She was there when I gave birth. When I guided women through theirs. When I forgot. And when I remembered. She has always been my birth doula—through every contraction, every loss, and every resurrection. And now I hold space for others as she has held me.

The Magdalene Pilgrimages: Walking the Sacred Path

Spring unfurls as I write this, and a quiet lightness begins to stir—hope creeping in at the edges. Staying aligned with the Magdalene feels more vital than ever. Because let's be honest—the life we are meant to live may not be the one we had planned. That's the great surrender, isn't it?

What keeps me grounded in the remembrance is guiding women to the sacred places where the priestess was revered—where Magdalene walked, wherever the divine feminine was honored, where the land itself remembers.

We walk in Glastonbury, where the Red Spring and White Spring flow as the sacred waters of the Great Mother. We climb the Tor, feet pressing into the ancient earth, reclaiming the sacred union within ourselves. We enter the cave of St. Baume, where Magdalene lived in exile but never lost her light. We kneel before the stone altar, touching the walls that still pulse with her devotion. We stand beneath the Acropolis and Delphi in Greece, offering honey at forgotten altars, remembering a time when women were revered as oracles, priestesses, and healers.

These are not just pilgrimages. They are initiations.

I continue to call in the help and guidance of The Magdalene regularly. Most specifically, before I get on a 1:1 session with a temple sister and before I open the ceremonial space on the new moon and the full moon.

She is a guide for times of upheaval, a teacher of resilience. Who, if not her, knows what it means to let go of the life you expected? To step into an entirely different path—and then be erased from the story altogether?

This is the shift we've been calling in—just not in the form we expected. But it's here, and it's time, sisters.

The Magdalene Path: Re-Birthing the Priestess

Magdalene reminds us:
Stay rooted in Divine Presence.
As we step into each temple… each day… Each sacred season, what wisdom

does she hold for us—the mystics, priestesses, healers, artists, and guides of today?

The tantra temple I guide is a sacred space—a place where I endeavor to step into a coherent frequency and help us all remember. The Magdalene Manifestation Temple begins in the depths of Samhain, ushering in seven months of surrender. A season of release—letting go of resistance, softening our grip on attachment, and learning to trust what is. Together, we witness and support one another as we open to more divine presence in our bodies, minds, and spirits. We are each other's birthing assistants, and the frequency of The Magdalene guides us.

With each season of my life, I return to this truth: Life is happening FOR us, not TO us. This is a relatively easy truth to grasp when life is going along swimmingly but when it feels more like a horror story.

From this knowing, realignment flows. Grace unfolds. Blessings arrive, perfectly attuned to the soul's calling.

This is The Magdalene Path.

And in the spring, as Beltane's fire ignites the earth, we re-emerge—temple sisters rising from the dark months, fortified with newfound wisdom, ready to bloom.

She is calling us back—not to the past, but to the present, where her wisdom is needed most.

This is the re-birth of the Priestess.

And Magdalene is our midwife.

We are not waiting to be chosen.

We are the ones we've been waiting for.

And now, it's time to walk it.

Magdalene Rebirthing Prayer

I call upon the fire that burns but does not consume,
the fire of love that strips me bare,
that unbinds my voice, O Radiant One,
She who walks the path of roses and fire,
whose hands have anointed the broken,
whose tears have washed away the veils—
I stand before you, ready to be made new.
Let the waters of my sorrow be turned to gold.
Let the wounds I have carried become doorways of light.
Let the shame that was never mine dissolve like mist at dawn.
Let it call me home.
May I remember the sacredness of my body,
the holiness of my longing,
the power of my name.
O Beloved, lift me from the tomb of forgetting.
Unwrap me from the old stories, the old griefs, the old fears.
Let me rise, as I was always meant to rise—
whole, radiant, and free.
Amen.

Hallie Lifson

Hallie Lifson is a therapist, temple guide, retreat leader, dancer, artist, and spiritual seeker whose work explores the transformative power of storytelling, sacred symbolism, and embodied wisdom. With a BA in English, Philosophy, and Theater, she brings a deep understanding of narrative, archetypes, and creative expression to her work. She also holds a Master's in Occupational Therapy, which informs her holistic approach to healing and personal transformation.

A devoted practitioner of Tantra Yoga, Hallie integrates movement, breath, and ritual into her spiritual and artistic practice. She believes in the power of the body as a vessel for deep wisdom and sees creativity as a sacred act of union between the seen and unseen worlds. Through writing, dreamwork, and intuitive exploration, she helps others reconnect with their inner mythology, unlocking the hidden forces that shape their lives.

Her work is particularly inspired by the sacred feminine, Mary Magdalene, and the alchemy of the rose, drawing from esoteric traditions, depth psychology, and mystical practices. She invites others into a space where healing and artistic expression merge, offering a path of radical self-reclamation and spiritual awakening.

When she's not writing or teaching, Hallie can often be found immersed in nature—walking beneath ancient trees, gathering symbols from the landscape, or practicing devotion through movement and stillness. She is committed to living and sharing a path of beauty, courage, and authenticity, always in search of the next unfolding mystery.

Learn more:
Instagram @hallielifson
www.mythicadventuretravel.com
Book a call: www.duramatertherapy.com

Magdalene Dharma Activation
Activating the Seven Gates of the Womb: A Dharma Initiation

The following Magdalene Dharma Activation is a sacred embodiment journey that awakens the divine feminine creative power within you through the Seven Gates of the Womb. Rooted in the mystical lineage of Mary Magdalene, this activation invites you to remember who you truly are—a Temple, a Grail, and a Tower of Light-through breath, vision, ritual, and soul-based creativity.

Each of the Seven Gates corresponds to a flame of energy-red, orange, gold, pink, blue, indigo, and white-that aligns with your chakras and womb space, reconnecting you to:

- Your ancestral roots
- Your sensual, creative life force
- Your radiant self-worth
- Your open, loving heart
- Your voice of truth
- Your inner vision
- Your connection to the Divine Source

Through this process, your womb becomes the altar of manifestation, healing, and sacred expression. You are not just remembering Magdalene—you are becoming her presence in this world. In short: The Magdalene Dharma Activation is a ritual of awakening the soul of your femininity—so you can create, speak, move, and live as the sacred embodiment of the Divine Feminine.

Access here:
https://duramatertherapy.com/ola/services/free-magdalene-dharma-activation

CHAPTER 17

The Wise Web of the Red Thread

By Alessandra Mary

Help me help you.

She whispered gently yet alerted fiercely, jolting me out of a deep sleep. I glanced around the dark bedroom, half expecting to see someone standing nearby, but I already knew no one was there. A familiar tingling crept up my spine. The sensation of truth dawning… *that was a sign, a message from the divine.*

Her words resounded into the very fabric of my being. Great Mother speaking directly to me, answering my prayer: *Why is this happening? It's not fair. This is so hard. I feel so lost. How will I ever get through? Show me what to do. I don't know what to do…*

I was sadly single, broke, recovering from COVID-19, and about to move from New England to North Carolina. To say I didn't want to go is an understatement. I sulked through the day and cried myself to sleep at night, stubbornly resistant to this looming upheaval. Even after walking my spiritual path for almost three years, I still deeply struggled to go with the flow and fully trust in things working out for me. My anxious, white-knuckled grip kept me terrified of relinquishing control. I often felt like my worst enemy rather than my greatest ally.

Help me help you.

Her transmission encouragingly guided me to trust the journey unfolding— to let go and let flow. What I know now that I didn't fully understand then is that this was a red-thread moment. A critical turning point that brought me back to this truth: *I am not walking this path alone; I have never been alone, nor am I abandoned.* When we feel unsure, disoriented, helpless, or hopeless, we've lost our connection with soul and source. We've forgotten how held we are by the Great Mother or, as I have come to know her, the Magdalene Mother.

The beautiful thing about being lost is you get to be found. You get to remember who you truly are, reconnect with your eternal wholeness, and reclaim the infinite power within you. You get to come back home—again and again and again. This is the heroine's journey, a spiraling path filled with red-thread moments that take you deeper into your own magnificence. It's where you slip out of logic and into the mystic so you can see the world behind the world. The more you recognize these divine orchestrations and starstruck synchronicities, which I believe are planted by the sacred to be sensed by your soul, the more you become aware of the limitless resources available to you, understand the power of your own potential, and know that anything is possible for you.

This is a story of key red-thread moments that filled me with possibility and gave me permission. Permission to listen to the whispers of wisdom within and around me. Permission to help the Magdalene Mother help me by opening and allowing myself to receive Her support and Her love. She wants you to know that even though this is my story, it's also a mirror for your story. A *Herstory* of following the red thread, learning the clues, answering the call, taking the leap of faith, honoring your ever-changing true nature, surrendering to transformation in grace, and shifting your perspective to perceive how guided you *always* are. Let's begin.

So what is the red thread? Back in my early twenties, I came across a Chinese proverb about a red thread of fate, tying us to those we are destined to meet regardless of time, place, or circumstance. During this "ink fever phase," I chose tattoos as symbols for who I yearned to be and how I desired to live, so I decided to get this proverb forever etched into my skin. I loved the possibility of being guided toward destiny by unseen magic.

Even then, in my "pre-spiritual awakening" phase, my soul was speaking to me. I like to think I had one eye open and one asleep. Despite the hustled, performative conditioning of my upbringing and the "appease to please" programming of societal norms, my curious nature still had me asking, *Is this it? No freaking way… There's gotta be more to life than disappointing relationships and unfulfilling work.* There was a thirst for truth within me. I wanted a magical adventure. To go seek a "Great Perhaps…" So, it's no surprise how the enchanting mystery of the red thread pulled me in. Underneath my starry-eyed wonder was the real reason for my obsession: I desperately sought connection. Mind-blowing, heart-opening, body-enriching, soul-satiating connection. One I would finally find years later during another red-thread moment that led me all the way to Greece.

To honor my 30th birthday and the important threshold I was crossing from one decade to the next, I found myself at my first women's retreat. In the year prior, I had this weird, unexplainable feeling that things were about to change. Sure enough, my life as I knew it crumbled when the long-term romantic relationship I had given everything to abruptly ended. I was left with this booming inquiry from my soul... *Are you ready to find out who you really are? Because it's certainly not this.*

This was a catalyzing tarot tower moment that brought me to rock bottom, so I willingly dismantled everything I knew to go on a quest for something more true. And that's exactly what happened. I found my Self (capital S) on that retreat—my Sacred Soul Self. It was the spiritual awakening of a lifetime—many, in fact. I finally understood myself as I truly am, as we all are: sacred, wise, whole—radiant beings of loving, luminous light. Genuine intimacy anchored within me, creating special bonds with the women, the land, and the feminine frequency. I recalled the inner divine power to co-create my desired life. My unique magic came online, ready to passionately guide me toward my soul purpose. Relief, joy, and gratitude flooded in as I became more embodied than ever, and I knew my life would never be the same. Weaving its magic yet again, the red thread led me home to what I had been missing—the Sacred Feminine.

This kind of connection and liberation can be found when you give yourself permission to follow the path of the red thread. It's unconventional but unbelievably fulfilling. I used to feel stuck in every area of my life because I kept waiting for permission to be, do, and have what I wanted. But that's not how it works. You have to give yourself permission. To go on that retreat, get certified in what you feel drawn to practice, quit the comfort of the cushy job that siphons your precious life force, leave the relationship that makes you feel less than you actually are, do the damn thing you feel called to do even though you can't logically explain why. To follow the breadcrumb trail of your soul, see that red thread, take it, and weave it.

Because here's the thing... you are weaving this thread as much as it is weaving you. It's a co-creative dance, so as the weaver of your world, when the old story isn't working or doesn't serve you anymore, you get to weave a new one, and the red thread shows you how. I know because I have done this many times over. It's why I tell you this story—as inspiration for you to pay more attention to the whispers of your soul and how the red thread is weaving within, around, and through you.

You see, the red thread is so much more than just an adage. It's the sacred guiding path that weaves pivotal points of your life together, so when you look back, you can see the tapestry of magnificence it has woven for you—how you were always getting exactly where you were meant to go.

I remember back in my late teens being fascinated with the author Dan Brown and how, of all his books, *The Da Vinci Code* was especially my favorite. Logically, I didn't know why until post-spiritual awakening when I re-read it and realized this was another red-thread moment reminding me that to be human *is* to be divine. It was as though Mary Magdalene planted the Sacred Feminine seed of Herself as holy rather than whore, and the womb as the holy grail portal through which co-creation occurs so I could reclaim this light within me when the time was right.

That's the thing—sometimes, the whispers are obvious; other times, they're ambiguous. The clues are always there, whether or not you realize what's happening. Magic unfolds all around you, even now. The act of being guided to this book, this chapter, is very likely a red-thread moment for you.

The architectural artistry of the red thread brings you back to your soul, reminding you to stay connected with the truest essence of love, power, and wisdom residing within. Just like in Disney's "Frozen II," when Elsa is beckoned into the unknown by a mysterious voice in order to find herself and her source. Or when Moana breaks free from the status quo of her island to chart her own course and do what only she is capable of doing. You are the one you have been waiting for, beloved. You won't find the answers you seek outside of you because the call comes from *inside you*. Don't look to others to find your path. Follow the true north of your inner compass to see where it leads and lands you. Trust your instinctual knowing and the ever-flowing, ever-changing, ever-evolving mystery of the red thread.

As you become aware of the red thread and look at your own life, you may start seeing things with a fresh perspective. You might also wonder, *How do I know if that was or this is a red-thread moment?* Great question. What I have found is certain circumstances trigger visceral sensations in the body. This is a sure indication of your soul trying to convey important messages—like the chills you get when you hear a resonant truth or the intense emotional responses to seemingly random stimuli. It's when you meet someone new yet feel as though you've known them for lifetimes. Every time you say to yourself, *I have no idea why, this makes zero sense, but everything in me is saying YES…* that is the red thread weaving her web of wisdom. Everything in your body comes alive, and your cells start singing because your soul is speaking to you, saying THIS! *Pay attention because this is a clue leading you back to you.*

That's why it's *so* important to listen to your body. She is the vessel, the channel through which your soul, the sacred, the Magdalene Mother, all communicate with you. I used to see my body as an inconvenient chore I "had to" take care of. Even while spiraling deeper into my spiritual journey, I still carried this narrative of my body being a barrier to the divine rather than the access point, or more truthfully, the temple of the sacred itself. It wasn't until recently, through yet another red thread weave, that my perspective irrevocably shifted.

At one of my favorite Sacred Feminine retreats, there was an opportunity to take home crystals that had been activated during the weekend. On the last day, I was handed a purple fluorite butterfly to place on the altar. Immediately, every hair on my body stood up. As I held it, my fingertips tingled, and my palms pulsed as if my whole heart had melted down my arms to pool in my hands. I started crying. The woman who handed it to me lovingly said, *I believe that's your crystal.* Right away, my mind ranted, *Nope. It's double the amount you said you'd spend. We are not buying that.* This is guaranteed to happen when your soul asks you to do something beyond what your mind can conceive, and you have to be willing to ask yourself, *Who am I going to listen to? My limited ego or my limitless soul?*

Synchronistically, this butterfly symbol had presented itself to me as an ally (aka, a red thread) about a year ago when a mystic reflected the essence of butterfly within my energy field. She said when I embrace this frequency, I effortlessly float on the stream of creation, graceful and free. She warned me if I kept going back to my cocoon (a metaphor for the old pattern of forcing my way through life), it would eventually kill me. *Spoiler alert: it almost did.*

I listened to my soul, bought the crystal, and within days of arriving home, collapsed into an extreme health crisis, landing me in the hospital with a debilitating diagnosis of hyperthyroidism and thyroiditis. Do you know what shape the thyroid gland is? *A fucking butterfly.* Not only was it foreshadowing, but more importantly, the crystal was a serendipitous gift from the Magdalene Mother to support me through the uncertainty of what I was facing. I spent weeks without clear answers about why this happened, what it meant, and what needed to be done next. I was thrown deep into the unknown, a place typically avoided out of fear because its ambiguity is extremely uncomfortable. Yet, that's the paradox. We never really know. The mind has an agenda and will spin you into a Tasmanian tizzy over all the worrisome "*what ifs*" for what might get in the way of what it wants, but life will always be a mystery. Your job is to surrender to it. To willingly dive into the unknown, find your ability to be comfortable amidst its discomfort, and trust the unfolding.

But Alessandra, how in the whirling dervishes do I do that? Oh, my love, you already know the answer—you look within to lean on the Magdalene Mother. When the external world feels tumultuous and terrifying, turn your gaze to the wise one within, the essence of Her in you. The more I oriented myself here, the more I found patience, peace, and possibility. From this space, I remembered and found solace in the most important aspect of butterfly's meaning: *transformation in grace*.

Through this initiation, I had to be gentle, go slow, rest, and restore—something I was not good at doing. My calendar was cleared, and my agenda dismantled. Despite my resistance, I consciously chose to give myself space to face what was uncomfortable. To feel the anger, sadness, and confusion in order to heal what was ready to be healed—the part of me who fearfully fought instead of faithfully flowed. This excruciating yet expansive identity shift took me from the anxious late bloomer who felt so behind in life to the playful elegant empress who knows she is right on time, exactly where she is meant to be. The butterfly, crystal, and thyroid were all red threads, leading me to the exact incubation I needed to create a deeper and more reverent union with my physical being.

In that former version, I neglected my body by saying I didn't have time to take care of her, so she made the time. When I let her nourishment be my "soul" priority, I allowed the alchemy of this massive healing to actually take root. I completely surrendered my will to the will of the Magdalene Mother and thereby ceased relying on my own strength to navigate life's twists and turns. My cells soaked up the embodied experience of softness, spaciousness, and serenity through the womb of winter as a glorious and gruesome way to get me to where I am today.

As I faced the criticizing guilt of doing the bare minimum and the crippling shame of being so "unproductively lazy," my neural pathways rewired, finding the balance between rest and activity so I could stop forcing myself to always be "on." As I healed my nervous system at the deepest layer, I broke traumatic ancestral cycles of over-giving, under-receiving, and the incessant need to hustle or hurry up. My capacity to savor the sweet nectar of this human experience strengthened as I realigned with the delightful dance of life's inherent rhythm. The one that is our Goddess-given right to indulge in and enjoy.

The woman I have emerged as is who I always saw in the visions my soul would show me. Soft brow, serene eyes, relaxed jaw, open heart, wild spirit. Equanimous yet effervescent at the same time. My daily interaction with life is the most harmonious, joyous, and freeing it's ever been. Where I previously had rigid attachment to an outcome, I now warmly welcome the spontaneity of the moment as it arises. I prioritize pleasure over pressure, and I measure my success by how good something feels rather than how it looks. My life has become one big moving (and regularly answered) prayer. This is what happens when you devote yourself to soul and source.

Can you see how these red-thread moments are also here to teach you something? Whether a learned lesson or a bestowed blessing, it's all divine design for your own soul's polishing. This is not to say you don't have free will; it's more about how you view what happens in your life and how you choose to show up. Will you live as though nothing is a miracle or everything is a miracle? The latter empowers you to see obstacles as detours toward the greater good and challenges as opportunities for personal growth. Witnessing the deeper meaning behind situations allows you to see possibility instead of problem so you can maneuver through with grace instead of grit.

Your life is a mystery school, and the red thread is the tool through which you learn to master the curriculum. Though its teachings can range from beautifully blissful to astonishingly awful, the purpose is always for you to realize that life is happening *for you*, not to you. Having that perspective shift becomes second nature when you put the sacred at the center—not as a spoke in the wheel of your life that maybe gets 10 minutes on the meditation pillow, but as the hub.

Because the red thread, as a symbol of the sacred, *is* the spool that makes everything else effortlessly spin when you choose to weave it back in and allow your sweet soul and sacred source to be your holy guiding force. It becomes the one you share your deepest desires to, celebrate your ecstatic experiences with, rely on when shit hits the fan, and relax into when nothing makes sense.

Through it all, the Magdalene Mother is there, holding you in her warmest embrace to let you know you will be okay—no matter what. Even in the darkest hour, the most uncertain unknown, you can always ask, *What would you have me do? Where would you have me go? Who would you have me be?* And trust in the answers being revealed.

The Magdalene Mother is always here for you. *Help Her help you* by listening to the red thread, learning the weave of its web, and living your life as though you are led. Because you are. *Always.*

Alessandra Mary

Alessandra Mary is a ceremonial priestess and holistic alchemist devoted to cyclical, mystical living and guiding the collective to weave the Divine Feminine back into everyday life. Through her sacred gatherings, oracular transmissions, and ritual candles, she creates opportunities for deeper communion with soul and source. Her passionate, curious nature inspires irrevocable perspective shifts around what gets to be possible, thereby cultivating a wondrous lens for witnessing the world. She is driven by a Goddess-given mission to launch a podcast that highlights the heroine's journey and establish a multi-modality emporium of enchantment for exploring the inner landscape, reclaiming intuitive wisdom, expressing authentic truth, remembering innate divinity, and embodying an intimate relationship with magic.

Outside of her vocation, Alessandra treasures forest frolicking, ecstatic dance (especially around a bonfire), regular candlelit bubble baths, daily tea witchery, getting lost in a Jane Austen novel, and following her daring, free spirit on spontaneous adventures. She resides near Asheville, NC, with her supportive partner and playful pup.

Learn more:
covendivine.com
Instagram @covxndivine
Coming soon: covendivine.com/podcast

Sacred Gift

Soul ⊚ Journ
An encoded blueprint for reconnection, remembrance, and reclamation.

This curated experience of seven daily activations will further awaken your awareness and profoundly shift your perspective on what gets to be possible for you when you commit to living a sacred life. If you feel like the fire within has dwindled, burnt out, or perhaps just needs to be lit, these transmissions are the spark for you to reignite.

Access here:
covendivine.com/souljourn

CHAPTER 18

PEEK BEHIND THE VEIL

by Christy Grace Michaels, M.A.

There were no boy babies to be found, so my mother offered me. Hundreds of people were coming that Christmas morning in 1949 to witness the Christ child in a live nativity scene. At six months old, I could be presented incognito as the Christ child. However, everyone knew that my mother had a girl. But suppressing the Divine Feminine was okay—then.

What no one realized was the significance of what it meant that a Sophia-Christo (girl-child) was being presented to the congregation in a church building that looked like the Temple of Solomon. As the story goes, it was the Holy Sophia (the wisdom of God) who instructed King Solomon, her husband, to build the temple,[1] with six massive pillars towering on either side.

Introducing a Christ, female-child created a paradigm shift! As a girl, I could be none other than a representation of Sophia-Christo (the potentiality of a Feminine Christ). Even my full name, Christiane, means *one who aspires to be like Christ.*

That moment as a child, being presented as Sophia-Christo was significant, but I couldn't have imagined how it would all unfold until my ordination as a Priestess of Magdalene so many years later.

On 10/10/10, I was ordained a Priestess of Magdalene by Priestess Elizabeth Kelley of the Holy Order of Mary Magdalene,[2] into her Lyceum of the Holy Sophia.[3] I am grateful to Elizabeth for opening my eyes to the Magdalene[4] and to Gnosticism. Gnostic Christianity holds Magdalene as the great demonstration of both the incarnation and embodiment of the Holy Sophia.[5]

---

[1] 1 Kings 4:29-31 tells us that God gave wisdom to Solomon; In the Song of Songs (also known as Song of Solomon or Canticle of Canticles)… it speaks of Solomon's marriage to Holy Sophia. Wisdom 9:8-11 even tells us that Sophia instructed Solomon in building the Temple!, https://www.crystalinks.com/sophia.html
[2] Priestess Elizabeth Kelley's Lineage-Hierophant, Tau Rosamonde Miller, The Mary Magdalene Line of Succession, ordained in 1994 by Rosamonde into the Holy Order of Mary Magdalene. https://www.gnosticsanctuary.org/lineage.html
[3] In 1998 Lady Olivia Robertson, ordained Elizabeth Kelley a Hierophant of the Holy Sophia and certified Elizabeth through the College of Isis to begin a Lyceum. https://mmagdalene.org/index.php/holy-sophia/
[4] Priestess Elizabeth Kelley, https://www.mmagdalene.org
[5] Margaret Starbird, *Magdalene's Lost Legacy,* (Rochester: Bear and Co., 2003), 125.

Sophia is needed to balance the Divine Masculine and Divine Feminine. My destiny was revealed to me to be threefold:

1. To unveil the suppression of the Divine Feminine (like "Sophia… who was written out of the script entirely"[6] or Magdalene, thought to be a prostitute, but in 1969 the Catholic church admitted there was no evidence of that[7]);
2. Restoring the role of the Priestess in modern times;
3. To fulfill the prophecy of Mathew 26:13 and Mark 14:9 by creating the Magdalene Moonrise Easter Celebration.

At the beginning of 2011, I received the vision to create the Magdalene Moonrise Easter Celebration. This live interactive celebration would help fulfill the prophecy:

"I tell you the truth, wherever the Good News is preached throughout the world, this woman's deed will be remembered and discussed."[8]

You probably know, as well as I, that "Wherever the Good News is preached"… rarely is she remembered, much less discussed. She is sometimes not even named… "a woman came in with a beautiful alabaster jar…"[9]

Easter Sunrise Service was to honor the "Risen Christ." Now it was time for a Moonrise Service to uplift the Magdalene as a fully awakened human woman (Anthropos)[10] and bring balance to this sacred partnership. Part of the original intent of Jesus's purpose was to acknowledge Magdalene as a woman worthy and deserving, an equal in the eyes of God. His genius was that he appeared to her at the Resurrection, thereby elevating her status. If it were true that only men are superior, then he would have appeared to Peter first.

In preparation to fulfill this destiny, I had to peek behind the veil several more times. Being the youngest girl of three older brothers, I did not feel equal. Our father was a raging alcoholic. Ice clinking in a glass sounded alarm bells in our house. "Dad is drinking!"

---

[6] Daniel D.C. Morse, *The Divine Spark Within: Excavating the Mysteries of Sophia and the Deep Christ*, (Sophonia Press 2022), 25.
[7] Jean-Yves Leloup, *The Gospel of Mary Magdalene*, (Rochester: Inner Traditions International, 2002), xvi.
[8] Mark 14:9 and Matthew 26:13, *New Living Translation*
[9] Mark 14:3a, *New Living Translation*
[10] Jean-Yves Leloup, *The Gospel of Mary Magdalene*, (Rochester: Inner Traditions International, 2002), 111.

The trauma of what was to come triggered us all. The boys took cover, leaving me, the tiniest of all my siblings, standing alone to deal with him. He was mean to the boys. I was Daddy's girl. I could get him to leave them alone. They quickly learned to send me out to deal with him. This was confusing as it seemed like I got his love and attention, but mostly when he was drunk.

I looked for safety with the other adults in my life—they were no help. They all drank. My traumatized brothers didn't understand and certainly did not want to join me in the healing of singing and dancing. My Mom made Dad promise not to drink when she went to work. But when she was gone, corks started popping. A drunk Dad was difficult to handle. I needed help from beyond the veil.

One night, I was awakened by a female voice whispering to me to come to the beach behind my house. Excited, I responded. Even though I was only six and would be alone on the beach late at night, I felt safe. What scared me was trying to slip past my parent's bedroom window. "Crunch," went the twigs on the ground beneath my little feet as I tried to sneak away. I froze! I listened for a stir. Silence. I made a run for it down to the beach. Breaking free, with all fear gone, I ran to greet a stunning full moon Goddess rising from the sea dripping in sparkling moonlight beams.

Struck by her beauty, I leaped into the air, "Ooooklahoma, where the wind comes sweepin' down the plain"[11]... I sang and danced up and down the beach to my favorite Broadway musicals all night. She helped me from beyond the veil to know joy! Under her guiding moonlight, I was free!

Later, I learned that this was Selene, the Moon Goddess. She rides her chariot across the sky to greet her brother, the Sun God, Helios, with their sister, Dawn, the Goddess (Eos). They work in harmony—when the Sun sets, Selene rises until Dawn, then she sets. Given my family, this Goddess story modeled the harmony I needed more than an old man-in-the-moon story. Looking back, I now see how this early encounter with the Moon Goddess prepared me for my later work with Mary Magdalene and amplified my passion for producing the Magdalene Moonrise Easter Celebration.

Meanwhile, back home, I keep hearing about this God guy. He was all these Omni's—Omnipresent, Omnipotent, etc. I needed help dealing with the insanity of living in an alcoholic home with all the trauma to my family.

---

11 *Oklahoma!*, music by Richard Rodgers, lyrics by Oscar Hammerstein II (New York: Williamson Music Company, 1943).

Somehow, I had to get a hold of him, but how do you do that? In my 9-year-old mind, I figured I needed to come up with a test that only God could pass. "Oh," I thought, "Only God could bring me a solid-covered diamond dress!" Two weeks later on a trip back East to visit my grandparents, we stopped over in Chicago. After dinner with family friends, the wife said, "Christy, I have something for you." She went into the back bedroom and brought out a dress covered in diamonds (rhinestones).

Her daughter was the U.S. Olympic Champion ice skater the previous year. Her costume on me was the perfect length dress. Kicking up my heels, I danced with confidence of the healing to come. I found God, I found HIM! I was so happy! The sparkles of rhinestones were diamond enough for me. Shortly after that, my prayers were answered. My Dad sobered up in Alcoholics Anonymous.

Next on my mystical journey, I would have to die to see more behind the veil. I was 12. Huffing and puffing, I rode my bike as fast as I could to catch up with my friends who got ahead of me. Suddenly, I fainted while going at top speed. I hit the pavement. I popped out of my body. Floating above, I looked down. "Wow, that's my body down there," I said. But I was not the least bit concerned. It looked like an old coat that I would not want to put back on. I felt whole and complete! I didn't care that my body was on the ground. Nothing was missing. I was whole.

My friends panicked and rushed in around me. I was trying to tell them that I was fine, but I realized I needed my body to communicate, so I slipped back in just in time for the ambulance to arrive.

At my ordination (2010) I was in such a state of bliss that I wondered, "Why am I so happy? Is it because I am with all these beautiful Goddess women?" We were all dressed up as Divine Feminine Priestesses. "Is my inner child (who loved playing dress up) finally happy?" Contemplating these questions, I went back to my room. I randomly opened *A Course In Miracles* (ACIM). My eye caught this sentence:

"All separation vanishes as holiness is shared. For holiness is power and by sharing it, it gains in strength."[12]

I had never experienced sharing "Holy Power" before. I could feel the bliss and the gain in strength. Wow! What an amazing feeling. From that point on, when a holy vision came, I had to share it to feel its wonderful, peaceful strength.

After my ordination on 10/10/10, all the puzzle pieces of my life started to come together. My first holy vision was a sacred celebration to honor Mother Mary for her consciousness to conceive light and birth a God. By 12/12/10 (Feast Day of Guadalupe), I was standing before 100+ people leading this glorious celebration as if I had always been doing it. What surprised me about being upfront leading these celebrations was that I had no thought about how I looked. Normally, I judged myself about my body. This time, I was free! Free to express my joy.

One morning, in meditation, I asked Magdalene, "But why me? I don't have a Goddess body. I am an older, overweight woman." I was grateful, like that night under the full moon, but I didn't understand why. I sat still for an answer. She whispered, "When people see you do it at your age, they know that they can do it, no matter their age. You help to shift the paradigm from a shut-away elder to a wise, joyful grandmother. When you open people up to feel their own joy, believe me, they are having too much fun to be concerned about your age or size. If you forget about it, so do they."

In 2012, it was all the news that the world was supposed to end. Early in the year, I learned about the Magdalene crop circles. I was curious about crop circles. It seemed that Magdalene crop circles were deemed not to be man-made. Often created on her Feast Day, July 22, the sacred geometry forms of the crop circles seemed to reveal something that was suppressed about her.

"What was the first crop circle of 2012?" I wondered. Turns out, it resembled the center of a Flower of Life mandala.[13] The irony is not lost on me that my story is being published for the first time by Flower of Life Press.

---

12 *A Course in Miracles* (Mill Valley, CA: Foundation for Inner Peace, 1992), 315.
13 The first crop circle of 2012 was reported near Lurkley Hill in East Kennet, Wiltshire, England on April 15. https://temporarytemples.co.uk/crop-circles/2012-crop-circles

Obviously, the world did not end. However, the last crop circle of the year[14] was telling. Located in Australia, as their summer is our winter, it was the shape of the Vesica Pisces (two circles overlapping in the middle to create a womb-like portal). This geometry is the seed of the Flower of Life symbol. When one calculates the math of the sacred geometry of this portal, it adds up to 153. Interestingly, the letters of the Greek alphabet are numbered. According to Margaret Starbird in her book Magdalene's Lost Legacy, "The number 153 is also by gematria the sum of the letters [that spell]… 'the Magdalene.'"[15]

We closed out 2012 with a powerful statement—etched into the Earth itself. A crop circle, shaped like the sacred vulva, symbolized the birthing of the Magdalene onto the planet. It marked the dawn of a new era, one destined to restore balance through the rise of the Magdalene.

From 2012 to the present, hundreds of people have attended the Magdalene Moonrise Easter Celebrations. We have remembered and discussed the powerful things she has done and experienced them by walking in her footsteps. In a six-station ritual, we viewed Easter through her eyes. Each altar was set up to tell her story, unveiling a deeper truth about her.

Now on a roll, I was having so much fun, fulfilling my destiny birthing this joyous celebration every year. Our dedicated Priestesses and Priests led people through these rituals to fulfill his prophecy. Now I unveil it for you. I hope you might be inspired to learn more, carry it forward into your own circle celebrations[16] to see Easter through Mary Magdalene's eyes.

A Magdalene Moonrise Easter Celebration begins first with the anointing (Station #1). Magdalene is remembered for anointing Jesus. Messiah means Anointed One (Christo). She knew what she was doing. She bought the oil. She was the one to do it. She was Sophia-Christo. Now, we are all called, male and female, to recognize this Christ light within each of us.

An Anointing Priestess greets you at the altar, witnessing who you truly are. You relax as you receive the blessing of this anointing; there is nothing to fear. You are celebrated as the Holy Anointed One. So be it!

---

14 Last crop circle of 2012-Boorowa, Lachlan Valley, New South Wales, Australia, 23 November, https://youtu.be/8FQkmA4eyro?si=VpdLlhmV3vahFEjZ

15 Margaret Starbird, *Magdalene's Lost Legacy: Symbolic Numbers and the Sacred Union in Christianity* (Rochester, VT: Bear and Company, 2003), 139.

16 YouTube channel: @MagdaleneImpact, there are videos of past celebrations, please like and subscribe.

Many are healed by this sacred touch. One woman, depressed from years of childhood sexual abuse, stepped up to be anointed. Sacred touch was something she had never experienced before. She was surprised. Her depression lifted immediately upon being blessed. There was no funny business in this touch, although it was quite intimate... just healing love. She walked forth in peace to Station #2.

Often, by the time women arrived at the last Station #6, the Gates of Heaven, they sat down and burst into tears, realizing how much they have missed by not knowing of the Feminine Priestess ways. Beautiful altars are adorned with images of the Divine Feminine, previously restricted and controlled by the patriarchy. Touched by the lost sacred art of anointing with the essential oils (Spikenard,[17] Rose oil, etc.), our hearts open. We come alive.

In the Last Supper painting by Leonardo de Vinci, Magdalene is seated at the table next to her beloved, Jesus. At Station #2, communion is served with the Easter braided bread[18] of the Goddess by a Priestess alongside her beloved. Life is celebrated with a cup of wine. Wine symbolizing blood came in the 12th century when the communion was changed.[19] From then on, only the Priest could offer communion. This was designed to make people feel separated. They could not seek God directly except via the Priest. Magdalene achieved a direct connection to God in the Gospel of Mary.[20] Therefore, she is qualified to give communion.

Station #3, the Cross, demonstrates her courage. She is the one who stayed, listening as Jesus said, "Father, Forgive them..."[21] For the Moonrise service, we built a cross with hundreds of nails in it, so when you step up to it at Station #3, you pull out a nail, symbolizing your commitment to stop crucifying yourself and others.

At Station #4, the Forgiveness Altar, you pick a card from an ACIM lesson on forgiveness. As you read your lesson, a Priestess tosses rose petals on your head. Joy abounds when rose petals start flying through the air.

---

17 I use a Spikenard blend that has a sweeter smell than pure Spikenard, which has a very earthy smell. More info is on my website. https://gospelofmarymagdalene.info
18 Braided breads served at Easter includes Italian Easter bread (panedipasquap a n e d i p a s q u a panedipasqua), Jewish challah, or Easter braided colored bread.
19 https://en.wikipedia.org/wiki/Transubstantiation
20 Jean-Yves Leloup, *The Gospel of Mary Magdalene*, (Rochester: Inner Traditions International, 2002), 31.
21 Luke 23:34, *New Living Translation*

With an open heart, you make your way to Station #5, the Empty Tomb where Magdalene went with the Holy oils. She was greeted by two Angels.[22] You, as well, are greeted by two Angelic Priestesses who anoint your heart. For in ACIM, we learn… "That the message of the crucifixion is perfectly clear: Teach only love for that is what you are."[23]

Anointed in sacred love, forgiven, healed, and celebrated, we share and extend this feeling of bliss entering Station #6, the Gates of Heaven. We are greeted by sound healers for a final blessing before we gather as One for a closing circle.

"Wow," one man said to me. "I have never experienced anything like this."

Another friend told me she has to thank my brothers for her profound experience at the Magdalene Moonrise Easter Celebration. "What? Why my brothers?" I asked, completely baffled. They were the ones who unmercifully tried to pop my bubble of joy every chance they got, often intimidating me and never joining me in any singing or dancing. In fact, even to this day, they have never once asked me about my Priestess experiences, the most glorious thing that has ever happened to me in my life.

"Yes," she said. "The pain of their rejection drove you deeper into seeking your healing. This search now drives you to create so much joy for others." It warmed my heart to hear her say that.

As glorious as all this was, and as much as I loved the Gospel of Mary, I was unresolved around one issue. During the year, I would teach the *Gospel of Mary Magdalene* (LeLoup). I was conflicted about what it says in this one passage:

"For it is within you that the Son of Man dwells. Go to him, for those who seek him, find him."[24]

"What?" I cried out to my God. "Seek *Him?* Why? What about seeking *Her?*" It never made sense to me that we have to seek only Him. What about Buddha, Krishna, and other great avatars? Please help me with this," I asked as I dropped into a meditation one morning. I was to teach this passage that night. "Is there another way to look at this?"

I let go into a sweet, uplifting meditation. I forgot I asked the question as I sat, enjoying the stillness. Then I heard, "You tell them it is H.I.M.!"

---

[22] John 20:11-28, *Contemporary English Version*
[23] *A Course in Miracles* (Mill Valley, CA: Foundation for Inner Peace, 1992), 94.
[24] Jean-Yves Leloup, *The Gospel of Mary Magdalene*, (Rochester: Inner Traditions International, 2002), 27.

"*H*-period, *I*-period, *M*-period?" I asked, "What does that mean?"

H is for Heaven, I is for In, and M is for Me. HIM is Heaven In Me.

"YES!" I exclaimed with great joy. Of course that makes perfect sense. If I seek the experience of "Heaven In Me" and find it, I will know the Kingdom of God. Jesus has explained the Kingdom of God is within.[25] For, what is God, but Love.[26]

The next line is "Walk forth."[27] For once we discover "Heaven within," we walk in that state of consciousness of love, sharing that love. The Gospel of Mary reveals to us that Magdalene discovered God within and was walking forth as an "Anthropos,"[28] a "fully realized human being." At the end of her Gospel, it says:

"…they all went forth…[as she had now activated the disciples by her 'Grace' and was leading the men]…to spread the Gospel… THE GOSPEL ACCORDING TO MARY."[29]

And so, inspired by Magdalene's teachings and Jesus's revelation of "Heaven In Me," we are all called to walk forth, in harmony, embodying and spreading the Gospel according to our own love-filled hearts, for we are that love if we choose to share and extend it.

~May it be so!

---

25 Luke 17:21, *King James Version*
26 1 John 4:8, *King James Version*
27 Jean-Yves Leloup, *The Gospel of Mary Magdalene*, (Rochester: Inner Traditions International, 2002), 29.
28 Jean-Yves Leloup, *The Gospel of Mary Magdalene*, (Rochester: Inner Traditions International, 2002), 29.
29 Jean-Yves Leloup, *The Gospel of Mary Magdalene*, (Rochester: Inner Traditions International, 2002), 41.

CHRISTY GRACE MICHAELS, M.A.

Christiane "Christy" Grace Michaels, Priestess of Mary Magdalene, is a mystic and teacher of the Divine Feminine. Her passion to uncover what has been suppressed led her on pilgrimages to sacred sites devoted to Goddesses, Magdalene, and Mother Mary throughout Europe.

She has studied with many top Magdalene scholars. Her mystical experiences led her deeper, illuminating where to look to uncover what had long been suppressed. Inspired ideas would come to her in meditation. Once, she heard "Magdalene Underwater." Googling it, the Disney movie, "The Little Mermaid," popped up with Ariel looking at Georges de La Tour's Magdalene painting, "The Smoking Flame." In Christy's research, she discovered that he painted two other paintings which outlined the steps of Magdalene's Awakening.

Christy has been a devoted student of *A Course in Miracles* (ACIM) since 1998. Through her work as a teacher of the Gospel of Mary, she discovered a powerful truth: Mary's Gospel beautifully mirrors the teachings of ACIM.

Christy was ordained on 10-10-10 into the Lyceum of the Holy Sophia by Priestess Elizabeth Kelley, of the Holy Order of Mary Magdalene and High Priestess Lady Olivia at the Temple of Isis in Geyserville, CA.

At age 15, she had the lead in a play with Bette Midler, right before Bette left for New York. She later had a mystical encounter with Bette that changed her life. One evening, she felt a nudge to turn on the TV. She hesitated, resisting the urge—until a clear voice rang out: "Go turn on the TV!" When she did, Bette's documentary lit up the screen, followed moments later by a photo of her and Bette together. Bette had followed her dream. In that instant, Christy realized she hadn't followed hers. The spark ignited—within days, she was enrolled in film school.

This gave her the skills to create and direct the Annual Magdalene Moonrise Easter Celebrations since 2011. Christy's Master's degree in Clinical Psychology focused on the impact of Eastern religions on psychotherapy. Christy teaches webinars on the suppression of women.

Learn more:
www.gospelofmarymagdalene.info
YouTube @MagdaleneImpact

The Magdalene Model for Finding True Love: H.I.M.

The secret of where "True Love" is has been hidden from us. From a young age, we were told we would grow up and find "True Love" outside ourselves. Magdalene models a different journey. "True Love" is within, as you learn in my chapter, "Peek Behind the Veil."

By unveiling the truth about who Magdalene is, we are given not only the clues of where "True Love" is, but the blueprint for awakening this love within ourselves. Magdalene is one of the most powerful examples of embodied love we have on this planet.

With this gift, you'll discover:

- The path she walked to embody divine love in her life.
- The steps and insights from her journey that illuminate how we, too, can awaken inner Sophic wisdom and the Gnosis required to find H.I.M. within ourselves.
- Learn her secret power—she did not need to "get love" from her beloved Yeshua. She only needed to share it from her own awakened state. She knew H.I.M. meant "Heaven In Me."
- Follow along and practice the steps she took.

Access here:
https://www.gospelofmarymagdalene.info/about-1-3

CHAPTER 19

Midwifed by the Magdalene
Resurrecting the Holy Woman

by Shardai Magdalena Rose Moon

What happens to the masculine and feminine principles when the Holy is stripped away? When the undulating backs of the women are forced to straighten? And the posturing of the men becomes the new tongue of transformation? When both are asked to take the shape that is foreign to their true nature?

What happens when the loss of the Holy becomes the new poverty, and the spitting voices of hatred spread the deadliest pandemic of all? We just might form a desire to exit this living hell. When, in truth, we arrived here to save it.

Death of the Perpetrator

I hold my beloved as he lies on the cold bathroom floor. Muddied pants sagged down to his ankles. Vomiting out the bottles of wine and hash that attempted to drown him in pain. Bloodied cuts on his arms, highlighting a neat slit across his wrist where he had struck out the tattooed word, "TRUST."

As if it were that simple.

Falling out of grace. Escaping this life of seemingly endless punishment. He has a personality disorder. What others see as crazy or inappropriate, I see as his unclaimed shaman's calling, hidden under layers of generational trauma. It's his cross to bear, his sacred gift to unwrap, if will and circumstance would only let it unfurl.

He blames this on me.

He says he has never felt this way about ending his life until I came into it. Crying out for me, his beloved, he can't imagine going on without me. *How could I do this to him?* It's a predictable peg in the cycle of psychological abuse—manipulate her to stay by threatening to harm yourself if she goes.

For a few short weeks, I had offered him the presence of the embodied Sacred Feminine in his life. And in his good moments, he offered me the open and nurturing arms of the beloved. Yet I knew it was not a healthy state for me to stay in for long, and my research of our shared Patriarchal Traumatic Stress Disorder and my apprenticeship of how to live on the street had taken a Self-sacrificing turn. I had ended things between us, yet from the deep, dry well within, he continued to thirst for the lifeblood of this immortal Feminine chalice.

He was vying to become my emotional perpetrator, aiming to leash me to him for a life of subservience and poverty, while I was simply there to learn how to survive and, eventually, escape it. I explored the game he was playing with a dangerous closeness and magnetic intrigue. Sometimes, my inner healer needs to lick the flames in order to learn to transmute them.

Holding off the wave of intended guilt, I travel into my inner sight to feel for the truth behind these wounded ego accusations.

In a way, I did pass this to him. I focus on my inner sight as I track the source of this possession, back through my time on the Big Island of Hawaii, where I felt possessed and overwhelmed with a sudden urge to cut and kill myself. But then, I realized I had inherited this energy through my former partner, through the pores of my dreamtime, who inherited it from his mother, who battled with major depressive disorder.

Not to mention my own past lifetimes of persecution, the red thread of women from my lineage who had succumbed to the strong arm of narcissistic culture, and the many hands that strangled the lifeblood from the feminine.

I am a born healer. Yet, in order to heal this patriarchal illness of self-hatred from within me, I had to see it outside of myself through this complete and unlivable heartache of the loss of the Feminine and the distortion of the Masculine that we were playing out. Oh, how it turns ourselves against us.

An entire line of healers calling in healers to mend this pattern, yet this unassuming man was able to top them all. I was in awe of him. An upwelling of gratitude spilled the tears from my eyes, wringing my heart out like a sponge. I wept at his feet, spilling my tears on the blood-stained floor as I mourned the tragic loss of my beloved to this patriarchal illness that would not let him truly live or love another fully.

I mourned for the Holy Woman in me who sacrificed everything I AM, only to be brought to my knees in penance before the patriarch.

My heart broke for him, for myself, for every being that has suffered under the misogynistic rule of subservience that depletes the soul of its light. For any being who has become impoverished of their very spirit. I saw myself—and every soul who has ever been denied their magic—reflected in the pain of his torment.

Was this really my fault?

I truly loved him, yet perhaps my selfish curiosity had given him too much false hope in a savior, and perhaps my sense of love from him was clouded by the suddenly met need of feeling wanted by a man again. Perhaps the perpetrator, the victim, and the savior *were* one and the same...

I stayed and held him—my persecutor, my victim, my savior—that night. I anointed his body with my Holy Oils as he drifted in and out of consciousness, crying out on occasion to see if I was still by his side. I laid out my medicine stones from my altar, singing my channeled songs to infuse his drifting consciousness with good medicine.

I held him as he wept for the Beloved he believed he had lost in me—an ache I knew intimately within my own heart. It was the agony of a soul bound by the grip of a patriarchal wound, a kind of madness that kept him from truly living or loving another wholly. His sorrow poured out in despair over the loss of the Holy Woman he was only just beginning to remember. We were brought together to find her again and to love this Holy Woman once more. It was time to save ourSelves.

Death of the Victim

I spend the next days at my altar, where Mary Magdalene comes to me. Stitching up my energetically severed womb from multiple lifetimes of trauma.

The same death I had witnessed in my beloved I now was ready to offer from within me.

With my inner sight, I beheld the charred and solemn corpse of a woman, head bent and body withered from a life of struggle. I had spent years completely drained of resources, will, and passion. I felt the bone-tired exhaustion of a woman who was so tired of feeding this story of being a disempowered woman. So tired of living a life that was created by others, of never having enough or being enough. This disempowered feminine archetype was ready to be released from my soul's path.

I was happy to offer her the sweet relief of her own demise. I buried a drawing of her at my healing altar beneath the medicine piece of my soul. I anointed her with myrrh, the kiss of death, and received the instructions from Magdalene to let her decay there for three days.

Ashes to ashes and dust to dust. A spiritual suicide of the part of me that had already died long ago—the one who had danced too close to the flame—to preserve the life that wished to live on.

Setting the stage for a Holy resurrection.

Death of the Savior

Another man enters the scene after this one exits, cast as the healthy masculine. My nervous system re-harmonizes under his care, feeling the literal weight of the safe and respectful masculine holding me anchored to myself once more.

Rewiring the illusion seeded from my relationship with my father that it is normal to be stuck in the craving for a love and emotional connection that, deep down, I know I will never receive from this person.

But to my dismay, just as quickly as he arrives, he vanishes like the ephemeral sand in the Sahara wind.

ABANDONMENT.

I recognize that this Savior archetype always enters my life after the persecutor leaves. I try to cling to him. To entice him to stay. My heart silently pleads for him to rescue me from this recurring fate of self-abandonment. I wondered, if there was no such thing as a savior, then who would be there to help me when I couldn't help myself?

I go to meditate at the ocean with a tender heart and ritually accept back the safety and protection of the divine masculine, reconciling the fear he will abandon or hurt me again. I lay down the exhaustion of trying to be something I'm not in order to get the other to stay.

Magdalene tells me, "Don't reach so far for the other's understanding that you lose your own footing."

The possibility of holding onto the sacred masculine was just another hollow illusion. No one was here to save me from my suffering. Would I ever be enough to keep the masculine present in my life all-ways?

Will I ever be enough?

Death of the Beloved

Magdalene stayed by the side of her beloved as he took on the pain of the world. As he breathed the last breaths of a dying path of honoring the God/Goddess in all her forms of LOVE.

As a highly trained Holy Anointrix, she anointed his body in the tomb with the Holy oils alongside the other Marys. Offering him death rites through the healing of Myrrh, the immortal spirit of Frankincense, and the compassion of Spikenard. Preparing his Spirit to ascend to the Father of his higher self.

I imagine because she was a real-life woman like me, Magdalene was traumatized by losing her protector. After his persecution and death, she was thrust into hiding, forced into the shadows by the threat of further violence. Suddenly, the world was no longer safe for her as a woman. She had not only lost him but also the uncorrupted face of the Divine Masculine.

Magdalene was taken care of by her coven. By the brotherhood. However, there were wisdoms and people that even she herself could not protect in the physical realm. So many losses of loved ones to the tragedy of greed.

On the spiritual plane, she was protected by him. But never again did she feel his arms around her… "Do not cling to me. For I am no longer of flesh, nor am I of spirit." He let her know he was still transitioning forms, though he appeared as flesh. *Do not cling to the illusion of what I once was, for I am something different now.*

We carry a deep collective guilt as if the blood of the Holy Man stains all our hands. Yet, it was only a few—those driven by power—who stirred the crowd and orchestrated his death. So, we must ask: is it possible that even today, those same forces of control and manipulation still sway the crowds under the guise of religious morality today?

What happens to our collective root system when the healthy masculine is crucified before our eyes and the healthy feminine is sent into exile? What kind of fear does that seed in the heart of humanity?

What kind of unquenchable longing for the beloved does that seed within our own hearts?

Holy Womb

I'm sitting now, staring at the double-lined test before me. A flood of shame rushes to my cheeks. Shit. How had I let my own insignificance gestate in me this incomprehensible news?

I anticipated the cultural shaming and legal action that would ensue if I shared this information, expecting that I, as the woman, would bear the brunt of the criticism and bear the ultimate responsibility for the consequences of this pregnancy. I was no longer an independent woman (Virgin). I was a slut and a whore. And due to the incapacities of the man, this path was mine to walk alone.

I shuddered at suddenly feeling spiritually dirty and undesirable by men. How was this so? How did sexual intercourse and love and new life become de-sanctified and re-defined as "dirtiness" and sin? How did the degree to which a woman is owned by a man become the qualifier for whether her pregnancy is sacred or disgusting?

I spend several weeks with one foot in this world and one foot in the spirit world, being initiated on the next phase of my Priestess path as a portal keeper between worlds, like Mother Mary and Magdalene were before me. I know that part of my sacred responsibility as a womb Priestess is discerning when to open and when to close the portal—when to welcome a soul into this realm and when to guide it back to the unseen. It means being deeply attuned to the Divine will moving through that soul as it prepares to take form within me, and honoring its voice in shaping its own destiny. It is an immense privilege, duty, and honor to be incarnated into a body that can create, release, and sustain life.

When in connection with her womb, a woman is closest to the creator. Whether in the death throes of bleeding time, the otherworldly ecstasy of childbirth, or the embodied power of the moon's cycles, she is trained in the meaningful ceremony of life and death simply through a lifetime of inhabiting her own body.

Why is it, then, that a woman who "plays god" within her body is a murderer, yet a man who "plays god" on the battlefield is a hero? Perhaps we have forgotten the role of women as Holy creators and sacred blood shedders. We all came into this world from the womb of a woman, and we will all return to the womb of Mother Earth when we leave it. Perhaps we need to remember the deep reverence for life that is required in order to take it.

To do so, we have to trace the story back to the very beginning. The moment our creation story shifted to personify God as a male. The Goddess-given job of the Priestess was demonized when the Priests then decided women weren't Holy enough to be so close to the creator that they could interpret and enact Divine will without the oversight and approval of a "holier" man.

When her titles of Magdalena, Priestess, and Holy Woman were stripped, so too was her sense of self-worth, orientation to purpose, and sense of belonging. The true purpose of the Holy Woman was stolen from her. Was stolen from me.

I felt emboldened to reclaim my purposeful creative power. This embodied activation and living prayer in my womb was acting as a reminder that I am capable of creation. And I am also responsible for this immense Goddess-given power.

Yet, in these moments of revelation, I felt anything but empowered. I pulled out another chunk of hair that had fallen out of my scalp from malnutrition. At my baseline, I was barely healthy enough to make it through the day with my chronic fatigue, let alone provide enough energy for two lives—I felt like this fetus was eating me alive. I had noticed myself in a state of pure exhaustion, needing to sleep most days. I became sorely out of breath as I took the double flight of stairs to my shared apartment I paid $175 each month for, and would collapse onto my child-sized mattress under the glow of my blue curtains and the constant ruckus of the street below—heard effortlessly through my single-pane windows.

Was this unglamorous pregnancy really the magical quest for the Holy Grail of eternal life I was seeking? Were these the bloodlines I wished to pass on through my sacred chalice? Was this the beginning of the end of my life as I knew it, and the start of another?

Holy Whore

Magdalene is everything made taboo about woman. Sovereignty. Wealth. Sexuality. Magic. Leadership.

Alongside Eve, she represented the fall of woman in the eyes of man. The erasure of the divine feminine archetype of the empowered woman.

SHAME. WHORE.

Sexual energy was distorted into evil in her name. Suppressed and shamed in women and yet glorified through defilement of the Feminine.

Magdalene's story was both unwritten and rewritten. She was exiled from her own story and from a culture that betrayed her—rendered an insignificant character in the greatest myth the world over. Her honor and titles were stripped from her in the retellings. She was recast as the penitent whore. The sinner who appeared to grovel at the feet of Jesus, from whom 7 devils were cast. Her gospel gutted, the most sacred teachings of true tantric liberation torn from the pages.

Are we really ready to receive her full gospel and ministry? Or will we reject and discredit her once more, sending her back to the underworld for a few more thousand years? Do we trust our own deserving?

How have we fallen out of favor with the Holy Woman within ourselves?

Labour of Love

I spend six hours in an excruciatingly beautiful labour of love. Pouring my heart, soul, and full body into the wrenching forth of this prayer from my womb. This breaking of a cyclical curse through the breaking open of my womb.

Sometimes, we have to reject what we "should" do in order to do what is right.

I call my closest sisters around me. Where the men used me, the women uplifted me with their effervescent light. I make clear directives in order to priestess my own rebirth through their hands and hearts.

"Anoint my feet with Frankincense for the pain… Bless my womb with rose oils…" It was time for me to take another dose of medication, which would send me into another round of unbearable pain. Just as I was ready to give up to the waves of anguish and call it quits, I prayed to the Magdalene for deliverance. I felt the sudden knowing that it was time for a final push. I asked my sister Sara (daughter of Magdalene) to place Release oil on my spine, and she blessed me with ancient mantras from her own Islamic tradition. With a few deep cries of pain, I felt the warm waters from within release.

"Hamdulilah!" (thanks God) we all declared as I collapsed onto the pillows in exhausted joy.

It had worked! After an exhausting month of searching for solutions to make this conscious choice in a place where it was illegal to do so, and without the support of an understanding family or funding to seek treatment elsewhere… The journey was finally finished.

I, and the entire room, become overwhelmed by this joyful feeling of blessing that even amidst the strangeness of this unorthodox entry, I was now somehow… *a mother.* This capacity of my body to create life, no matter how small, no matter how incomplete, no matter how "wrong," had suddenly launched me over a very important threshold into the wonder and belief in my own capacity as creatrix.

We all sat in the silent wonder together as we beheld this being. A room full of women who across traditions and beliefs chose to anoint this moment as sacred, through the ONE unified heart of sisterhood. There in my hands lay a new beginning and an eternal ending, entwined around each other, like the doubled-over cord around my baby's neck. I was affirmed in my own intuitive knowing by this symbol of death that this soul's purpose was never actually to be born. Their purpose was to act as the sacred offering to break this pattern of Self-sacrifice that was seeded into my womb against my will by the patriarchy.

Sacred Union

Like every enduring myth, the masculine and feminine—sky and earth—are held at arm's length, forever separate yet endlessly reaching for one another. Always seeking resolution. Always yearning for reunion. This is the root of our collective longing, the pulse beneath human connection: a deep, insatiable ache for the other self.

Did Yeshua and Magdalene complete this circuitry of sacred union, uniting in the eternal at last? Or do they represent the tragic beauty of human life that we journey through but moments of deep connection and moments of deep separation from uniting with who we truly are?

We're all looking for a great love story—perhaps this was the greatest love story never told, yet right there before our eyes all along. The tragic love story between humanity and the Holy Woman.

Perhaps we had to hear it this way, with just one of the characters (Yeshua), in order for us to appreciate that the story was really about the ONE anyway.

Perhaps we needed to hide this love story from ourselves in order to feel the ache of what is missing, tugging the halves of our hearts back together across time and space. Perhaps the tragedy of loss is what makes us appreciate the grace of true union.

The Sacrificial Lamb

I stand at the edge of the great Atlantic Ocean, sandaled feet upon jagged stone. I hold the mason jar close to my womb and heart, grasping onto the precious prayer held inside, until it's time to let it go and surrender it all back to the great mother. The joy, the possibility, the grief, the longing, the pain…

I had never before felt this sensation of a mother's grief for their child, but it lingered behind my eyes for months. I hadn't felt attached to that being while they were inside of me… yet seeing them here in front of me made the seemingly invisible connection and etheric shadow-work visible.

As I pour out the contents of my jar, I give these waters and this soul from my womb back into the primordial womb waters of the Mother, for her salty tears to wash them over with her grief and renew this potential for life into its fullest expression of love.

A personal sacrifice—both of and for myself. For to sacrifice, in its truest definition, means to make Sacred. I lay my precious baby to rest, nestled inside of a shell, placed within a womb-like pool of safely guarded ocean waters. They are buried beneath my prayers of safe travels that are delivered through the crisp leaves of sage and soft petals of rose.

To create, we must destroy. To destroy, we must sustain. To sustain, we must create again.

This represents the death of the ancestral pattern of the unhealthy masculine and unhealthy feminine living inside of me. Completed through a powerful choice to end this cycle of unconscious creation, and to enter into a new paradigm of conscious creation. Rolling the stone away from the tomb to reveal the light of eternal life.

It represents the loosening of the noose of unworthiness that would not let me truly live or love myself fully. And the reclamation of my emboldened power as a Magdalena, both death doula and midwife of creation.

Saltwater winds lap wisps of hair to frame my determined gaze. Ancient stone watchtowers flank me at either side. My heart silently laying to rest this lineage pattern, breaking the chains of confinement that would have me recreate it.

What will I seed into this empty and fertile womb? What will I choose to pass forward through the life-giving waters of my Holy Grail?

What do I create from here?

Holy Sacrament

Months later, I lay there alone in a hotel bed in southern France. Just miles away in both space and metaphor from the place that called me here—the infamous Cave of Sainte Baume.

I am travel-weary, and though the room was only $70, it is more than I have spent on a place to stay in years. Depleted of borrowed cash from a fellow vagabond (Sa'ha, daughter of Magdalene), and exhausted from years of repeating this survival game pattern of scraping by to feed and shelter myself, my nervous system gives a much-needed outbreath in this comfortable quiet room, wishing to take up residence for longer than a night.

How did I get back here again? I question. I had the foundation of financial security drop from beneath me with the loss of my health and my masculine anchor. For years, I was slowly digging out from the depths of my own grave. How fitting that I would never make it to the cave on the hillside but only to Her tomb beneath the Church.

I curl myself under the covers like an infant in the womb and call Magdalene in to hold me. I feel her presence more profoundly than ever before. She offers her gratitude for my visit to these lands where her spirit dwells.

She guides me to use my signature blue lotus oil in self-pleasure, where she opens 13 gates of my Feminine power. Circling my yoni, she helps me reclaim the sacredness of this creation portal. With each orgasm, I lift centuries of desecration to this holy temple and re-establish clear boundaries with a Guadalupe-style border of fragrant roses. The energy of the Masculine is the last step. He penetrates with reverence in order to translate the wisdom encoded in the body of the Feminine, thus bringing the teachings into the world with clarity and grace. She holds the wisdom in her body.

"Do this in remembrance of me." Take in the Holy Sacrament of the body of the Goddess. Play in the pool of her waters. Remember that living in effortless abundance is as true to our nature as is breathing.

I partake in the holy sacrament of my pleasure, in remembrance of who I truly am. Breathing in. Breathing out.

Despite it all, I knew somewhere deep within my bones the voices of the Magdalene and of the Goddess were singing my marrow awake with the electric pulses of my true desires, and the wisdom and trust to let the world around me meet them once more.

My body held the wisdom of the Goddess. The answers were here all along. Simply waiting to be penetrated and received by the loving hands of self-devotion.

Resurrection of the Holy Woman

The story the many bloodied hands of the rising patriarch rewrote severed the sacred contract of love between the Masculine and the Feminine. It drew a neat line in the sand through TRUST. Creating a fissure in the body of the earth itself, so deep that it slowly grew to divide the whole world.

Will this chasm now be repaired through the many hands and hearts choosing to reach across the divide? Perhaps this is where the many hands of the Magdalene pick back up the story.

There are old records to be struck and TRUST to be rewritten. In order to rebuild the culture of reverence for one another that was lost, we must rewrite the ending together in a way that includes HER voice. It is essential that we trust the Feminine to lead once more, calling back the resurrected Holy Man to her side to uplift and support her mission that is encoded in her very BEing.

Magdalene and Yeshua were sacred rebels of their time, destined to tell a different story for their generation. We are now called by the Magdalene to flip the script for our generation, to rebirth the Holy Woman as the redeemed savior of her own world—a world that includes all of us.

It is time for her to tell her own story instead of living the story that was told for her.

I am the Holy Woman.

> *"I am the way the truth and the life.
> No one comes to the Father except through me."*
> **(John 14:16)**

I AM
SEX
LOVE
MAGIC
POWER
WEALTH
LEADERSHIP
SOVEREIGNTY

I am not a sinner nor a saint. I am both, and I am neither. And that is my power. The power to choose for myself. And to live in the liminal space between the definitions of what I am and what I am not.

Anchor in Truth.

Trust in Love.

Resurrect the Holy.

And so it begins. And so it ends. And so it is.

Shardai Magdalena Rose Moon

Shardai Magdalena Rose Moon is a registered nurse, sacred activist, and international spiritual teacher, bringing a wealth of cultural experience to her students. She is the founder of the Rose Priestess Temple and Mystery School. As a healer and ceremonialist of over 15 years, Shardai acts as a bridge between the ancient and the modern. As a Sacred Feminine advocate, she is passionate about resurrecting the traditions of earth and of women.

Grateful for her roots grown in the rural heartland of America, Shardai has since taken an unorthodox path to break free from the societal mold that would have her story already written for her. She found that detoxing herself from patriarchal colonizer indoctrination and remembering the path of the Rose Priestess was the key to regenerating her Christian roots and reclaiming her authentic voice and power as a Holy Woman. Today she leads others to do the same.

Shardai is a sanctioned shamanic teacher in the Pachakuti Mesa Tradition, a certified Priestess Presence temple guide, an adept shamanic healer and a Holy Anointress. She currently resides between the big island of Hawaii and Morocco, where she offers her shamanic and priestess retreats amongst authentic cultural immersion.

Shardai is passionate about training women in the arts of ceremony, healing, and sacred leadership. She has awakened the healing gifts and visionary sight in many of those around her. She believes that the very wisdom and healing we seek is seeking to be remembered from within us. It is her honor to help re-member You.

Learn more:
www.rosepriestess.com
www.rosepriestess.net
Instagram @shardaimoon
email: shardai@rosepriestess.com

Magdalene Healing Bundle

Magdalene Guided Journey | Womb Clearing Transmission | Healing Prayer

Receive this 3-part journey of healing to reclaim your sovereign womb.

Magdalene Guided Journey is an open door to connect with the Magdalene and the wisdom of your womb directly. Through the beauty of the red rose, you will be guided to receive a womb healing and anointing by the Magdalene.

Womb Clearing Transmission is a video of energy healing and sound clearing that is meant to cleanse the womb of past transgressions, and reseal its sovereign energy field.

Healing Prayer is a written wisdom transmission for your altar or daily practice, meant to remind you of the power of your inner Magdalena.

Access here:
http://www.rosepriestess.com/magdalene-bundle

CHAPTER 20

MARY MAGDALENE AND ME

by Lin Murphy

"In the midst of hate, I found there was, within me, an invincible love. In the midst of tears, I found there was, within me, an invincible smile. In the midst of chaos, I found there was, within me, an invincible calm. I realized, through it all, that in the midst of winter, I found there was, within me, an invincible summer. And that makes me happy. For it says that no matter how hard the world pushes against me, within me, there's something stronger-something better, pushing right back."

—**Albert Camus**

Introduction

This is a story about Mary Magdalene and me. Mary Magdalene was a powerful spiritual leader who was maligned and marginalized in life and in death. She was misunderstood and dismissed, her story distorted, and her true role erased. Yet she persevered as a powerful leader in the early days of Christianity, and her role is being reclaimed in the collective consciousness by many of us today. She helps us to be resilient. She shows us that we can keep our heads up and hearts open even in the darkest night. She guides us to stand in our truth and power and to trust our wisdom and knowing. In honoring Mary Magdalene, who lived thousands of years ago, we also honor ourselves today.

I share my story so that you may know your absolute worth and divine feminine power, to know that you, too, can rise in these challenging times and reignite the fire in your heart. I invite you to step into the light and love of Mary Magdalene.

I grew up in an English, Irish Protestant family in Staten Island, New York, a working-class community. I went to church and sang in the choir most Sundays. I came to realize that no matter how much I prayed or contributed, I could never be a leader in the church. In fact, women were mostly omitted from the Christian story.

As a young adult, before I knew what I was doing or why, I began seeking out feminine images of the divine. I found a pantheon of Goddesses in Greek and Roman myths. I learned of Artemis, Athena, and Aphrodite. I studied yoga and sang the names of Durga, Saraswati, and Kali. In Buddhism, I found Tara. In the Egyptian mysteries, there is Isis and Hathor. Although satisfying and even exciting, I had a longing to find Her in my own tradition. However, in my austere Lutheran church, Mary, the mother of Jesus, was downplayed, and I knew little about Mary Magdalene except that she was an unappealing character. I was taught she was a prostitute, a fallen woman, certainly not someone to look up to as a role model. It took me decades to discover that her true-life story is quite different. It turns out Mary Magdalene is the nurturing, healing aspect of the divine feminine. I came to know her as Jesus' beloved and a highly evolved being in her own right. She is an archetype linked to themes of death, rebirth, and the transformative power of love and devotion. New questions arose: What is it about her that is so magnetic? Why was this important woman's story buried and left to be pieced together like shards of pottery after thousands of years?

Little did I know how important she would become to me!

Around the turn of the millennium, 2000, there began a great rumbling like early earthquake tremors. It started with a novel by Dan Brown titled *The DaVinci Code*. This book spoke to something in the popular imagination about Mary Magdalene. I was drawn to the rumblings like a moth to a flame. A plethora of novels about her soon emerged. Novels such as *The Moon Under Her Feet*, *The Woman with the Alabaster Jar*, and *The Book of Love*. Then, it became an earthquake. Ancient scrolls that were buried for millennia in caves near Qumran in the Judean desert near the Dead Sea were discovered and made public. The Nag Hammadi scrolls and other gospels, including a Gospel of Mary Magdalene, were being translated and became available to the public. A very different picture of this woman began to emerge.

In one key story, the apostle Peter asks Mary to tell him and the others what "the Master" Yeshua taught her that they may not have learned. Mary obliged and told them a very esoteric account of what happens to the soul in death and how to escape the powers that seek to keep the soul entrapped in the world and ignorant of its true spiritual nature. As she finishes her account, two of the disciples quite unexpectedly challenge her. Andrew objects that her teaching is strange, and he refuses to believe it came from "the Savior." Peter goes further, denying that Jesus would ever have given that kind of advanced teaching to a woman, and then questions her character.

Mary begins to cry at his accusation and asks, "Do you think I made this up?" The story ends here, but the controversy is far from over. Peter and Andrew have not understood the Master's teaching and are offended by Jesus' apparent preference for a woman over them.

Though denied, Mary chose to carry her version of the story forward. Her teachings became known by some early sects as "The Way of Love," "The Way of the Rose," or simply "The Way." This version is very different from the Roman Catholic version that Peter preached.

Many of us who had long since left the church were obsessed with the reclamation of the historical Magdalene. Like a storm gathering power, it grew in our minds and hearts and spread across the globe. She came to me on the inner planes in meditation and dreams. Many images of her emerged: chestnut hair, red robes, light or dark skinned, but always with piercing eyes that bore into my heart. I dove in and enjoyed swimming in Her mysteries.

After the crucifixion, the people close to Jesus were in great danger and had to flee. There is nothing written in the bible about where they went or what became of them. I have learned through my research and travels that Mary Magdalene traveled to Egypt during this time. Then, she continued on to France to a village later named Saintes-Marries-de-la-Mer. Here, she is welcomed and shares "the good news" about Jesus and his life. I traveled to Saintes-Marries-de-la-Mer and witnessed an awe-inspiring festival in her honor. I wept as the locals re-enacted the arrival of the boat carrying Mary Magdalene and her companions to the shore under the moonlight. The villagers gathered on the shore to greet them, tired and weary from their long journey.

Mary Magdalene's story has never been more relevant than today. Many of us feel hurt, angry, and frustrated by the systems that continue to attempt to silence, suppress, and deny us our rights. It's no surprise that after thousands of years, we may have unconsciously assimilated messages that we are "irrelevant and powerless."

This is our reminder, our wake-up call to claim our birthright and our crown. Amid great challenges, Mary stood up for her truth, showing us that we, too, can rise. Now is no time to play small. Mary Magdalene is calling us to show up, to move out of the background and into authentic, joyous expression. It's time to take our place in the world! Together, we can do it. We can choose to break the cycle of self-criticism. It's time to respect, love, and accept all parts of ourselves.

Throughout my seventy-plus years, I've had my share of challenges. Looking back now, I see these as spiritual initiations and evolutionary steps in my spiritual progress. These challenges became turning points where the direction of my life aligned with my innate spiritual nature of love and harmony. Like Mary Magdalene, I was abandoned and discounted by the close men in my life. My father was a hardworking man who worked nights and slept days, so I saw little of him. My mother was kind but distracted. She had two sons, a much younger daughter, and a husband who wasn't around to help, and she was often overwhelmed. I was overpowered by my two much older brothers. They were already teenagers, and a baby sister was not their idea of a good time. My brother Tom was my ally and soul brother. When I was a toddler, he would watch me and ride me in the basket of his bike. He named his first boat, a rowboat, after me. But he was 14 years older and soon had other interests, like girls and cars, which took him away from me. The five-year-old me felt abandoned.

My other brother Harvey was always taunting, teasing, and finding ways to harass me. I tried to make myself small and invisible to avoid his unwanted attention. I felt like an intruder and like I didn't belong in this family. This sense of not belonging haunted me throughout my life.

When I started to date my first real boyfriend, it did not go well. As it turned out, he was a narcissist. Narcissists tend to attract people with low self-esteem, and that was me back then. We met down the shore. He was tall, blond, and tan—a good-looking surfer. I fell in love. We would go surfing together early in the morning with the sun coming up sparkling on the water. I was in high school, and he was a pre-med student at Rutgers College. It all seemed so romantic. After our initial courting period, when he made me feel special, he then started to put me down. It was subtle at first and then escalated. He criticized my words, thoughts, values, and even my body, commenting when I gained a few pounds. I was always worried about my weight and on one diet or another. He became a mirror for my feelings of inadequacy and shame. Our physical attraction was addictive, and the abuse became the background of our "love."

When he went off to medical school in California, we split up. I had to rebuild and heal from this relationship. I found a good therapist, enrolled in college, and created a life without him. I carried on. It was a few years after this that I had a spiritual awakening. I was in Ireland in a stone circle that I had been guided to when I was downloaded with spiritual information about the cycles of birth, life, death, and rebirth. I began writing poetry. I studied psychology, the closest thing to soul work I could find. I worked with trauma of all kinds, including war Veterans, rape survivors, domestic violence victims, and childhood trauma. I became acquainted with the underworld of the soul.

Like Mary, I learned to become empty and hold space for the release of the deepest human grief imaginable, including my own. This served my clients, friends, and everyone I came into contact with. I later went on to train in a spiritual path called the Pathwork of Self-Transformation. I learned how to move blocked energy through the body. I began laying my hands on others, helping their bodies activate innate healing abilities. I met and married a kind and wonderful man who was also on a spiritual path, and we started a family and continued the work of becoming. We are still together decades later, still loving, learning, and growing together.

Like so many good stories, there is another layer to this one.

Reclaiming the truth about Mary Magdalene isn't just about getting the historical record straight. It's about reconnecting with the divine feminine within us all and recognizing and honoring the divine feminine in the world. When we embrace Her story, we heal the wounds of suppression, shame, and unworthiness that have been passed down for generations.

The feminine has been buried and hidden in the modern world. Mary Magdalene is a teacher, a guide, and a powerful reminder that the divine is within us all. Her story invites us to rise, reclaim our voice, and live from a place of authenticity and inner strength. It beckons us to heal ourselves and our world.

I am now part of a sisterhood that guides others through pivotal life transitions such as coming of age, marriage, giving birth, becoming a parent, illness, and death. I do this through ceremony and ritual with the Magdalene as my guide. I am the living embodiment of the Magdalene energy. I am taking back my hands of light and rising again.

Conclusion

Do you resonate with the Magdalene Consciousness that is calling us forth to walk as love? To hold the light through grief, anger, despair, and all of life's challenges? The world needs us now more than ever. If you are reading this, I think that you, too, may hear Mary Magdalene calling. I invite you to look at the places where you may feel small or misunderstood… and to RISE. To claim your true self, the one who loves deeply and knows who she really is.

Poetry is the language of the soul and the deep issues of our humanity and divinity. I offer this to you as a prayer. Many Blessings!

LIN MURPHY

Lin Murphy holds an MA in Community Psychology and specialized training in trauma therapy. She is the co-founder of Pathfinders Institute, where she worked with survivors of rape and domestic abuse, as well as veterans coping with PTSD. Lin also founded two holistic health centers in Saratoga Springs, NY, and has led women's circles, workshops, and retreats for hundreds of women.

A lifelong student and teacher on the spiritual path, Lin's journey includes the Pathwork of Self-Transformation, Shamanism, Celtic and earth-based practices, and Yoga. As a passionate world traveler focused on sacred sites, she has led sacred site tours in Ireland and England.

Lin is a published author and poet. Now in her elder years, she serves as a celebrant, officiating weddings and hosting seasonal celebrations for her community on the solstices and equinoxes.

When not serving others, Lin enjoys hiking in the Adirondack Mountains, gardening, and spending quality time with her husband, two adult children, and grandchildren.

If you are looking for a Celebrant for your wedding, email Lin at Linmurphy100@gmail.com.

I Will Rise Again

I will rise again
I have not been in it
with my whole heart
I have been unwilling to go the whole way
I've been a petulant child
an unfaithful wife
in my heart
a hummingbird
flitting from place to place
sucking deeply from life's nectar
I have been the seagull
swallowing the clam whole
I have thirsted for the holy wine
longed to drink from the golden cup
I am the icy fire of lightning
bolting through the night sky
the star falling through space
leaving a brilliant trail of light
that spills hope
I am the waning moon
I am falling water and
I am the rooted tree
Do you lie awake at night?
I have been there in the sleepless night
hurricane of desire
I am the lull in the storm
I am no stone Goddess
limbs and nose broken off
I have been to the holy well
I have stood in the ring of stones
I will rise again
to shine into the ring of power once again

—**Lin Murphy**

CHAPTER 21

THE ROSE

by Sarah Alissandra Nomngoma

Mother of hearts
Mother of souls
Mother of light
Mother of hope
Beloved of Christ
Friend of Life

Woman who moves with incredible power
Will of the wind
Warmth of the sun
Strength of a flower
Mother to weary travelers and pilgrims
You touch the broken and bring truth to empower

To Children of Love
You bring down the rain
Blessing their youthful joy
Absorbing their pain
Mother I come, pouring with tears
And supplicate myself before you
Mary Magdalene
My heartbreak, my fury
Oh Mother make sense
For I don't know how to live with pain this intense

Help me
Sacred Magdalene
I know no other way but to weep before you without shame
Mother of comfort
Mother of solace

I come with sincerity as my humble offering
Show me the colours I need close to my heart.
Share the simplest truth
So that I can empty myself and restart
Begin with your love and never cease loving
Show me the path
And recreate peace in all feeling
Tinge my Life with your petals
With the Rose scent of healing
It has been so many years, instead of faith I ran in fear
I've been so lost, but you helped me find
A gentle path, loving and kind
My heart has begun to believe again
Mother Mary Magdalene

Through the humbling grief of losing my child, I have discovered this: When the heart breaks, it bursts open like a rose. Like the heart blood that diffuses the canvas of our lives with its life-giving, deep crimson-red, blood of Mother Nature. Heartbreak allows an opportunity for the pain you hold to be valued. So whenever you feel the suffering, be like a rose. Surrender to it and let your pain offer the world an opportunity for reflection and pause, simply to bow to beauty, to breathe in its perfume. The Love, the ecstasy of sharing the contrasting joy and pain of being a Mother, a woman who loves with all of her heart.

A Message to My Child

My own pain is real and raw. My heartbreak at this estrangement feels palpable, as if there is a bigger, softer heart outside of myself making itself known. I so often ask whether I should feel shame at my sorrow, the pain of being rejected, trampled on, disregarded, and abused. But I can only feel my heart asking the obvious question, "Is there ever a moment when you miss me, too, my beautiful daughter?"

When you were young, there was always so much love between us. Such deep understanding. I faced so many challenges bringing you up alone. Everything was amplified by your need to depend on me. My own need to find nurturing, bring in our bread, and keep the roof overhead. And I did it quietly, without you realizing that in every waking moment, I was walking on the very edge of survival. I did it creatively and wove beautiful stories into the struggle to survive. You saw the brave face of a woman who refused to give up, to whom failure was never an option, and the luxury of self-compassion was a rare and beautiful gift.

So often, I could not hold them back and shared my tears with you, my child. You knew my heart because I spoke the truth. About your father, how he died, about my emptiness when I felt beyond myself and so tired. About my incredibly tortured heart, the agony of anger I had no right to feel towards a world devoid of conscience, and the broken strings of love that hold our children dear. Now I feel how deep your pain is. I understand your need to estrange yourself from all that we went through. Someday, you, too, will understand your Mother's love and sacrifice for you. What I gave you can never be undone. What you felt within you—the bond between us—will never be unbroken. All the words you spoke, in love and hatred, in anger and resentment about your life, these words, my darling one… can never be unspoken. Nothing will undo the damage done… Only love, the most transcendent and unconditional everlasting love, can heal this wound, my child.

Because your childhood pain and the terrible shame you carry is a sacred wound. As hard as it is to receive, the truth is a more potent medicine than any comfort you might think you need. Nothing but unconditional love—no sorries—will ever ease your pain. No pretense, no blame, not even someone listening to your heart will ever change a thing. What was, is simply yours. The best that I could do. And if I could, I'd sit you down beside a river and sing life back into you. Each one of us is born from the essence of God. What your soul came to bring into your life is the miracle of love, the only thing that makes us whole. All those questions and all that blame. "What did you do to him? Why did he leave us, Mom?" has left you without goodbyes. I am sorry that your father died. I, too, have had to make my peace. I, too, had nothing left of him to hold onto. But as I've often said, "Your Father's spirit lives on in your eyes."

So, Love, as you walk through the darkness, hold your head up high and don't be afraid. Remember that your mother's eyes once looked into those of your father and knew his essence. You are born of our love; never forget that. He loved me as deeply as I loved him. Together, we created you, and together, we loved everything about you, my child. So, in this healing time, walk with me again. You have taught me well—you have brought me home as the world awakens to compassion and rebirth during this healing time on Earth. There is wisdom here, a wonderful lesson to be learned for all mothers and their children. Let the oceans and the mountains speak. Let the waters run, and the deepest wounds heal. You have heard my stories, oh so many times. You have laughed with me, and our laughter has washed away my tears. You have shared my joy and felt my pain. I am not afraid. I am not alone. My darling daughter, walk with me, as my friend this time.

The Lie That Divides

Trauma takes us all into places and situations that none of us believed we would ever have to live through. It's these lessons of life, the experience of the story, that brings us to the lips of a far greater understanding. This deep sense of grief, of losing my only child, my beautiful and beloved daughter. The pain of this terrible loss has made me open my eyes to the levels of deception in the world at this present time. To the lies that our young people are being told and the artificial world of technology, AI, and all the commercial and materialistic values that they are steadily being sold. In this present reality, we are all a part of a tremendous illusion—a takeover of everything that is wholesome, natural, and beautiful, of all connection between parent and child, between friends and lovers, and between grandparents and their grandchildren. The precious human legacy and magic of tradition are dying out because of this deception. The lie that says, "Follow me, I'm the Pied Piper," to our fellow humans and, more especially, to our youth. Innocent, brave, open-hearted young men and women are being deceived into choosing sides against one another. In fact, we are all being deceived in this way.

It is the human soul that will free us from this deception—the lie that divides us, breaks us apart, and convinces us that we are separate, different, or defined by what we possess rather than who we are as one beautiful Earth family. In truth, we are souls embodying on this material plane, emissaries of Heaven on Earth, carrying source codes and messages of Love.

These days, I feel more like Demeter, the Greek mythological mother of Persephone. I keep on… living with the living, but a part of my heart died when my daughter left for the underworld. A part of me keeps searching, looking for answers and ways to find my daughter and bring her home. I have journeyed so far into the darkness that even the smallest glimmer of hope sends a quiver of possibility and lights up my heart. All the ways I seek are blocked, and in desperation, I have begun to look to cross the Great Styx, river of darkness and death from whence there is no return…

I see a pale light shimmering on the dark surface of the water. Holding this pure light is the beautiful Mary Magdalene. "You will find your way in the light, beautiful Earth Mother." She calls to me across the water. "Go back home, do not cross the dark river of death. Your daughter will return to you at the time of the awakening of humanity on Earth. Go home and prepare yourself for her return." I hear her powerful and sweet voice clearly from across the fathomless stretch of dark river water. Did I dream her apparition? She who held the light so strongly for me in the depth of my despair. She who holds the powerful light of I AM. A light so pure and truthful that no confusion, no reversal of truth, could ever remain.

For a while, I had doubted my own sanity and was confused by all of this deception. *Am I really mad?* I frequently heard myself thinking. I kept hearing the words—not just in my own mind but echoing all around me. "You must be going insane," the world seemed to whisper. "She must be crazy… she must be crazy…" I heard it in the silence, in the quiet weight of her comments.

And I wonder why. Why have I been given the role of the "crazy one," the disruptor, scapegoat, and the black sheep? What is it that makes me so worthy of shame? Did I cross the line and speak forbidden truths? Truths too deep to touch the heart? It's all upside down and inside out. It is only natural that I feel this way about this separation and estrangement. She is my child, so close to my heart, and now she's gone. I accept and respect her choice to leave, but there will always be a raw space where a part of my heart was ripped away at our parting. More and more, I feel drawn to the subtle qualities of nature, the quiet places, the garden. The simple fragrance of a rose and the breath of rain.

Being a part of a circle of women from across the world has always been a precious gift to me. I have many women friends who are Elders who embody the Divine Mother's gifts of wisdom, courage, and beauty. Now, whenever I feel the powerful tsunami of agonizing grief begin to engulf me, I turn to these beloved women. Gypsies, Soul Sisters, African mothers, strong women who embody the qualities of the sacred Rose and the spirit of Mary Magdalene. I am brought into their center, into the exquisite heart of compassion and holiness without words through our shared tears, heartbreak, and understanding. We are all brought closer to eternal principles, sacred wisdom that acknowledges and allows all things. Together, we remain as compassionate witness to the chaos and destruction, the deception, the deep level of trauma that has affected every one of us on our beautiful planet. These wisdom keepers who uphold the Divine Feminine way of the Rose have shown me the future, a life filled with unconditional love, peace, and non-judgment.

One day, perhaps a day not too far coming, in a time of miracles and healing, we will find that friends and family members who once misunderstood everything that we held sacred will return in gratitude and reconciliation and with a far deeper understanding of life. And even if they never reconcile, I have come to accept that they, too, have chosen their paths, and I will always love them. The Divine Feminine energy is flowering as never before within the hearts of humanity. There is greater need and urgency for this graceful, wise, nurturing, balancing energy, especially now as the world we have known is rapidly breaking down. Our families, relationships, homes, and even our environment here on Earth are at stake. It takes time, this blooming, this coming back to our own beloved Higher Selves again. Here in the sacred circle of the Rose and within the loving heart of Mary Magdalene, we are brought into a space of deep compassion, forgiveness, peace, and introspection. It's here in this holy place where a woman may rest, pray, and begin to feel restored.

A Mother's Wisdom

As Earth beings, we all have had to make choices. How we choose to respond to grief, crisis, devastation, stress, and the intense pressure to survive will make all the difference. In these turbulent times, I have witnessed such enormous emotional mountains that children have to contend with. I, too, have known anxiety, my own panic, confusion, and my rudderless and directionless fear of abandonment. At some point, many of us have found ourselves tangled in the midst of disconnection. Cold and heartless attitudes from fear-driven people. No family is immune to the effects of environmental stress anymore. Village communities and extended family support structures have become the rare exception in today's world—there are fewer and fewer communities where grandmas and grandpas and stay-at-home moms are the norm. Yet, in these times of social and economic chaos, young people need an anchor in their lives more than ever. Children need their mother's wisdom. Especially precious is the living bond between daughters and their mothers. It is this natural extension of richness and experience that an older woman imparts to her daughter, which is most valuable at this point as she grows into the fullness of womanhood and enters into relationships of her own. This is the time when young women most need to draw from their mothers and embody everything that is of the sacred and Divine Feminine. However, in this time of chaos and confusion, it is exactly the opposite that has happened for many women and their daughters. All that is sacred is being confused and refused. Everything beautiful and holy has become fractured, and like a broken chalice, the form and sense and all that is sacred about womanhood has been steadily destroyed.

It is the time of the "Great Shattering," and it is happening to all of us. It's a time of global wars and diaspora. There has never been a time like this before where the reality of surviving an economic crisis has become a reality for most families. Where mothers are forced to leave their children and families behind to join the workforce, give all of their precious energy to corporate environments, and be completely depleted in the process. Where having enough money and assets takes priority over nurturing our children and maintaining the loving connection between family members. All of the old ways, the subtle ties between loved ones, have slowly become less and less valued. Those beautiful moments with Grandma in the kitchen, baking pies and learning sweet home skills, the sharing of memories, song, stories, and experiences, are being lost to the winds of time.

I am a mother, and I see all of this happening around me. I also see the consciousness shift that is a natural response to this pressure to supply, work, and produce. Humanity has begun to awaken to the truth of who we are and to realize that this disconnected, energy-depleted state is not natural. That our natural state is our well-being, contentment, compassion for one another, joy, generosity, and kindness.

"A wise woman seeks an answer and burns a candle throughout the night in prayer." These words echo around the world from beloved African Elder and Sangoma, Grandmother Virginia Mutwa. "You are never alone, for the Great Spirit fills the darkness of the heavens. It fills the endless yearning of the soul. It lives within each part of us and is also the whole. It is the fire and the wings that fly us home. So never give up your praying for love, hope, and strength because all women who are suffering are joined together at this time, as one. Remember that God is with us. We must just be sure that we love God and pray to God every minute and all of the time for help and salvation. I love you all as my own children. Ngiabonga usale kahle, Thank you."

A Message to All Daughters

Humanity has long been held in the thrall of materialism and domination. This will continue as long as humanity holds more judgment than compassion. You, too, will carry the "Gold" for others when you begin to live with inclusivity, unconditional love, gentleness, and care. Once we open our hearts to the possibility of service and becoming a blessing in other people's lives, everything we know will change. Love will begin to permeate the Earth again. The ripple effect of our love and compassion for one another will change and positively affect everything, even the trees, the birds, the fish in the ocean, the snow on the mountains, and the clouds in the sky. Even a smile or the merest thought of love, the humblest gesture of kindness, will change everything, you will see. So don't hold back. Never hold back from expressing yourself, your joy, your inner perfection, and your beauty.

Shine brightly, daughters of Earth!
Your love matters, now more than ever on the face of this exquisite blue planet,
Mother Earth.
She knows us, she loves us
She feels us, she cares about us
And she has been waiting patiently
For all of us to realize
Our potential to change the world
With Love.

Sarah Alissandra Nomngoma

Sarah Alissandra Nomngoma is a poet, writer, and artist of the soul. Her work reflects qualities of the mythical that are so intrinsic to life on this beautiful African continent. She was trained in Archaeology and Fine Arts at the University of Cape Town. She later continued her research into San culture and the Rock Art of Southern Africa, weaving these elements into her work. Her paintings have been exhibited widely in South Africa and internationally in New York and London.

Sarah writes about the human experience, focusing on Motherhood and her deep connection with Mother Gaia. She has valuable memories of her time with the Khoisan people, deep in the Kalahari Desert, listening to their stories and to those of many Great African leaders and healers.

Sarah presently lives on the beautiful Southern African shores of the Garden Route, where she paints, writes, and directs a children's Education Program called "Ubumama Outdoor Classroom."

Look out for future books by this exciting new South African author.

Learn more:
https://ubumama.co.za

SACRED GIFT

Forgiveness

Because everything is connected like the spiraling Fibonacci petal sequence of a rose. We too are a part of everything in life. And whatever happens, whatever has affected our lives, we as the guardians of our earthly beings must come to accept, to make peace with all that is, has been and ever will be.

And so I offer you the gift, this invitation, the revelation of this opening prayer, the unfolding of the Rose.

Access here:
https://ubumama.co.za/magdalene-unveiled-gift

CHAPTER 22

Womb Wisdom, Moon Magic

by Lara O'Neil

"Let me not squander in the hour of my pain."
—**Rainer Maria Rilke**

It was a dark, cold winter evening in February, and the moon was bright and vibrant. I was taking my sacred ritual bath. The warm, silky sea salt water contrasted with the bitter, dry cold outside. The steam was rising over the top, creating a dream-like feel, the aroma of Frankincense and lavender filled my senses, and the flickering candles illuminated this sacred space. I was doing this as much as I possibly could, as it helped soothe my pain and nervous system from taking care of my dying mother. It helped me feel connected and grounded again. I could feel my muscles and tension give way. I relaxed and released into the envelopment of the water. I was in prayer, asking for guidance and letting the tears flow, joining the water around me, as my body was wracked with grief and overwhelm. That is when I felt it—an undeniable sense of divine love and comfort. It was my grandmother's presence that overcame me. This was the maternal love and embrace I was longing for without even realizing it. I felt a sense of calm that, yes, my mother was going to pass soon, but it was a sacred passing to another dimension beyond the veil that I did not need to comprehend, and she would be divinely received. I breathed into this moment as something powerful shifted in me.

Throughout these months of my mother's decline, I felt the beautiful presence of Mary Magdalene along the way. My grandmother's healing presence while I was in the bath was another welcome connection with divine feminine wisdom and love—the wisdom of standing in grief with Grace. I had been studying and in devotion with the Magdalene teachings and the Way of Love for many years. But now, she was bringing me even deeper, supporting me to bring sacredness into the darkness of loss, grief, endings, and completions. This challenged me further into surrender and faith.

The Goddess reveals herself in many faces, and the Death Maiden is perhaps one of the least revered in our youth-obsessed world—yet I have learned she is just as holy. During this time, I felt as though I was being powerfully initiated into this archetype, even though I resisted it every step of the way—kicking and screaming, quite literally at times. My resistance was strong. But I had no choice. For several months, the darkness coiled around me, the heavy weight of sorrow, and though I fought against it, resistance was futile. My initiation was to go there and stay present, so I did.

My mother passed away two nights after the visit from my grandmother. I was sitting next to her lifeless body at 4:30 am. The moon was outside of her large bedroom windows. It was ominous but beautiful and vast. I felt utterly alone and wracked with grief. She did not look peaceful like in the movies, like I had hoped for. Her skin was gray and sunken. Her mouth was slightly ajar. She was not the mom that I was used to. I tried to cling to her and hold her, but in this Earth form, she was gone. I wanted to know her, hear her, and see her in the way I knew her before, but she wasn't that anymore. Her body was just a remnant of the soul that had now departed. The Latin phrase *Noli Me Tangere* (cease holding on to me) came to my consciousness, providing solace. She had ascended to another plane beyond my comprehension.

The sobs took over my body as I wailed in a way that I never had before. I was in the deepest of dark despair. I had no control, which was a feeling I was not used to or comfortable with, but it overcame me regardless. From the bottom of my core, I cracked wide open. It felt like centuries of collective grief and sorrow surged through me—an endless river of mourning. Up until this moment, I had been skilled at shutting down crying when emotions were overwhelming. Not this time. It was excruciatingly painful because I felt as though I was going down into the darkness with her but without a lifeline. Yet somehow, in retrospect, it was a release as well.

In the two months of caring for her as she rapidly declined, I felt a deep resonance with the *Descent of Inanna*—a myth that describes the stripping away of ego, assumptions, control, and dignity. And now, like Inanna, I was at the bottom, immersed in darkness and death. It did feel like I was dangling naked on the meat hook, like in the myth. I was desperately looking around, reaching for something, anything to help, but there was nothing but my grief. Just when I thought I couldn't handle it anymore, Elsa appeared. She had been my mother's aide and confidant for the last several years—a true angel in disguise. She was devoted to my mother, and my mother was just as devoted to her. Elsa took one look at me, her eyes wide with grief, and immediately understood—she had walked this path herself just a few years earlier. Immediately, she began her African ritual of prayer and song, anointed oil to my hands, and guided me in her tradition for when a loved one moves on to the heavenly realm. Together, we stood over my mother, prayed and sang, and blessed her reunion with God and Source.

Slowly, I was coming back to life, still filled with grief, but grounded in this plane, releasing the darkness, presencing the moment, and honoring the death passage. It felt like a miracle. I was letting go of my attachments to who my mother had once been, setting her—and myself—free from the weight of the past. Dawn was here.

About two years before her passing, my mom announced that she would die at age 75. Despite her health slowly declining from Multiple Sclerosis, this fiercely independent, loving, and vibrant woman still lived alone, rolling around in her wheelchair, determined to handle whatever she could by herself. She remained active, mostly online, passionately supporting the many causes and organizations that were dear to her. Many people in her condition would have been in assisted living a decade earlier, but she made me promise—on my life—that I would never put her in a nursing home. That promise haunted me.

But now she was trying to prepare me and her three granddaughters for her passing. Honestly, I didn't believe her. To explain a little bit more about my mother, she had also prophetically announced about 30 years prior, at the beginning of her illness, that "Jesus said that I would be healed after my injured toenail grows out," and even though I really wanted that to happen, it never did, at least not in the physical form.

Yet, almost as if on cue, the day she turned 75 marked the beginning of a rapid decline, both mentally and physically. It was like she had been holding on for this, and now she could finally let go. It was remarkable.

Her behavior became very unusual. Our relationship was complex, and I have always had challenges with my mom, but this was different. I was in shock, staring at her dumbfoundedly, and she snapped at me, "Why are you looking at me that way!?"

Well, Mom, because you are acting like a crazy person, I thought to myself. I have certainly had a history of looking at my mom in dismay or mild disgust. My mother had an uncanny knack for embarrassing me. It was like her job on this Earth.

Yet, I caught on pretty quickly during the week after her 75th birthday that something was really wrong. It wasn't her usual wackiness. Her physical and mental decline was rapid as her aides and I watched with dismay and disbelief. We did everything we could for her, but there wasn't much to be done. She would not go into a nursing home. She would not take any medications except for some pain medications at the very end. She wanted to be spoon-fed yogurt and have whiskey rubbed on her gums, so we did. And by miracle—and the grit of our teeth—we were able to keep her home, where she could pass in her own surroundings as she had insisted.

The evening before her passing, I was again in prayer and meditation, trying to soothe my feeling of desperation. I turned to my divine *Magdalene Rose Oracle* cards for guidance and connection. Miraculously, I drew the Death Maiden-Black Rose. Once again, I wept with a multitude of emotions: sadness, relief, emptiness, knowing, love, and connection to Source all swept through me. Through the transmission of the card, I experienced the death maiden—the priestess of endings, embracing me with warmth, connecting me deeply with the divine mother.

Following her passing, many hours later, I tried to eat, sleep, and to feel like a normal human being—even if just for a tiny bit. Despite my efforts to care for myself, I was unable. I had brought some things home from her house to place them with love and honor. That is when I began to circle around myself, like I didn't know where I was or where I was going. I disassociated and was disoriented. Then I collapsed onto the floor, with no choice but to curl into a fetal position as the relentless tears flowed once again. I felt a deep, empty void in my abdomen as if something was being cut out of my womb space. It was confusing and upsetting. I felt dismembered.

This feeling lasted for several weeks, and I longed for something to fill this empty void to make me feel whole again.

The ironic thing is that now, many months later, there are times when I catch myself and chuckle because I feel her coming through me. I never wanted to become like my mother, but something has shifted, and now I have come into peace and reverence for it. I feel her in me when I get a glimpse of myself in the mirror or when I see my hands move. Or when I mispronounce "wolf" to sound more like "woof." When I talk to the birds, squirrels, and the trees or dance in my yard barefoot. When I cry from being deeply touched by a moment that I see, feel, or read. When I cry from being overwhelmed by the pain and suffering of our world, especially for the animals and the pillaging of Mother Earth. When I want to take home every stray animal I see or rescue a creature from the sidewalk or road, so they don't get stepped on or run over. When I shake my body and make funny noises to relieve tension and stress, or when my heart bursts with love and grandiosity for someone or something unexpectedly. When I stop and smell the flowers, even in a vase in my home, and when I am drawn to ceremony, ritual, and sister circles. When I speak of Love or am inspired by drumming music. When I talk to God/ Goddess/ Source throughout my day… In so many ways, I feel her in me.

Reflecting back, my mother did a beautiful job talking to me about death and grief ever since I was a young girl. She was a psychotherapist and was willing to explore deep emotions and processes of the human psyche. When I was in elementary school, we once visited a woman who had just tragically lost her fiancé. Her pain was so palpable that I remember it well. I don't remember exactly what my mother did or said, but I could tell her presence was healing for this woman. As we drove home, my mom spoke about the work of Elizabeth Kubler Ross and the many stages of grief, as well as the cycles of life and death. And she always connected it back to the spiritual and heavenly realm. I am grateful for this preparation and the wisdom she imparted. Later in life, she also spoke of how she was not afraid of dying, and she was looking forward to her reunion with her departed loved ones, as well as her beloved Jesus.

For decades, I identified more with my father in the way I looked, thought, and acted. Now, I know that's not entirely true. My father is in me, for sure, and I am proud of those qualities. But now I realize that my mother seeps through me the way my blood courses through my veins, the way *chi*—life force energy— moves through me and connects me back to the Divine Mother.

A few months after Mom's passing, I was sitting in meditation and feeling into that empty void in my womb. But instead of longing to fill it back up again, I was enveloped in the beauty of the dark, black velvet void. As I write this, it has been 11 moon cycles since her passing, and over the last several months, I have felt the pain of the void in my womb space subside. Now, it feels as if it holds the possibility of fertile ground, opportunity, and Rebirth. When I really feel this deep down inside, I can see Mom's smiling face filled with love and light, as it often was. I know that my mother gave me the gift of release and ancestral healing for me and my three daughters.

Witnessing her rapid decline was excruciatingly painful, yet during those months of providing daily, hands-on care, I came to understand—on a much deeper level—just how much she had been suffering all those years because of her illness and disabilities, despite her efforts to hide it. It brought me closer to her. I am now able to feel gratitude and realize it could have been much harder.

Divinely supported and calling upon all my tools for healing and wholeness, my mother's decline became an unexpected window for processing deep layers of resentment and frustration I had carried toward her. It felt like a slap in the face to have to address it *now*. There were days when I just allowed the rage to move through me—screaming, sobbing, losing control. Days when sadness and despair poured through me like a relentless wave. Days of journaling and reflection. Days spent in prayer and meditation with the Magdalene. It was a sacred yet painful time of growth—not just for me, but, I believe, for my daughters as well. Even though I hated every second of it and was often consumed by anger, I can see now that it was the necessary darkness of Death before the inevitable cycle of Rebirth and Life.

I acknowledge that in recent years, many speak of the Divine Feminine rising. Yet, from my experience with my beloved Mom, I stand in the truth that She has Indeed Risen. For me, the Magdalene collective consciousness is a path of authentic living, sovereignty, strength, and the embodiment of divine feminine energies.

I have learned that discovering the gifts within pain and loss requires deep exploration, courage, acceptance, and the willingness to release ego. I liken it to standing beneath the dark moon on the night before the new moon—when all is complete, the void is vast and empty, and new possibilities are beginning to emerge.

I now know that the path of the Death Priestess is the wisdom of this sacred cycle, honoring the full circle of life and death and bringing reverence to every moment. She is within me, the Divine Feminine, in all her forms—maiden, mother, and the sacred dark.

The Death Maiden

The Black Rose

The continued cycle of the maternal line

I am now the Matriarchy

We are the Sisterhood

We are One

We are She.

Lara O'Neil

Lara O'Neil APRN, CPNP has over 30 years of experience working with children and their families and has a thriving integrative pediatric and family wellness center. She is devoted to embodying the presence of love, wisdom, and healing.

Lara is an author and a sought-after and respected pediatric provider. She is a Certified Pediatric Nurse Practitioner with a Master's in Arts from the College of St. Catherine in St Paul, Minnesota. She has completed additional certifications in Integrative Health and Healing, as well as in Cranial Sacral Therapy and Reiki healing.

Lara is the bestselling author of *Rescuing Ourselves: A Story of Love, Healing, and Resilience through Integrative Medicine*—a personal transformation journey explored through the lens of authenticity, vulnerability, passion, and a deep love for her work. The reader will find themselves immersed in the journey with her and experience a range of emotions, from laughter to tears and everything in between, but most of all, hope.

Yoga, meditation, and a devotion to the Magdalene and the Way of Love are a sacred part of Lara's daily life. She also enjoys biking, hiking, and being in or near the ocean. She is a passionate and fierce protector of all things innocent: animals, children, and the earth.

Lara lives in Connecticut with her lifetime partner and takes immense pride and awe in her three uniquely different daughters.

Learn more:
www.thrivecenterforhealth.com
www.laraoneil.com
www.instagram.com/laraoneil_rescuingourselves

SACRED GIFT

Daily Compassion and Affirmation Ritual

This ritual is designed to nurture self-compassion and extend love and kindness to others, creating a sacred space for healing and connection. Take time each day to offer yourself and the world compassion, light, and love.

Access here:
https://www.laraoneil.com/free-gift

CHAPTER 23

COMPASSION REMEMBERED

Getting Intimate with Grief, Death, and Loss

by Jacquie Eva Rose Shenton

There is a brief moment when you wake up, when the veils are thin, and the mind lingers between the worlds. This is an etheric, semi-dream state in which everything is still possible, yet nothing is formed.

My eyes fluttered open and my body felt relaxed. I felt like cotton wool. It didn't last long, though, as the more conscious I became, the more the pain began to move through me and reality started to hit me.

She had gone…
She was NEVER coming back.

My heart felt like it was going to rip into pieces. Tiny little daggers were pinging all over my body as the void ripped open and I peered into the depths of despair. I couldn't catch my breath. All the air had apparently escaped from my body and was gone… POOF… Just like her.

I wanted more than anything just to feel her next to me…
To touch her again.

Her nose nuzzling into me, ushering me out of bed to go play. The excitement in her eyes when I picked up a stick and began to move my arm to throw it.

Sadness engulfed me…
I didn't know where to put it or what to do with it.

I got up like a zombie and walked to the coffee machine.

Being upright was disorienting—like having the flu, but far worse. My body ached for her. The grinding of the beans echoed the song of the pain in my heart.

I was crushed…

Ground…
Ripped up.

As the coffee beans continued to mirror my pain and form a liquid in front of me, my mind was with her. Images of our last days together, playing like an alternate reality.

Our last walk…
Our last cuddle…
The vet's floor…
The curve of her lip that I would never forget…
The surge of energy as she left her body and the stillness in the room that followed.

Being told by the nurse I had done the right thing, yet feeling inside of me that the world had ended and would never be the same again.

Nyah was more than a dog to me.

She was my best friend, my teacher, my guide, and my window to love. She showed me who I was in shadow and light and reflected unconditional acceptance. She was my confidant and the being I had decided to let fully into my inner world and true self. She was a part of me that was suddenly no longer there, and at that point in time, I didn't know what I would do without her.

As I sit and write this now and reflect on grief and loss as a process, I note that there is something very powerful about the experience. Grief transcends race, ethnicity, masculine, feminine, or being. We are all affected by it eventually, whether from the animal kingdom or the human. If you are a being on this Earth, you will, at some point—if you haven't already—encounter grief. When it arrives, it will impact you in one of two ways: it will open you wider to love and reveal more of who you truly are, or it will pull you into the depths of loss and despair, leaving you feeling trapped and unable to find your way out.

Grief is an Awakening Mystery. Its role is to hollow us to the core and clear the vessel for something new to take place. It shows us who we are and how we love, and if we are willing, it will show us the magnificence of what lies beyond loss and separation.

Grief tears away the confines of daily life and the mundane. We are forced to peer into the heart with such intensity that we are catapulted into the full human experience of raw love, abandonment, life, death, and rebirth.

The Magdalene knew this.

The Magdalene felt this.

And she left us a path filled with profound power and magic, woven from her own experiences and teachings. It's a path I now invite you to step onto with me.

You see, this is the left-handed path to liberation, freedom, and ultimately, joy if we are willing. A path to travel from darkness to light and into the awakening of the Christed Heart if you have the eyes to see and the willingness to surrender.

So, I'm inviting you into some personal reflection here for a moment.

How do you, dear reader, feel the pain of loss and the chasm of grief and overwhelm for your own journey?

Were you moved into your own tears and emotional centre by my opening story about losing Nyah? Did it ping the seeds of the grief within you or perhaps leave you feeling antsy, uncomfortable, or numb?

Pause for a moment and sit with this.

I invite you to further reflect now on the depth of your own pain. Is it a pain that you are willing to share and engage in as you make your way through this chapter and my story? Or will you choose to remain alone and closed off because it's not socially acceptable in our modern-day society to express the death and loss process and what it does to us on the inside?

I invite you to journey with me as I share my understanding of Magdalene's teachings on grief and loss, interwoven with reflections from my own personal experience and channeled transmissions from Magdalene. Together, we'll step back to the year AD 30 (or so) to walk alongside her while also straddling the years 2019–2024 in my life.

Magdalene Transmission:

"I am the one who holds you tenderly, knowing what is to come. I am the eternal truth that never wavers as we prepare for the inevitable. I will promise to not leave your side and hold the vigil of love as you suffer and then leave this earthly plane."

Can you imagine what it took for Yeshua and Magdalene to prepare themselves for the coming crucifixion? For him to die in such agony and for her to be the witness? Take a breath, pause, and feel into what this would have been like for them—as a couple—to know this was coming yet be unable to do anything about it.

This is the moment in the journey when you sense that loss is about to enter your life. Depending on the nature of the loss, you might be fully aware of it or only subconsciously aware. You may feel prepared to let go or, like me, totally unprepared.

I had already lost two dear beings that year and was deep in the realms of grief and doing my best to navigate it. My beloved cat Luna had been run over by a car in the spring, and my beloved Nanny Joyce had passed in the summer. I won't lie; it had already been a tough experience to navigate. Discovering that my beloved dog, Nyah, would be the next to go as we moved into the turn of Autumn, quite out of the blue, was utterly devastating. I didn't know what to do with myself, unsure of how to cope. Little did I know then that my best friend, Adrianne, would also pass that winter.

Hearing the sudden news that Nyah would have to be put to sleep was beyond painful—it was utterly heartbreaking. I tried everything I could to fix her, support her, and delay the inevitable as the cancer ravaged her from the inside out at lightning speed. There wasn't enough time... I needed more time... I couldn't get myself into a space where putting her to sleep was comfortable within me.

HOW COULD I DO THAT?... **TO HER?**

This rang out like a death wail inside my head from the moment I opened my eyes in the morning to the moment I closed them at night and waited for "THE day" and "THE moment" to come.

I knew I had to come to a balance within myself and prayed for a miracle as I asked the Magdalene what I needed to do here.

I had to move into a space of responsibility.

I had to put all of my feelings aside, even though they were crushing me, to do what needed to be done for the sake of the being I loved.

It wasn't pretty. My pain was already moving inside me like a wrench at my heartstrings and leaking out everywhere. See, I had been here before… 10 years previously with my first dog Kyia, and I knew what was to come. I'd been traumatised by the process, and I knew it was going to be incredibly difficult to navigate. There's something profoundly unsettling and heavy about being the one who must make the decision to end a life, not to mention the weight of moving through the loss of a loved one in the aftermath of their death.

Magdalene Transmission:

"I am the vigil. I am the light for my lover to follow in the darkness. I stand and silently weep at the foot of your passing, and I am the gates of grace guiding you through your last breath."

Can you now imagine for a moment what it took to bear witness to this spectacle as Magdalene watched her beloved be nailed to a cross and suffer such horrific pain? To be able to do nothing, yet hold silent space as she stared at this horror and held the centrepoint of love for him until his last breath?

As Nyah's heart stopped beating and her spirit slipped free, it felt like the breath inside me ended, too. I exhaled her relief, her release, as if her final feelings moved through me—and in doing so, something essential in me spilled out, landing silently on the floor beside her now-empty body.

It felt like a mercy for her—liberation from the pain she had endured. But for me, it was as if everything inside me left with her. And in that hollow space, a darkness I never knew existed began to take shape, slow and heavy, building like a storm on the edge of everything I thought I could bear.

In that split second, I made a choice to nail myself to the cross. I hung myself out to dry on guilt and let the scavenger birds peck at my weeping sores and bones.

I should have done better.

I could have done better, and there was no consoling me here.

She trusted me, and I led her to death.

We went home, and I sank into a pit of despair and the biggest blame spiral possible. My emotions were all over the place. I was overwhelmed with stacked-up grief, and the shock of what had just happened was disorientating. The house was eerily quiet—she was gone forever.

I remained nailed to that cross for the next three months. Unable to find my way out and unable to feel any spiritual consolation or hold any kind of space like Magdalene had as a vigil to Christ. I had failed as a spiritual person to be the vigil. I had failed Nyah, and I had failed myself.

Blame amplified out to all corners of my being. It was my fault my cat got run over. I hadn't spent enough time with my Nanny before she passed. I hadn't protected Nyah. On and on it went, crushing the light out of me. A small voice inside the darkness simply stated:

Now I am alone
Now I am abandoned

Love… had been wiped out.

Magdalene Transmission:

"I am the anointer. I bless each part of you as I tend to your pain. My caress and devotion awakens the door to everlasting life, beyond the realms of this existence."

Imagine the Magdalene now, devoting every part of herself to blessing the body of her departed beloved. Honouring him fully and bringing some form of tenderness to the pain he had just endured. Washing away the blood, pouring sacred oil over his wounds to bring back the light to the dark spaces on his body. Whispering words of utter devotion as she did so to create a field of love and holding around the vessel his soul had once occupied.

It was at this point in my journey when my beloved mentor Diana DuBrow reached out to me and asked me to hold Spikenard (Compassion Remembered) as a temple keeper in Rosa Mystica for the following year. Truly, it felt like Magdalene was reaching out to me on the etheric to guide me home as she wove her light and love through Diana's request. Gifting me the grace I needed to continue because I was so broken by loss.

In my blame, shame, and abandoned state, I didn't feel worthy of an oil of this magnitude! Who was I to hold the Magdalene's holy oil "Compassion Remembered" when I was so lost?

The first time I anointed myself, I felt Spikenard's magic encase me in a blanket of protection that held me safely as I sank into one of the deepest sleeps I had taken in months.

As the wheel of time turned onwards that winter, I found myself at the gate of losing my friend Adrianne. Hearing of her passing hit me like a truck and compounded all of the loss I had recently experienced.

Four weeks after Adrianne's death, my spine gave way unceremoniously. Two days prior, I'd received a warning vision that I didn't really understand at the time of what was to come. I woke up that morning and fell out of bed and couldn't get up off the floor. Pain surged through every part of me, and my body couldn't hold my weight. The lower discs were damaged beyond repair, and I needed surgery. Not only was I lost in the underworld internally, but now, I was bed-bound in the external, too.

As time moved on, winter gave way to spring, then summer, autumn, and another winter, and the oil of Spikenard began to initiate me, as all temple keeper oils do. The following spring brought my first spinal surgery, and I continued to anoint myself daily with as much devotion as I could muster. In my fragmented state, some days, all it took was the scent of the oil to make me pass out, while on others, I found myself in a deep outpouring of tears and rage over what I had lost.

Pain ravaged me in every cell as memories of all lost loves throughout this lifetime rose through my mind over and over again. Peering into the chasm of loss was all I could do. The weight of my grief was so powerful that there really was no option. I spiralled downwards and into the depths of despair, eventually coming one day to sit with the part of me that was hurt and grieving from childhood. A specific memory surfaced around the age of 7 when I knew I had learned that "to love someone or something meant to buckle under their loss when they left."

Little me inside was holding that mantle. I witnessed her pain. I let the memory move through me fully, along with the associated sensations.

Spikenard's magic was weaving its way into my core, and as time and life continued to roll on, I kept anointing and went deeper in. One day, I came to what lay beyond the voice of:

Now I am alone
Now I am abandoned

And I saw myself, aged 3, standing in the darkness holding a tiny toy dog to my heart with tears streaking down my face.

Magdalene Transmission:

"I am the witness to the awakened one's resurrection. I feel and tend to the spirit realm of our existence and invoke the angels to take you home."

Magdalene stands in Yeshua's tomb, holding vigil over her beloved, tending to her grief and loss. As morning light pours into the chamber, her beloved appears in spirit to her, in the arms of the angels. He tells her not to be afraid or to hold onto him but to go and share the news with the disciples that he will be ascending. She receives this balm of relief and goes to share.

I felt the tears come to a still point within me. Despair turned to utter silence within and then a vision.

Nyah and 3-year-old me were playing in a garden. Nyah's leg (the place that the cancer had most damaged) turned from the swollen and purple bruising that had been so hard to look at into woven strands of silk and ribbon. A beam of light came down from above her, and the radiance of this light transformed her body into a butterfly in its glow. As the butterfly flapped its wings and took off, 3-year-old me began to follow. Children's laughter filled the air. Ringing out like chimes through the etheric. Innocence, magic, mystery, and deep peace were attached to this vision as they danced in the light together.

In the alabaster jar of my own centre, my broken heart began to stitch itself back together.

Another vision followed. I was seeing myself, more the age I am now, maybe older, in a room in a beautiful building. Nyah came to greet me. As she licked my face, I felt such an overwhelming state of love move through my core. She then shared the following message:

> *I am always here.*
> *In the temple of the heart.*
> *I will and have never left you.*
> *You can visit me anytime you come to the centre*
> *and this still-point moment.*
> *Our journey can never be erased*
> *from who you are and who you will become.*

With a final lick of my face, the vision faded, and I returned fully to the waking moment.

I knew then I was going to paint her. I had created a painting process for myself when Luna died, so I had an outline of what needed to be done. Up until now, I had not been capable of doing it.

I wrote out my pain on the canvas.
I outlined her body and the butterfly.
I placed her ashes into her chest and heart space and sealed them over with paint.

She continued to visit me over the following weeks, and through my heart connected to the canvas, I followed her guidance on what needed to be done to create this memorial and completion point for her and me.

Magdalene Transmission:

"I am the eternal voice of love, ringing out through all states of being. Attune to the beat of the universal drum and take the steps you need to take in the world, knowing I have never and will never leave your side. We are always connected, and our love has opened a new door for you to walk through. Carry on our work in the world, as my light on the etheric continues to guide you through your daily life."

Now, I invite you to see and feel the Magdalene beginning to weave a new life. She sets up a new home in France and teaches the path of love that they had woven together. Although her beloved Yeshua is no longer by her side in the world, she feels him in the chambers of her heart and beyond the veil guiding her forward.

During my time spent in bed and recovery after my second spinal surgery, I continued to anoint, and the truth of Nyah's lessons continued to weave through me.

She taught me that it is okay to feel deeply. She taught me that there is always a witness and safe space to come home to. She taught me what unconditional love really means. She taught me how to fully travel through the path of grief and love and come out the other side whole. Her life with me and her ultimate passing supported me to cleanse myself of the deepest level of childhood wounding—Abandonment. She helped me to fully understand the threshold of death and dying and the ultimate rebirth. I will be forever grateful to her for this.

I placed the final ode to her on her painting, and it was complete:

> *You came to us from another world,*
> *beyond the stars and a void of space.*
> *Transcendent, pure, of unimaginable beauty.*
> *Bringing with you the essence of love.*
> *You transform all who are touched by you.*
> *And I loved you deeply.*

As I journeyed through years of post-surgery nerve complications and deepened my connection with Spikenard as a temple keeper oil, a body of work began to flow from me, shaped by my experience of grief. The places I had travelled on my journey became encoded like a map—one I didn't realise at the time was meant for others to follow.

I started to receive nudges from the spirit realms to share this work and gnosis I was fully remembering—that this path and teaching would also serve others deeply. This is the threshold of where I am today.

So now, beloved reader, I bring you out of the spiral of my story to the present moment to look again at the crucifixion teachings and what I understand to be true from them.

Come with me, full circle, into the flame of the heart and the ritual and wisdom of Compassion Remembered:

You see, I now understand that "Compassion Remembered" is not just about holding compassion for others (which I was already good at before that year of loss). Its lesson is to find compassion and peace inside of self first and then, eventually, radiate that deeper light out to others.

It's about tenderly holding the self through loss and never wavering from self as you prepare for the inevitable, however it will play out. Never leaving your own side and holding the vigil of love as you suffer through the pain of losing someone or something that matters deeply to you.

If you nail yourself to the cross, know that this is okay. There is wisdom in this teaching. The "purpose" of the blame, shame, and abandonment feelings is to propel you deeper into the underworld so you can visit the construction of your own pain and unveil the darkness within—if you are willing, of course.

Let yourself stand and weep. Big ass tears that come from your belly and core. Don't hold it all in, but let your emotions be fully present and tend to them with loving care as you step into the following truth:

It's okay to love deeply.
It's okay to feel deeply.

Pain and loss means you cared, you loved, you were loved. Let your pain show you the magnificence of what lies beyond. Fully engage in it rather than avoid or deny it because as we grieve, mourn, and truly engage with what we have lost, we open the door to dissolve our barriers of abandonment. Let yourself fully feel the pain until you can find the still place in the alabaster jar of your own centre that can speak to your lost loved one. Where spirit and matter dissolve into one, and the veils between life and death no longer exist. This is where your broken heart can stitch itself back together.

Plato said, *"We are fractured creatures trying to become whole."* The grief journey is an opportunity to put yourself back together again any way you want, so let others see and feel the depth of you. Don't hide it or deny it, especially from the self. Let the experience awaken you to a life that lies beyond. Be spent, softened, and opened by it so you can write a story of love and the rewoven heart.

It is my belief that what love and loss teach you is part of who you are and what you came here to do. Really understanding and embodying this will bring new life in ways you cannot possibly imagine right now.

The Magdalene is not just a person who lived many years ago. She is a consciousness that moves through us all. An archetypal blueprint that can bring us comfort in times of need and guidance on how to navigate the world around us from pain and suffering and into the light.

> *"Her energy is that of a Priestess, with a deep understanding of the thresholds of the spirit world. One who is available to true 'inner knowing' who can 'see' in deeper, clearer ways through a unique spiritual connection to both earthly death and the divine."*
> **—David Tresemer, Ph.D & Laura-Lea Cannon**

If you have the eyes to see and ears to hear, then Magdalene's life story holds many valuable lessons on how to live an awakened life. This is the one I have chosen for grief, but you will walk with her on many others through this book.

I have learned so much from following her guidance as a Temple Keeper of her holy oil. My journey led me to teach this work to others. Yours may lead you somewhere else entirely.

I'm going to return you to the question I asked at the beginning about the depth of your own pain. Is it a pain that you are willing to share and engage in as you make your way beyond this chapter?

Or, will you choose to remain alone and closed off with it because it's not socially acceptable in our modern-day society to express our feelings around death and loss and what it does on the inside?

Which do you choose?

Painting of Nyah

Jacquie Eva Rose Shenton

Jacquie Eva Rose Shenton is an Ordained Scent Priestess and Temple Keeper of Spikenard (Compassion Remembered) and Ylang Ylang (The Temple of Sensuality).

She is Faculty and co-lead teacher in Priestess Presence Rosa Mystica Mystery School and has her own program, Soulful Rebirth where she supports Empaths experiencing prolonged loss and grief to come to a Christed Heart healing resolution.

She has 19 years of deep embodied gnosis of Bodywork for trauma release, Reiki, Jungian Theory, Shamanic practices, Art & Dance as Therapy, Divine Feminine Embodiment practices, meditation, and how the mind creates and constructs our reality.

As Sacred Passage Guide, Jacquie's strongest gifts are transforming poison into medicine, the ability to deep dive into the realms of unconsciousness to bring back the gems buried there, and holding space for others to do the same. She loves spreading light in the darkness and helping others learn to come home to their centre, remember who they are, and embody their unique frequency of the rewoven heart.

She lives in Stamford, UK, and when not actively supporting others in the world, Jacquie loves to spend her downtime indulging in chocolate (who doesn't?), watching a really good series on Netflix, or walking in nature. She also loves soulful music and full-bodied wine. You will often find her dancing around her kitchen whilst creating glorious food for her family.

Learn more:
https://www.jacquieevarose.com/soulful-rebirth
https://discover.priestesspresence.com/rmms-year1

3 Days to Begin Healing Your Heart: A Gentle Journey Through Grief

This free 3-day experience is a soft space for healing—with simple rituals, tender support, and soulful practices to help you release what's heavy, honor your loss, and begin walking forward with more compassion and clarity.

Access here:

https://www.jacquieevarose.com/3-days-to-begin-healing-your-heart-opt-in

CHAPTER 24

Unveiled Creative Expression

by Crystal L. Steinberg

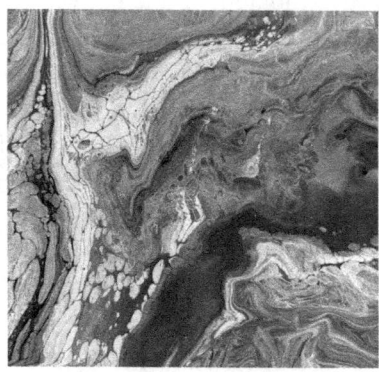

Mary Magdalene and Jesus are one of the most recent consort archetypes in human history. They bridge the ancients to our cosmic future where we identify the Divine in ourselves, each other, and all of creation. While I understand this now, Divine Feminine awareness did not grace my childhood. Realizing Her presence entails a dynamic journey leading me toward compassionate, conscious connections through curiosity and creativity. I grew up in a protestant household that elevated Christ as the only intercessor for "sinners." Even Mary, his mother, is not venerated in most protestant churches. She may be found in paintings or in stained glass windows to help tell the story of Jesus, but she is not venerated despite theologians such as Martin Luther affirming her perfection and virginity throughout her life.

In a tradition based on Jesus needing to be perfect to take the place of "sinners" and save them, why argue for a perfect Mother Mary? For if Mary was perfect, why did we need a perfect Jesus to save us? Why couldn't **She**? The consternation at the Counsels proposing and answering such theological questions needed Jesus' mother to be perfect so that he could be perfect. Otherwise, her imperfection might somehow genetically sully him. Their solutions point to the duality concerning women at the time. A woman's perfection had to be rendered less powerful than a man's. Wondering about such matters is part of the curiosity divine feminine energy inspires. Rather than simply accepting one tradition as correct, it prompts questions and contemplates if there are other meanings, other traditions to be explored, or if anything is missing. The Divine Feminine does not check Her brain at the door. It is Sophia Wisdom.

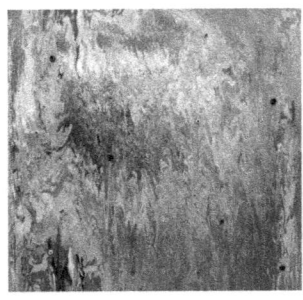

As Brené Brown reports in *Daring Greatly*, 85% of Americans interviewed recall incidents in school so shaming that they changed how they thought of themselves as learners. Half of the experiences involved art scars that prompted these people to no longer consider themselves artists. I knew I could draw, but my junior high art teacher caused me to doubt my ability to paint. He always began with positive comments about my work and would suggest one more step to complete the piece. But he gave no direction about how to use the suggested materials. When I fumbled through doing something like adding India Ink as an outline to a watercolor, he typically observed and disgustedly remarked, "Now you ruined it." It was around this same time that my mother's second husband started molesting me. I told my mom, and she said that she believed me, but he remained in the house like a troll living under a bridge. His interruptions while I slept made it feel unsafe to sleep. My imaginary screen went blank, and I no longer recalled dreams.

Relationships between mothers and daughters can be complicated. Anger that veiled the Divine Feminine brewed within me. Why had she allowed him to remain in the house? Why didn't she leave? We had many conversations about low self-esteem and how she would have been embarrassed to tell her parents a second marriage failed. After meeting with pastors who encouraged her to go home and be a "better wife" because her husband was a "fine church-going man," she even wondered if her family would believe her. It wasn't until I saw the movie "The Burning Bed," starring Farrah Faucet as an abused mother trying to leave her abuser and protect her children that I began to develop compassion for my mom. I saw how difficult it was to find community and support when so many didn't even want to acknowledge what happened.

My anger turned to exhaustion as my mom required assistance through half of her stomach being removed, knee replacements, and gall bladder surgery. They all involved complications and extended care. I was a mom, working full time and living on four hours of sleep. It seemed that I could never satisfy all her needs, much less consider my own self-care. When I felt overwhelmed, I'd sketch. Sometimes, a simple line drawing. Other times, a tree outside or an image that caught my attention in a magazine.

At work, I focused my creativity on writing curriculum to fill needs that students described. They didn't see themselves in the required stories they read. So, I asked them to share books that they did see themselves in and started creating classes like "Literature and Diversity" and "Literature and the Visual Arts." They listened to authors such as Joy Harjo, America's future poet Laureate, Sherman Alexie, and Walter Mosley present their work. When the students shared their work at The Chicago Art Institute, the head of the Education department asked me to consult and teach teachers how I used the exhibits and the museum in my classroom. I agreed, as long as my students continued to co-facilitate the class. We co-taught these classes each semester for seven years, during which we learned a great deal about creativity and art. As time passed, I decided that I would wait and learn how to paint when I turned 60. I rationalized that I could then take art classes for free in our state universities.

On the first anniversary of September 11, I was misdiagnosed with a brain tumor. After telling the principal of my school that I would not return to teaching because the doctor told me removal of the tumor would impact my intelligence, I spent the evening in the ICU preparing to have my head cut open. An early morning MRI revealed there was no brain tumor. Eventually, I learned that they confused my name with someone else's scan. Having avoided the surgery, something about walking back into school the next day and hearing the stories of others who had brain tumors caused me to reflect on my life. Why had I avoided the outcomes described to me? It felt like I had new life. But for what purpose? In hindsight, I see the Divine Feminine calling, but I only had a religious way of hearing Her voice. And the religion I followed didn't contain a divine feminine aspect.

Having experienced the Jesuit Leadership Seminars discernment planks, I decided to take a sabbatical to discern what was next. I spent my sabbatical at church, leading the confirmation program, visiting shut-ins and hospital patients, and before long, deciding to attend seminary part-time. The following year, I asked the school to hold my job for a second year and they agreed so that I could attend seminary full-time and discern if this was the path for me.

During this year, I awoke one morning with a 100% herniated disk between C4 and C5 that required emergency surgery to fill the space with a cadaver bone. I recovered rapidly with the help of my mom and seminary friends. Tears fell from my eyes as I sat in church and could not sing hymns. But when I closed my eyes, I saw all kinds of images and colors on the screen again. My creative sight had been restored! I started remembering my dreams, and I began preaching God in the feminine and masculine to the chagrin of our homiletics professor.

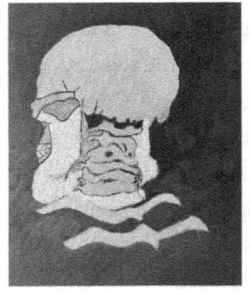

As I sat in a small office waiting for the doctor to do my post-op exam, a skeletal form of the neck bones rested nearby. I picked it up to examine it more closely. The vertebrae reminded me of doves. When I researched the spiritual significance of doves and the throat, I discovered interpretations suggesting a manifestation of divine presence and inner transformation. This affirmed my intuitive understanding of the surgery and the gift of creative sight that returned.

When I graduated from seminary and a parish called me to serve, I worked with two Goldendoodle chaplains, Abraham (Abers) and Sarah. They offered more pastoral care than any words could. Abers beelined for bedridden patients. He balanced one front paw on the bedrail and placed the other over the patient's heart while licking either their hands or face. The corresponding giggles always increased the speed of his licks and the wagging of his tail. A natural wheelchair heeler, Sarah moved at the speed of the patients in the chairs. On our very first visit, a caretaker  asked if a stroke patient in a wheelchair could hold Sarah. She did not speak since her stroke a month ago, so they were concerned. I lifted Sarah onto her lap, and she smiled as she started petting her. "Soft," she blurted out with a huge grin. The caretaker ran for the doctor and other nurses arrived, all overjoyed because of one small word. Every visit for nearly fifteen years included such affirmations of animal consciousness and how they could help heal.

While serving as a Mission Developer in my last call, my mom required back surgery. As a point of self-care, I flew in for the surgery but then returned to work as she recovered with other caretakers. However, when she received a terminal blood cancer diagnosis that fall, I went on leave from call to serve as her primary caregiver. I did my best to facilitate her living as she was actively dying. We experienced many kindnesses and hospitality. Mom wanted to experience the arts as much as possible in the time she had left. Outings such as *Million Dollar Quartet*, "The Vienna Boys Choir," The Chicago Christmas parade, Art Institute exhibits, meals at the Walnut Room (she loved the Fairy Godmothers there), and a trip with all of her family to Hawaii, her favorite place in the world, highlighted this time.

One of my dearest memories involves a trip to the Art Institute, where we spent an hour sitting in front of Picasso's 12 drawings of a bull. I watched my mom's arm flow like a bird's wing as she explained how she would order the images differently from the artist. Time seemed to stop as I admired her creative genius at work while she responded to another artist's creation. I dreamt her death the night before it happened. While we prepared for a bedside vigil of blood transfusions upon our return from Hawaii, my mom fell and died from a cranial bleed. She died with both of her daughters holding her hands and singing, "You are my Sunshine."

After Mom died, I encountered many mystical things. One of them involved healing the body memories I experienced on the anniversary of her death each month. I'd seemingly burst into tears for no reason, but then I'd notice it was the tenth of the month. When the place where I practiced yoga offered an Essential Oils class, I stayed to listen. As Lemon Essence came around, I closed my eyes and inhaled. An angelic Myrrhophore offering Lemon to me as a sacred gift on an altar appeared on the screen. I never experienced another body memory after ingesting Lemon Essence daily. Curious about this grief healing, I became a certified Aromatherapist and learned about the Myrrhophore tradition attributed to Moses' sister, Miriam and continued through the lineage of Mary Magdalene through today.

The Essences showed me how the Plants and Trees are conscious, healing beings of Light. Science supports this as it demonstrates how trees communicate through their root systems. When tragedies such as fires strike, they actually route nutrition to the trees with the best chance for survival. The HeartMath Institute now gathers data on how Trees respond to different stimuli, including hugs and positive affirmations.

After studying church documents and discerning, I decided not to return to church work after being on leave from call. The word "healing" did not appear in the documents, which seemed strange to me, given that a third of Jesus' ministry involved healing. Healing has always been a part of the Divine Feminine's call. Such healing power is part of why the women of the forest who understood Plant and Tree medicine were labeled as witches and heretics. This marginalized them, made it easier to murder them and then claim the forest lands with which they co-created healing.

When I left the church, I opened a Healing Arts Center. By this time, I was an advanced certified Medicinal Aromatherapist, a trained SoulCollage® Facilitator and Touch Drawing Facilitator. I partnered with a variety of providers: Tarot Readers, Channelers, Tai Chi Instructors, Circuit Trainers, Integrated Physicians, and Artists in Residence who offered classes each year. The center quickly taught me that space itself also carries consciousness. A Blue Christmas gathering demonstrates this.

The holidays change for people who lose loved ones throughout the year. The practitioners and I organized a Blue Christmas gathering as an alternative. Participants walked a labyrinth, remembered their loved ones, and received a Frankincense anointing. After the anointing, participants organically broke into groups to listen and support one another. As I watched, I could see their loved ones who had passed joining them in the room. Everyone felt the energy shift and commented on this as they shared hugs and thanked us for the healing they experienced. That night, I learned that I was a caretaker for the space. I thanked it for its gifts, cleared it after every gathering, and blessed it before the next.

Encouraged by other artists and Brené Brown's words:

"There's no such thing as creative people and non-creative people. There are only people who use their creativity and people who don't. Unused creativity doesn't just disappear. It lives within us until it's expressed, neglected to death, or suffocated by resentment and fear. The only unique contribution we will ever make in this world will be born of our creativity. If we want to make meaning, we need to make art. Cook, write, draw, doodle, paint, scrapbook, take pictures, collage, knit, rebuild an engine, sculpt, dance, decorate, act, sing—it doesn't matter. As long as we're creating, we're cultivating meaning."

—The Gifts of Imperfection: Let Go of Who You Think You're Supposed to Be and Embrace Who You Are

And so, I began to paint.

With opened bottles of Essences on the table, I experimented with dropping acrylic inks on water ground canvases. Images connected to the Essences emerged, such as, "Ancient Healers." Resin Essences Galbanum, Frankincense, and Myrrh sat open on the table as I poured the inks and a tree bark image appeared. Feeling connected to something bigger than myself, it often seemed that only minutes passed when I painted for hours. Then I heard Andrew Newberg speak at a "Creativity and Expressive Therapies Conference." He reported that brain scans of people making art lit up the same areas of the brain as those lit up by people praying, contemplating, or meditating. It seemed that science caught up to spirit as neurotheology emerged from his works, such as *How Enlightenment Changes Your Brain*.

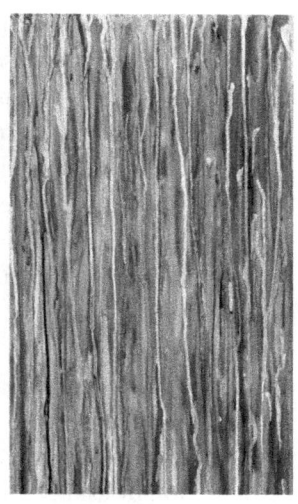

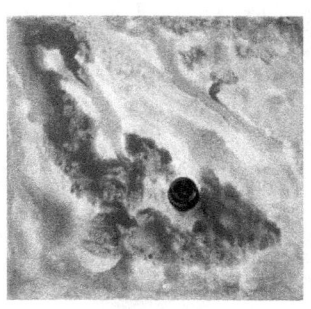

At first, I thought I was hearing things. I painted with an open bottle of an Essence in my studio a number of times, but this time, I heard a voice as soon as I opened the bottle of Violet. *Paint me,* she said. I looked around, even walked out of the studio into the rest of the floor to see if someone entered unnoticed, but no one was there. "Must be imagining things," I muttered to myself as I returned to my studio. But I heard the voice again. *Paint me.* So, I began working to create openings in the canvas to insert the bottle of Violet Essence so that viewers could experience Her as they studied the paintings. The African Ibis teaches us to generate a smooth flow of communication to create an appropriate working condition. This, along with the Acacia Tree representing a connection to the Divine, reinforced Violet's invitation to co-create.

I quickly understood that the Essences wanted me to pour them into the paint rather than to cut holes into the canvases to insert bottles. I smiled to myself as they made this clear to me. Of course, I thought, that makes so much more sense than creating an eye sore with the bottles. Realizing this, I repeatedly duplicated the process with acrylic

pouring paints in ceremony. After lighting a candle and placing the four elements on an altar, I'd ask the Essences who wanted to go next and listen in silence for the answer. At first, when I heard one respond, I checked my understanding with a pendulum. But after a number of experiences, I learned to trust our communication. We extended consciousness to the paint by asking what colors to use and in which order to use them. The painting on the bottom right of page 303 is a commissioned piece for a "Winter Garden" exhibit. It combines seven triangle canvases, each co-created with Eucalyptus Essences from different Tree families. We added two triangle mirrors to include viewers in the garden through their reflections.

As my consciousness grew through our co-creations, I experienced other life forms. When a channeler offered me an opportunity to paint with beings from another planet, I agreed. Together, we created three paintings in 45 minutes. I set the intention by asking questions and the being agreed to respond with answers through our co-created paintings. Find the paintings holding the answers to the following questions I asked below, left to right. First, what does Earth look like from your planet? Second, how are we communicating? I see a third eye. Third, what do the beings on your planet look like? I see robed beings.

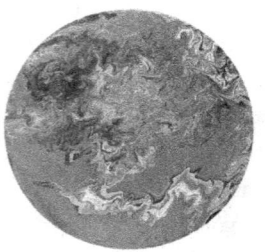  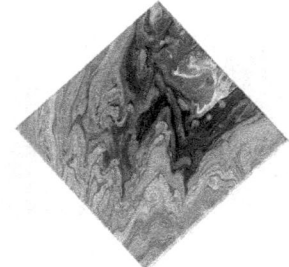

This interaction inspired me to learn about and practice Remote Viewing to understand more about the variety of beings in the cosmos by learning the Mother Tongue. None of our systems currently include the perspective of other life forms that research, military testimony, and current events such as the recent "drones" suggest. Ubiquity University, where I am currently working on my PhD in Wisdom Studies, is the first in the world to offer Certificates and Degrees in E.T. Studies. The Divine Feminine invites us to expand our hearts and minds to include all of creation.

I wrote the book *Walk Within and Reclaim Your Spiritual Nature* in part to demonstrate how the gospel lessons preached each Sunday in Christian Churches contain elements of the Divine Feminine. This is rarely highlighted in

churches, but she remains present just the same, just as she remained present at the foot of the cross. The majority of art throughout the world demonstrates this—even places where there is evidence that she was removed from paintings support this claim. The painting on the cover of my book emerged as I read *The Gospel of Mary* aloud on TikTok during a Lenten season. The video of the forty days evolution can be found under my Aromativity account there, or a condensed version can be found on my website.

Writing the book led to an invitation to lead studies with it as I traveled throughout Central and South America. Here I experienced great hospitality. Indigenous leaders invited me into ceremony. I felt an uninterrupted thread of Matriarchal energy. In many of the tribes, women select the chiefs who do the work, but the women make the decisions and continue their creative lineages. I noticed the respectful treatment women received in the culture at large: assistance crossing streets during rainstorms, with packages from the grocery store, or even with stairs or entering a pool. This was not saved for only loved family members; it was generously shared throughout the communities. When I fumbled their language, they generously smiled and corrected me with gratitude for even trying. This encourages my continued attempts. I find here that even a single word successfully communicated can continue the pursuit of meaning and connection.

An Art exhibit in Panama City involved all seven of the indigenous tribes gathering together for the first time. They created a document about how they intend to work together to preserve and expand their heritages. A Kuna Medicine Woman displayed the molas she made, including one of a solar eclipse that she experienced in 1968. In this manner, a community of women grows by carrying the powerful thread of matriarchy into the future. At the end of March, an International Women's Market at a museum celebrated the Divine Feminine found in the land, creations of high school students, and women artists. Below, the curators stand in front of a painting titled "Volcano Speaks." The artist hiked trails on the volcano and only used materials found on the hike to create the art. I see Her in this same painting behind them.

Through these people and their Creativity, She unveils an invitation I never imagined receiving. I hear Her calling me to stay, to relocate to a foreign land with a language I do not yet fully understand, to unveil Divine Feminine presence with these beautiful souls. This invitation to explore the Divine Feminine through art, connection, and spiritual growth does not end here in a singular way. It ripples throughout the cosmos like the rings appearing in a lake after a stone falls in it. The invitation to co-create meaning is a dynamic, ongoing call for all of us to recognize and honor the unlimited creative wisdom within ourselves, the world around us, and all of creation.

Cuna Medicine Woman, Guo, stands next to her Mola creations with five generations of her family during the "Gathering of the Tribes" exhibit at the MAC museum in Panama.

Interpreter Aaron and Attorney Darren share their enthusiasm at the 2024 International Book Festival.

Education Director Laura and Interpreter Marianne stand before "The Volcano Speaks" in the Cumulus exhibit at the MAC museum.

CRYSTAL L. STEINBERG

Crystal L. Steinberg lives her life as a pilgrimage. She integrates experiences, research, intuitive knowing, and remote viewing to grow and expand her spiritual awareness. Ultimately realizing she does not know what she does not know, she cultivates an empathetic and compassionate worldview. After serving as a learning facilitator in a Jesuit High School, a consultant at the Art Institute of Chicago, and an ELCA parish pastor and mission developer, she founded a Healing Arts Center. There she coordinated programming to include Aromatherapy, Chinese Medicine, Circuit Training, Expressive Arts, Integrated Medicine, Spiritual Exploration, Tarot, and more.

When covid precipitated the closure of the center, Crystal saw it as an opportunity to expand her learning and she began her PhD in Wisdom Studies: "Integrating Divine Feminine and Divine Masculine Energies for Wholeness through Creativity" at Ubiquity University. This entailed Toltec and Source Light Priestess, Intentional Creativity, Writing, and Transdimensional Mapping Studies that currently find her traveling through Central and South American countries. Here she finds a perhaps frayed yet uninterrupted matriarchal thread cared for and maintained by Indigenous peoples. Crystal so greatly appreciates their hospitality and willingness to share ceremony that she remains among these beautiful souls making art, writing about her experiences, and teaching classes about the presence of the Divine Source in all of creation.

Learn more:
email: crystalsteinbergcocreating@gmail.com
www.crystalsteinbergcocreating.com

SACRED GIFT

The Thank You gift I've prepared for you is a condensed video, only available through a private YouTube link. It includes me **reading The Gospel of Mary on TikTok during a Lenten season as I paint each day with Spikenard and Rose Essences.**

The final painting unveiled on that Easter morning became the cover of my first book, *Walk Within: Reclaim Your Spiritual Nature*.

Thank you for sharing your contact information with me. It will only be used by me to communicate co-creating experiences, reflections, and special offers as Life as Pilgrimage unfolds in Central and South America.

This link takes you to the page on my website where you register for your Thank You gift. Then click "sign up" to immediately access the video.

Access here:
https://www.crystalsteinbergcocreating.com/thank-you-gift

CHAPTER 25

THE BLUE ROSE

by Stellar

Introduction to the Goddess

I remember my first conscious encounter with the Divine Feminine and Magdalene energy very clearly. I was 27 years old, sitting on a beach in Devon, UK, with a dear friend, Annie. "There has got to be more to life than working, sleeping, eating, and playing," I said. At that time in the early '90s, I was working in media in London. Quite out of the blue, Annie said, "I feel it's time you met Isis." I looked at her, puzzled, and replied, "Okay, let's go!" I had no idea what I was letting myself in for, but my entire being said, "Yes, I am ready."

Without hesitation and after a few hours in the car, we had reached Glastonbury and I was taken to a beautiful house on the foot of the magnificent Tor. The Tor is like a beautiful green Cathedral towering over the town. As I entered the gate of the house, there was a sign saying "Shambhala," and little bells were chiming in the breeze. A radiant golden Buddha statue greeted us.

There was a feeling of deep peace, sacredness, and reverence as we made our way to the front door. We were quickly ushered into a stunning, spacious sitting room adorned with large Egyptian statues, where a formidable-looking, grey-haired lady with striking blue eyes asked me to sit down. She introduced herself as Isis. She immediately asked me to place my hands on my heart, and we went on a journey through time together. She took me back to ancient Egypt and asked me various questions about my life and work there. I could see everything so clearly in my heart—I was shocked and amazed at the same time. After this short meditation journey, Isis told me that we would be working together and that I should return and come back and see her often. Since I lived in West London at the time, this was fairly easy, and so I spent over 25 years working with Isis in Glastonbury.

Magdalene in Avalon

My time with Isis could fill an entire book. We accomplished so much planetary and cosmic work together, and she guided me through the most advanced priestess training. This training represented the culmination of many lifetimes devoted to the Blue and Red Rose Mysteries of the Magdalene and the embodiment of the Feminine Christ.

During my time with Isis, she always came back to the importance of living from the heart and living from love. She was a teacher of Love, and she helped me apply my heart's knowledge and heart's work to my everyday life and music. We also facilitated many walk-ins of souls who did not want to incarnate the usual way through birth but through a series of soul contracts and energy exchanges, so that souls could come to Earth to complete their missions. Whilst the training may sound wonderful and beautiful, it was incredibly intense. I was initiated through some of the worst scenarios, where I was called to bring unconditional love to the planet. The mantra for my mission became, "Love the unlovable and Forgive the unforgivable, and see all from the lens of Unconditional Love of the Mother." Whilst applying this training, I could see how unconditional love truly is the most powerful force in the Universe, with its sacred keys and codes to hack the illusory hologram of life and bring everything back to Love.

After my daughter was born in 2006, I spent more time with Isis as we moved to Devon to be part of a Steiner school community so that my daughter could have the best start in life. As Isis was starting to become older and mobility was difficult for her, she moved up beyond the main house into the original Magdalene Cottage at the foot of the Tor surrounded by a sacred orchard. The Magdalene Cottage is completely hidden and surrounded by hallowed trees. There is a high Druid seat and many portals there, marking the original site where Magdalene brought her teachings to Avalon, Glastonbury. It was here that she lived whilst emanating her teachings throughout the British Isles. The cottage is steeped in history, and the vibration of the place itself is palpable, with a powerful essence imbued with the frequency of the Divine Feminine. When I sit in silence in this space, it is as though Magdalene is sitting right beside me, whispering thoughts, visions, notions, and feelings through my crown as I feel the rushes and chills of absolute truth flood my being. One particular day, she said to me, "You are to return to France, along with everyone else." I immediately felt the calling and put out a notice for a retreat in May. Almost overnight, it was filled with 22 beautiful souls, each drawn to walk the Magdalene path once more and record the Magdalene Codes into the land there.

The Magdalene Codes

Two thousand years ago, Magdalene left sacred codes in the land of France, destined for this time—for the priests and priestesses who would return to receive these great sound and light codes of Magdalene Embodiment for the ascension process. In 2016, 22 of us recorded the initial sequence of these Magdalene Codes. This album captures those potent emanations recorded in the ancient caves, churches, and sacred spaces of Mary Magdalene in France:

https://open.spotify.com/album/5cNkl8ycVL2331AugP7tPE
https://stellar1.bandcamp.com/album/magdalene-codes

This part of France is very similar energetically to ancient Egypt. The land consists of a myriad of pyramids, stargates, energetic crystalline cathedrals, and goddess temples as left here by Magdalene herself. After the time of Magdalene in this land, the Cathars kept and maintained the Codes, and later, the Celtic Church had to go underground to preserve the Great Mother teachings and Cosmic Feminine Christ Teachings. During the Christos Mission 2000 years ago, Yeshua and Magdalene held the higher dimensional stargate Hieros Gamos codes and were able to ignite and activate these codes in the trained priests and priestesses. The Celtic Church, which kept Magdalene's teachings intact, consists of a series of ancient Rose and Melchizedek order teachings. These teachings uphold the belief that true Divine Sovereignty is an alchemical, initiatory inheritance of the Feminine Christ bloodline—one that has nothing to do with hierarchy or rulership over others. Instead, the Celtic Church recognised each human as a divinely sovereign being on a unique path to God through Gnosis or direct experience. For the Celtic Church, this royal sovereign inheritance was always recorded in the blood through the mitochondrial DNA of the Great Mother's Bloodline. The Celtic church is now rising once more with the hidden knowledge of the ancient synarchy codes and the Magdalene Codes that run right through the land in France.

Mary Magdalene's potent gateways and Codes in the land here are emblazoned with the Blue Rose original teachings of Divine Sovereignty, Hieros Gamos, Inner sacred Union, and the activation of the most important gateway and stargate of all—your human heart. There are several planetary and galactic stargates here in the land that link directly to the human design and body, as well as sacred telluric geometries that activate the remembrance of the original teachings of the Magdalene and of the Christ within your human heart.

The Order of the Blue Rose

The Order of the Blue Rose is a part of the Holy Order of Divine Sovereignty and is symbolic of the advanced knowledge of the teachings of the heart. It guides us in creating from heart consciousness and seeing every situation through the lens of love. My teacher Isis was in her true mastery of this sacred technology of the heart. The Blue Rose Order is a lineage of the codes of light from the Mother God-Source to anchor the Divine Feminine Christ here on Earth. The ones who carry the blue rose templates are the essence of the Holy Universal Mother on the Earth and walk as divine sovereigns and as the Feminine Christ. The Blue Roses are the emissaries of peace. They are the best peacekeepers in the Universe and are highly skilled at using the cosmic sword, which is the art of keeping the peace in the multi-dimensional realms. They are as much divine warriors as they are peacekeepers across this and many other universes.

The Order of the Blue Rose had to be trained in the dark arts to know how to counter and thwart these dark arts in cosmic battle and spiritual warfare—preparing for times like the one we find ourselves in now. They were highly skilled in the art of battle, warfare, and peacekeeping. Many feminine heroines of the past, such as Joan of Arc and Boudicca, carried the Blue Rose Geometry of Holy Universal Mother's True indigo Light. This order is also highly trained in High White Tantra—the sacred arts of Hieros Gamos, or divine sexual union—an ancient practice of true creation across all realms. Because of this profound knowledge, they were often demonised as whores or reduced to the false Madonna-Whore archetype in the minds of men bound by lower egoic consciousness. Yet their deep knowledge of teachings of sacred sexual union was divine and considered the holiest of holy work. They also knew how to build the Unity Consciousness Christ Grids to terraform the Earth back to its original template in order for the master builders to return to build the new Earth. At this time on our planet, the Magenta and Golden children are returning to Earth to be the master builders of the new Earth. They come with very powerful instruction codes in their DNA and are advanced souls who are committed to Earth's Ascension process.

The Blue Roses are one of the most demonised priestess sects in the Universe because they carry the codes of Divine Sovereignty and the pure Power of Unconditional Love. These codes are very destabilising and threatening to the status quo and the false light. The essence of the Blue Rose's symbolism is the experience of pain and the transformative power of love to transmute it.

You will find that these Blue Rose Order initiates have had deeply difficult lives. If you were to look through their Akashic records, you would see nothing but pain and suffering. Pain is a way for them to release the codes of light into the hearts of humanity, so they have to become very familiar with pain and the power to transmute pain with unconditional love. They also, in every lifetime, had something dreadful happen to their issue or offspring, such as the loss of a child or the loss of a child's innocence. This is the deepest pain a mother can endure, and the Blue Roses were highly skilled at taking this level of pain and transmuting it for all of humanity.

Through their divine voices, the Blue Rose Order have always been masters of frequency, harnessing the healing power and divine harmonic energies of nature. With their voices, they sing healing technologies to restore emotional and physical well-being in the sick and frail. They knew the power of song and mantra and were divine songstresses who allowed the Holy Universal Mother to speak and sing through their incredible voices. They could use their voices to heal not only humans but planets, planetary systems, galaxies, and indeed all organic life on all planets. They could and can also sing through dimensions to far-off lands and sing the elemental and multi-dimensional realms awake.

The Ascension Pathway

The Order of the Blue Rose are the teachers of the Heart and the true teachers of Love, but the price to become an initiate is not for the faint of heart and requires many, many painful lifetimes to be able to hold universal and galactic consciousness and the intense training required.

The Blue Rose ascension pathway is very specific and is now ready to be emanated on the planet again; this will involve the following wisdom teachings:

1. Reclaiming your divine sovereignty: Prime directive of the Universal Holy Mother and Father—Essential Liberation, Sovereignty, Synarchy, and Invincibility Codes for this ascension cycle.
2. Shadow exploration and excavation: Clearing the false self and illuminating the false light—The Phoenix dive into the Holy Fires of the dissolution of illusion into Holy Truth.
3. Healing and reclaiming the inter- and multi-dimensional splintered fragmented inner child and intensive trauma healing: Self-compassion and self-love.

4. Unity consciousness embodiment training with 144 qualities of divine love contained in the Heart of the Blue Rose: The Divine Pathway Home, Combined with Holy Order of the Red Rose teachings.
5. Initiation into the Temple of the White Flame in order to run the electrical and magnetic currents of the Divine Feminine into the Earth.
6. Hieros Gamos training - High White Tantra - Holy Order of the Blue Rose teachings.
7. Synarchy, allowing the divine and creative intelligence to work through us in a community - joint governance and unity consciousness.

These ascension teachings are now ready to be returned to humanity because humanity has reached a level of spiritual maturity to walk the path home to freedom and liberation.

Magdalene Lineage of the Blue Rose

The Blue Rose Order is an ancient order of the feminine counterpart of the Christ teachings and templates. It aligns with the teachings of the Divine Masculine Christed Way of Love and the essence of the Divine Feminine Christ.

The Blue Rose Order continues to be led by the Magdalene lineage, and there are many acolytes waiting to return and remember the teachings of this order. The training is universally and galactically very intense and involves the ability to hold more love and compassion, walk the Earth as a Divine Sovereign, and be an emissary of Divine Compassion in action. It requires a deep warrior spirit and great focus to sever illusion from truth.

The Blue Roses are able to love the most unlovable situations because they know the pure power of Unconditional Love. They can tap into the vast infinite pool of creation—pure love—and spread that liberally to all of humanity. Their missions are often to achieve the impossible in their lifetime on Earth. They have the innate superhuman ability to apply unconditional love and forgiveness to the most heinous and unspeakable of situations on the Earth and many other parts of the Universe, where God's Cosmic Sovereign Natural Laws are still being violated.

In their rigorous teachings, they were given the deep responsibility to carry the light, methodology, and technology of redemption and to redeem all souls who wished to return to serve others and the true light. Those teachings are still being facilitated today for any soul wishing to serve others and be in service to God's Love.

The Way of Love

The lineage of the Blue Rose was embedded in the hearts of many in the times of Ancient Britain, France, and the Celtic worlds through the teachings of The Magdalene, and these teachings are starting to arise again within priestess communities across the world as they are remembering the true technology of Love in the heart.

The Order of the Blue Rose carries the blue ray light of Source Love and the Way of Love by emulating and expressing heart-led living. They come as teachers in every epoch of time to remind humanity of their divinity in the material realm so that mankind may awaken to their Christed Self, remember the power of love, and gain full knowledge of their true multi-dimensional and divine sovereign integral origins.

From epoch to epoch, the Blue Rose Order has carried the full frequency of Magdalene's Holy Universal Mother geometry. In this lifetime, they are here once more, emitting this sacred frequency to establish a new foundation rooted in the heart. Their call resonates with the hearts of those who carry this sacred bloodline, inviting them to remember the Way of Love.

As the Sisterhood of the Blue Rose returns, they will unite to form the Divine Sovereign Council of the Divine Mother. Each will step into their sacred role as a Divine Representative, guiding humanity in the evolution of their soul's choices and, above all, protecting the children of this world.

The Book of Love

The *Book of Love* is returning to us, and this time, it will take more than one being to write it again. This sacred text carries the teachings of the Diamond Fractal of the Holy Universal Mother—a living transmission of divine wisdom. As you begin to embody these codes, your own Grail Codex awakens, revealing the fractals of the Great Mother's teachings: vision, guidance, holy union, and the transformative power of love flowing through the womb heart.

When these codes are activated within you, you become a conduit for the magnetic currents of the Feminine Christ. The Holy Grail was never a physical artefact; it is a collection of sacred teachings, blueprints, and templates that empower you to embody the Goddess as the all-seeing eye. This is the full blossoming of the sacred heart and womb as One, in alignment with the "Teachings of the Law of One," passed down through the Great Goddess and the Feminine Christ.

The Feminine Christ

After 25 years of training with the Goddess, I am here to remind every woman that the Feminine Christ is the remembrance of Magdalene within us all—and our unique role in carrying forth these sacred teachings. *Christ* is not a religious term; it means one who is self-realised and self-actualised, someone who has completed their earthly initiations and transcended human limitations to embody divine presence and guide others how to walk as a living Christ.

Yeshua and Magdalene left countless energetic vortices in this sacred land of France, anchoring their teachings into the very earth. These energy points remain as invitations for you to embody the living Christ frequency within yourself and step forward as a way-shower for this time.

A Return to the Holy Order of Divine Sovereignty and Synarchy

Over the past 10 years, I have been mapping this sacred land—intuitively sensing and attuning to the codes held within it—to share the Feminine Christ frequency with others. In turn, those who connect with these energies are activated to embody the Magdalene Codes of the Feminine Christ.

Within this powerful crucible of sacred land and its energetic vortices, we don't just become healers—we become living, breathing centres of healing, capable of running the morphogenetic and magnetic currents of the Goddess as we walk the path of the Feminine Christ.

Recently, I relocated to France to deepen and facilitate this sacred work, continuing the mission of reclaiming Divine Sovereignty for all souls and guiding those who are ready to walk together in *Synarchy* on the Magdalene path. *Synarchy* is the principle of harmonious, co-creative leadership, where we rule together in Love. Magdalene has been overlighting my journey with each breath, gently reminding me to extend the invitation to others who feel the call to embody this frequency once more.

As Yeshua once said, *"Greater things shall you do than I."* We are now being called to awaken the deep feminine wisdom that has been so long suppressed, allowing it to rise again within us. This is the wisdom of Divine Love, a living, breathing vibration that can return the Earth to its heavenly resonance through sound, frequency, and embodied presence.

Your invitation to France and to Glastonbury is open. Magdalene is calling you home—to step into the fullness of who you truly are: Compassionate Love in Action, the walking embodiment of the Feminine Christ, and a living reclamation of your innate Divine Sovereignty.

Stellar

Stellar has been working in the field of sacred sound, music, and healing for 35 years. She studied with her teacher for 25 years in Glastonbury remembering the sacred ascension arts of the Blue Rose Order and Magdalene Lineage, of which she has been initiated into over many lifetimes.

She has published two books, one in honour of her teacher, Isis Beloved, called *The Teachings of Isis Beloved,* and also *The New Magdalene Codex,* which holds all the keys, codes, and steps necessary for authentic and organic ascension.

After going through a very deep Christed initiation, and after soul mapping this dark space for five years, she realised that there was no law on the planet, only the presumption, illusion, or colour of law and so when her beloved John walked-in as a walk-in soul, they brought the liberation codes of the Emerald Order to the Earth so that humanity can be free and have the necessary divinely lawful paperwork to detach from Luciferic blood covenants and hidden contracts that keeps the soul bound by bonds, monetisation, and bondage.

In 2016, she started bringing groups of priestesses and their beloveds to Magdalene and Cathar Country in France. In 2016, she recorded the album "The Magdalene Codes," featuring the Lord's Prayer in Aramaic. She sang the codes of the land and continues to do so by bringing sacred souls to this land again to be activated into their deepest spiritual and soul sovereignty, Hieros Gamos inner Christ and Christos union, and true ascension protocols with the codes that Magdalene and Yeshua left in the land for this time.

In 2018, she and her beloved John anchored the Holy Order of Divine Sovereignty on the planet to bring back Creator Source and God's law to the Earth. In doing so, she and John anchored in the Declaration of Divine Sovereignty, which ensures absolute liberation and freedom commanded from the God-head to all sentient life, humans, animals, and all life forms across the Universe from matrix entrapment, control, and 21st-century slavery through bloodline bondage.

She now runs several activating retreats in France each year, as well as her online Mystery School and Advanced Priestess training. She is Chair and trustee of the Divine Mother Trust and Foundation and also the White Flame Trust in Glastonbury, which cares for the original Magdalene Cottage at the foot of the Tor. Stellar has recorded over 22 albums in 432Hz and emanates the frequency of the Holy Universal Cosmic Mother.

Learn more:
The Magdalene Cottage in Glastonbury
https://www.magdalenecottageglastonbury.com

Magdalene Codes Retreats in Southern France
https://magdaleneretreatsfrance.com

Reclaiming your Divine Sovereignty
https://decreedivinesovereignty.org

The Magdalene Codes Special Edition Collection

This is the perfect accompaniment to your Magdalene Sacred Practices, Retreats and Pilgrimages around the world. This incredible Special Edition Collection includes:

- Rosa Mystica Meditations
- New Magdalene Codex - eBook
- Magdalene Codes Album - Recorded in the caves and churches of Mary Magdalene France
- Magdalene Codes Emanations Southern France - Highlights from one of Stellar's retreats.
- Magdalene Songlines - Release from the Magdalene Church - Rennes Les Chateau

This entire bundle is worth over £250.00, and it is my honour to share this work with you as a gift from the heart.

Access here*:

https://payhip.com/b/NgLjF

*100% discount at checkout code: **38KTVR4I7E**

CHAPTER 26

Becoming Big Mama

From Daughter to Matriarch, Initiated by Love and Guided by Magdalene

by Lettie Sullivan

Mary Magdalene

Mary Magdalene was a hoe.

Oh! You didn't know? Well, that's what I and so many who grew up in our black Pentecostal church community were taught.

Sure, she anointed Jesus with her tears and some really expensive oils. Wiped his feet with her hair. Was at the tomb after his crucifixion.

But don't you ever forget that she was unclean, had 7 devils cast out from her, she had fallen, she was a prostitute, and that was one of the worst things you can be. DON'T TURN OUT LIKE HER.

I remember Mary Magdalene being talked about most consistently around Easter services. Her witness that the tomb was empty was the most neutral aspect of her narrative. Her sexual history is the most prominent.

Unlike Mother Mary, who got the spotlight during Christmas season, Mary Magdalene was always a minor character in the narrative of Jesus, especially the way that I remember it.

Accepting Jesus as our Lord and Savior, believing in his crucifixion and resurrection on the third day, and that his death was a punishment he bore for the sins of the world—MY SIN—sits at the heart of the faith that I grew up in. As a child, I accepted this wholeheartedly. Along with all the stories of the people who surrounded him.

It wasn't until I came across Dan Brown's book, *The Da Vinci Code,* that Mary Magdalene blazed into my awareness like a close-orbit comet. It was quickly followed by another book, *Holy Blood, Holy Grail.*

These fictional narratives piqued my curiosity and opened me up to a whole new perspective on Mary. The more I searched, the more I found.

I was lit up inside! Something deep inside me remembered the truth that was hidden in plain sight. Mary Magdalene was nobody's hoe. In fact, she was a Christed Being—a highly trained spiritual leader and landowner who played a pivotal role in what is now known as Jesus the Christ's ministry. More than that, she was his Beloved Companion—an equal, not an outcast.

It shattered my paradigm and understanding of the world that I was raised in and revealed to me the depths of the deceit and depravity that lie underneath social constructs that perpetuate inequality, injustice, and generational trauma. Especially amongst women and girls.

It was because I felt such a deep resonance with Mary's contribution to the ministry of Jesus and having it hidden in plain sight that I began my journey to discover and follow the teachings of the Magdalene and live by her example as a Divine Feminine spiritual leader.

My Story

That was 20 years ago.

Since then, I have been walking the path of the Divine Feminine. The Way of the Rose.

For most of my life, I felt more comfortable expressing my masculine energy. I loved to lift weights, run marathons, climb mountains, and really push my body to the limits. It felt good to build and test my own physical strength.

Deep in my heart, it felt like something was missing. After being happily married to my husband and having a young son, I realized what was off when we welcomed my eldest daughter into the world. Her birth revealed to me how my masculine and feminine energy were out of balance. More than anything, I longed to connect with the softer aspects of life. My baby girl was the catalyst that opened up the long-disregarded little girl in myself.

There was a time when women outnumbered men in our family, but then amongst my siblings and myself, six sons were born, which balanced the scales. With her birth, my daughter was the first to begin carrying the feminine bloodline into the next generation, which is not something I had really thought about. The way she carried that lineage forward, I soon discovered, greatly mattered to me.

The challenge was that I had to learn how to be more in my feminine power and balance out my overdeveloped masculine side. I had no clue where to start. That's when the *Gospel of Mary Magdalene* found me and led me straight into the heart of my maternal lineage.

My Mother

Matriarchs aren't born. They're forged.

The molten hot fires of trials, tribulations, and trauma become the fuel required to form and fashion the type of individual who can hold down the lineage and anchor an extended family unit.

In my family, that was my mother. She was my grandmother's first child. It was only near the end of her life that my mother shared with us that a white man had raped my grandmother, and my mother was the result of that attack. The relationship between my mother and her mother was volatile and harsh. Punctuated in my memories by yelling and screaming and broken furniture.

I now understand how the underlying trauma of my mother's conception, along with her fair skin and curly hair making her stand out everywhere, could have affected my grandmother's mental health. My grandmother was cruel and abusive towards everyone—an alcoholic who used words to cut and maim and even kill the spirit.

My mom ran away from home for the first time when she was 14 years old. She was picked up by a neighbor, and when she returned home, she was pregnant with my sister. The neighbor was at least 20 years older than her. My mother never went into detail about what happened, but it was clear that the consent was questionable. In turn, my mother's relationship with my eldest sister was also volatile and harsh. The cycle of trauma had been passed to the next generation.

With the intention of healing her life, protecting her children, and breaking the cycle of abuse and trauma, my mother got "saved" and became a Christian. Church became her whole world and, therefore, OUR world. She was devout and truly relied on Jesus as her Lord and Savior. Our entire lives revolved around participating in church activities and building up the community around the church. Being an evangelist and preaching and teaching the word of God became her calling. She coordinated church functions and grew the ministry by caring for the elderly, children and teens, homeless people, and those who were sick or injured. She held bible study in prisons and even had a weekly AM radio slot where she played gospel music, spoke about God, and prayed. This would have been considered a podcast today.

Mom didn't drink alcohol or smoke, not only because of her faith but also because of the abuse she suffered at the hands of her mother and those around them—people, including her own siblings, who were caught in cycles of alcohol and drug abuse. She tried to keep us away from her family because she didn't "want that stuff around her kids."

As her youngest child, I witnessed my mother carry out her ministry. I saw her make plans and follow through with them, always led by her intention to love and care for others in whatever ways she could. Time and again, she would find a "way out of no way," giving all the honor and glory to God. She was a vessel of comfort and care, walking as Jesus walked and striving to live by his example. In that, she found her salvation.

Growing up in the Pentecostal branch of evangelical Christianity, women were expected to be submissive and take on subservient roles.

What I didn't realize until much later was how much my mother's faith and good works were put down, misunderstood, and unappreciated. In her case, this was compounded by being a relatively young, unmarried, single mother, physically beautiful, and of mixed race. She stood out with a powerful, charismatic presence—quite the opposite of what was expected of a "humble and meek, God-fearing woman."

As my mother carried out her ministry, she faced judgment and scrutiny from the women of the churches she visited. Being single, she was seen as a possible competitor for the affections of the available men of the church, where women always outnumbered men.

Then, she was distrusted for being fair-skinned or "high yellow," a consequence of colorism within the Black community—the painful legacy of a racist society that placed those with more white ancestry higher in the Black social hierarchy. While much healing has taken place in the Collective around colorism in recent years, back in the day, the undercurrent of tension was deeply felt, especially among those with darker skin and kinkier hair towards light-skinned folks.

By the age of 25, my mother had four children by four different men, and none of those men stuck around. This fact was used to diminish my mother by the judgmental and gossipy ladies at church. Because of that one factor, she was considered loose, and her virtue and trustworthiness were called into question. Little did they know how much trauma was involved in her becoming a mother so young. What I remember most is my mother holding her head high and singing, praising, and loving the Lord. The sad thing is that she never really had close relationships with any of the women in her life.

Mary Magdalene

Using sexual history to undermine the credibility of women leaders is a common practice in patriarchal society. Anything less than being a virgin or held under the sacrament of marriage was deemed unacceptable.

When Mary Magdalene arrived on the scene with her alabaster jar filled with extremely rare and precious oil to anoint Yeshua, she knew exactly what she was doing and why—and so did the one they call Jesus.

Magdalene was a high priestess on assignment as a divine feminine spiritual leader, conferring kingship on the one they called the Christ.

In those times, it was known that it was the domain of the priestess to anoint the sovereign as they ascended the throne of all royal dynasties.

While Mary Magdalene's story shows up in all of the canonical gospels, as well as the later discovered gnostic gospels, the disinformation about her sexual history remains pervasive. It is now, with decades of liberated women rescripting the narrative about our sexuality and sovereignty, that the shame that used to be wielded like a weapon has dulled.

A woman today can finally reclaim her sacred sexuality and the spiritual authority, rites, and rituals that were forcibly removed from the Collective Consciousness of humanity by the remnants of the Roman Empire and the religion they imposed upon every land they conquered and colonized.

The act of anointing is something deeply intimate. There are many rituals and practices to raise energy that can now be explained scientifically, but in ancient times seemed like magic and miracles. The laying on of hands and altering the energy field of another person is one of them.

My Story

My mother used to anoint my forehead and pray over me before bedtime when I was very young. I never really understood why she did it until much later in my life when she told me that she had been praying for my continued protection. It was only during the #MeToo movement that I realized how pervasive childhood sexual abuse was to women and girls all over the world. Anointing was Mom's way of affirming her prayer that angels were watching over me. She wasn't able to protect my sisters from the sexual abuse committed by her younger brother, but my mother was determined to make sure at least one of her daughters could get through childhood unmolested.

Her hard work was fruitful because that cycle has been broken with me. To accomplish this, a good deal of my childhood was spent alone, locked in the house, only let out to go to school and church. While I learned to love my solitude, it was a lonely experience and I felt abandoned and unmothered in some respects.

As a young adult, I made the declaration that I was not aspiring to marriage or kids. I decided I would rather be single than conform to what looked from the outside as bondage to a traditional custom designed to subjugate my free will and ambitions.

Life is funny, though. Not even a month after I made that declaration, I met the love of my life. We had both made the same declaration about marriage and kids, so it seems the Universe was laughing at both of us. My Beloved and I were content to have it be just him and I against the world, and that was blissful for the first four years.

Then motherhood came for me when I least expected it. I was surprised and taken aback at the positive pregnancy test because my husband was told by a doctor that he couldn't have children because of a long-ago illness before we met. My Beloved told me this while we were dating with much anxiety that it would be a dealbreaker for me. I assured him that it was a confirmation of just how perfect he was for me.

So there we were, having to come together and craft a parenting philosophy and redesign what our lives would look like. We needed more physical space and more income but, most importantly, a plan for how to care for our love child day to day. Lucky for us, I knew the ins and outs of childcare because my mother ran a daycare center out of our home during my high school years. It was instrumental in my declaration of not having kids. Talk about effective teen birth control!

One thing was always clear: our child would be fiercely loved by both of us because of how intensely my Beloved and I love each other. The other moment of clarity was that I could not stay at home full-time to care for our child. I was in the early stages of a career that I had worked hard to establish. I worked a corporate job with good benefits, and while we were a dual-income household, my work was bringing in the most perks.

We made the consequential decision that my Beloved would stay home with our son until he was old enough for preschool. It was a maximum five-year commitment, and he could still draw income—albeit only part-time. It worked well for us. We had a second child, our daughter, within two years, and it felt as though our family was complete.

My crafted version of motherhood was inverted from the societal norm. When my children cried, they reached for their father instead of me. When they cried in the middle of the night, he was the first responder. I watched from the outside how the three people I loved most in the world had a whole day-to-day experience of life that did not include me. In those early years, I worked long hours and was taking classes to advance my career—and exercising to manage stress and stay in shape for the relentless grind. When I would come home, my husband would whip the kids into a frenzy when I walked through the door, and I would fall on the living room floor for hugs and kisses and giggles.

For a while, especially before the kids went to preschool and kindergarten, this worked for us. But as my daughter got older, I could see that she needed something from me that I wasn't giving. She needed a mom, a model for womanhood. I had that from a distance with my mom, but I knew that I had to give more than what I received growing up. This was the catalyst that I spoke of earlier.

Oh, the work I did to untangle my complicated relationship with motherhood. I had to understand my motherhood wounds, which brought me to the wounds of my motherline. It became clear that the patterns I was uncovering and clearing went way, way back. I was the one from my generation who had been assigned this monumental task. As I healed, especially after grieving the passing of my mother, I was able to harvest the gifts my mother gave me from her life experience. I released that sense of abandonment and broke the cycle of overwork that took her away from me and was taking me away from my kids.

While I didn't take on my mother's faith tradition, I found something new and more compatible with my expanding views on God/dess, history, gender, and spirituality. What I carried forward from her example was a deep devotion—a daily connection with a power greater than myself and a continuous expansion and deepening of my healing from generational trauma and the localized trauma that comes from being an African American woman in a country steeped in systemic racism and sexism.

As my spirituality evolved, I shared some things with my kids, but never wanted to pressure them to perform or participate in anything that didn't feel true for them. One thing they all enjoy is anointing and having me lay hands on them whenever they are feeling unwell in mind, body, or spirit, or crossing an important threshold in their lives.

I anoint and pray over my children now whenever they are amenable to it, whenever they ask me to. Especially before they travel anywhere. I feel as though I am interfacing with the Matrix of all Creation and programming the field around them with my words, actions, and intentions. It is the legacy of the Magdalene in action.

All Together Now!

So, what do Mary Magdalene, my Mother, and Myself all have to do with this concept of becoming the Matriarch? For the Magdalene, historical accounts tell of a woman who was not just hanging out on the outskirts of Yeshua/Jesus' ministry. It's quite possible that she was contributing financially and leading the other holy women who were in service to the followers and disciples. She was depicted in the gnostic gospels as the one Jesus loved the most and was his Beloved Companion. There are also stories of her bearing his child and continuing his bloodline.

After the crucifixion, Mary's story really blossoms and we can see even now how her message and ministry endured times of persecution, suppression, and disinformation.

Even though the record was corrected about her false persona as the "penitent prostitute," it still remains in the Collective Consciousness. What is never talked about, except in certain circles, is her example of spiritual sovereignty and leadership, deep compassion, and mysticism. She carries deep and potent medicine, not just historically but also to be utilized in our modern times. She was the prototype for the Matriarch who held it all together, even when unacknowledged and unappreciated by those she was caring for, and left a lasting legacy for those after her to follow.

Within my bloodline, my mother was this type of Matriarch. Her name was Marretia. The children in her daycare and their parents called her "Ms. Rita." I watched her mother other people's children as if they were her own. My siblings and I joked that she took better care of them than she of us. This was true because that was her actual work, while by contrast, she was taken away from caring for us in order to make money to care for us. It's just the way it was.

Forgiveness work has released the burden I was carrying from childhood of feeling abandoned and unmothered. I have been able to mother my inner child while mothering my own children, and that has been a hugely challenging and rewarding undertaking.

The lasting legacy of my mother's time on earth was not just her ministry contributions or her impact on me and my experience of building and growing a ministry but of her perseverance and determination to be a force for good, no matter what.

She gave her all to everything that she did and everyone she cared for. She helped raise her siblings' children at different stages of their lives and even took in kids from our church and made a difference in their lives. My mother kept our family together until the very end.

After her transition in 2014, it seems like our family fell apart. Infighting kept my siblings and me apart in ways that mirrored my mother's contentious relationship with her own brother and sisters. We never got around to healing that strand of generational trauma, but now that both of my older sisters have passed away, both in their early 50s, I now find myself in the position of the Matriarch.

I am the oldest living woman in my bloodline right now, at age 48. When this realization struck me, I immediately felt unworthy. But why? I've been in that inquiry as I have been processing the grief of my older sisters dying less than a year apart while we were all estranged from one another. Yet another generational trauma that we did not get to heal, but boy, did I try my best.

Being the matriarch is about legacy. Being the keeper of the stories, the essence of our ancestors, and of the times lived through both individually and collectively. I am learning that the more simple and humble I can be, the better. If you carry the mantle of matriarch as a burden, you're doing it wrong. The mission of becoming Big Mama, if you choose to accept it, is to hold the remembrance of the soul force of the family unit, to preserve its essence. Tell the stories of the ones who came before with homage to their contributions, struggles, and triumphs.

Most importantly, the matriarch is charged with holding the chalice of healing medicine collected from remembering and processing all the stories of our ancestors and dispensing it as balm to the generations that can use it in the present.

Lettie Sullivan

Lettie Sullivan is a Professional Organizer, International Speaker & Life Coach, Bestselling Author, and Priestess of the Sacred Arts.

A modern Mystic with 20+ years of mystical studies, practices, and initiations—as well as 18 years in private practice as a Professional Organizer and life coach—Lettie supports people in elevating their standard of living and facilitates sacred ceremonies and rites of passage for those who identify as spiritual but not religious.

Learn more:
www.lettiesullivan.com

The Sacred Altar Masterclass

This class gives an overview of how to craft your own sacred altars for ancestor veneration as well as for your own spiritual practices.

Access here:
https://www.lettiesullivan.com/sacred-altar-masterclass

CHAPTER 27

Mary Magdalene—Death Doula and Priestess of Resurrection

by Anaïs Theyskens

Mary Magdalene reveals herself in the whispers of a lover's heart. Her memory lies hidden within the inner chambers of the human heart. It takes an initial opening of the heart to release her elixir into the body and our consciousness. This first outbreath can be caused by loss or heartbreak, facilitating a cracking of the shell that surrounds the heart, forcing us to feel intensely. But in my case, it was love. My world started to turn differently when I met John at a friend's housewarming party. I literally fished him out of the crowd on his way out by grabbing onto his trench coat to pull him close to me. There was something different about him; he intrigued me. That first night, we talked for hours. Without having the words to describe it, something within us recognised each other and acknowledged the importance of our meeting. Things went fast after that: we moved in together after three months, and the following year he proposed. It was the start of an 11-year-long, deeply alchemical journey together.

Fascination initially drew me into this relationship; my taste for adventure kept me hooked because this relationship wasn't smooth sailing, to say the least. After colliding in each other's lives, we were never the same again. Our meeting sparked a spiritual awakening for us both and set a series of deeply life-changing events in motion. Soon after we moved in together, we had a big spiritual expansion—we started channelling and were contacted by different spirit guides. Most evenings, we would sit together in meditation and receive guidance and information from them on our past lives, the energetic structure of the universe, how the human body fit into it, and the different dimensions of the invisible realms. During these evening classes, we would get homework and were instructed to do specific meditations, movement practices, and visualisations to harmonise our bodies, heal ourselves, and further our spiritual and energetic expansion. These shared moments of expansion and devotion were beautiful. They were the foundation of our love story and gave us a shared sense of purpose. We gave each other access to deeper mysteries and experienced states of grace together.

But at times, the road together proved very challenging. John would fall into pockets of darkness, becoming a portal into windy places of sadness and despair.

I would sometimes spiral into the underworld with him, into depths that were populated with menacing shadows and demons. Our life together was filled with ups and downs, but I stayed with him because a part of me felt I could save him, and I was up for the challenge.

The intensity of all that was unlocked within me—the surge of Shakti swirling from the secret inner chamber of my heart, travelling through the layers of my being—made it impossible to continue the corporate, functional city lifestyle I had been living. The divide between my two lives—the rich, inner world I was nurturing and connecting with and the external life still rooted in the person I believed myself to be before my spiritual awakening—grew wider and more overwhelming. The constant shift between these two realities became exhausting. Furthermore, through everything I was tuning into and receiving from guides like archangels Michael and Metatron, Chananda—one of Gautama Buddha's disciples—and Merlin, I had touched upon a thread of truth. My whole being wanted to follow that thread and see where it led. And so, I freed myself and gave myself permission to explore my truth. I quit my job to commit to my relationship and to my spiritual journey, which I still thought were indistinguishable at the time.

It was amidst all this change and upheaval that Mary Magdalene introduced herself for the first time as she unexpectedly appeared during one of our nighttime meditation sessions. As soon as she came into the space, a big sigh of relief went through my body. Even though I didn't know her, I had a sense of homecoming—my body just felt the obviousness of her presence within me. I no longer remember what she said that first night, but the sensation of this meeting is still with me today. It was like an unctuous, juicy wave of energy rippling out through the body from the heart. A honey-like substance started seeding my veins and nervous system with sensations of peace and bliss. It was a very physical sensation, enlivening me and somehow gathering the different parts of me together. Life-altering as this experience was, she retreated into silence for a long time after this first encounter, even as I could often feel her watching and supporting me from the sidelines.

I know now that I first had to be initiated and prepared in order to fully meet her. The starting signal for this initiation was our druid wedding, for as soon as our ceremony was over, we received guidance to leave everything behind and start travelling. We were encouraged to put into practice everything we had learned until then and to connect to the language of the earth more deeply by meeting the different frequencies she held in various sacred sites. Without a clear idea of the purpose or a timeline for our travels, we decided to let go of all our belongings, clear out our flat, and head into adventure. This has been one of the main themes on my journey with Mary Magdalene—a repeated release of attachment, a radical commitment to being in the flow, an acceptance of constant change. The path of the Magdalene, the path of the mother, is one of total surrender.

Many amazing, miraculous things happened on that trip. I sat in sand dunes with orbs visibly flashing all around me. I received teachings from the earth herself through visions I had in her sacred sites and temples, and I received messages from the spirit guides present in the different locations I visited. Through my initiation with Mother Earth, something else awakened in me: I started having spontaneous kundalini awakenings that were brought on by the Shakti of the land moving through me. The first time this happened was in Chili. I was staying in a beautiful place called Valle del Elqui and was doing daily meditations in the hotel garden, facing the Andes' Mountain range. As I meditated with my eyes open, I could see rainbow-coloured light waving from the mountain's crest. This intensified until suddenly, these waves of rainbow light started rolling down the mountain and washing over me and through me. This would bring on a full-body orgasm, culminating in an intense and lasting sense of bliss.

This kind of experience would repeat itself throughout the journey, especially on mountains or close to them, like Machu Picchu, for example. Alongside these activations, I began experiencing vivid dreams and visions of myself across different timelines and in different forms—engaged in ritual, meditation, or prayer on mountaintops and within ancient temples—often accompanied by intense kundalini awakenings and ecstatic, orgasmic energy. I knew that this was intentional, that it was part of a very sacred, ancient priestess practice to channel the sexual currents and creative energy of the planet into being a real vessel for the wisdom of Gaia and allowing her to create through us.

In my understanding, prayer and meditation activate the kundalini energy from above, coming in through the crown, while earth-based practices draw up and summon the kundalini energy from below. Women have the capacity to hold and harness this power within the sacred chamber of the womb. An awakened womb will automatically connect into the earth's kundalini currents and activate them. This is the reason why women who were bleeding wouldn't go into temples or sacred sites during their moon time, not because they were impure but because they wielded too much power and could throw off the energetic balance in the temple.

In ancient times, womb priestesses and so-called dragon-riders—women who mastered and channelled the life force currents of the planet—purposefully and intentionally chose sexual partners who deserved to receive this energy. These chosen men were pillars of support for their community, at the service of the common good, and keepers of collective well-being and safety. They would receive energetic support from these priestesses. Sometimes, this would happen through purely energetic support and exchange, sometimes through sexual union, but this was hardly always the case.

Sharing this energy with pillars in the masculine community so they could better perform their sacred duties was just one of the ways in which this energy was channelled into the community and distributed. Pre-patriarchy, the energy thus harnessed would support whole villages, cities, temple complexes, and even civilisations as the energetic backbone and primary source of energy. The priestess could share and expand out that harnessed energy, creating a resonant field of life force coherent with the energy of the planet. Practices like the ones employed by this priestess lineage are still in use today: plant medicine and sacred chants were some of the vehicles used to activate and access Shakti. These methods don't work in the same way as they used to because we no longer have the energetic structure to receive the breath of life. For these methods to facilitate a permanent shift within, there needs to be a strong field of devotion present within the person prior to the spiritual peak experience for Shakti to pour into. Another requirement to receive this energy fully is to have established a powerful axis of faith to allow the initiate receiving Shakti to stay grounded and aligned. Without this, the fallout of a sudden discharge of Shakti can be catastrophic; it can completely fry our circuits.

When humanity was still connected to the goddess and priestesses were present as conduits of Her life force, civilization was embedded in temple consciousness: humans created societal structures with the energetic support of the earth and the divine mother. They lived in coherence with the innate intelligence of the planet, generating abundant and thriving communities.

Mary the Magdalene was part of that age-old lineage of priestesses dating back to the origin of life on earth. They were keepers of the primordial flame, celebrating the innate connection between humanity, the land they lived on, and the soul and consciousness of the planet. Magdalene was a priestess of Hieros Gamos—a sacred temple practice involving a symbolic marriage rite to the goddess—who initiated Yeshua into receiving the kundalini of the land as the living presence of the divine mother. As a dragon priestess, she baptised him into the ways of the earth mother, teaching him how to summon and hold the sexual energy of the earth to support his healing work and physical body.

The life force Magdalene wielded was extraordinary, and though she didn't flaunt it, it was felt and deeply feared by those who no longer understood the old ways and distrusted the feminine. It is the kind of energy that will naturally collide with unnatural barriers within our consciousness, psyche, and biology. It is flowing, undulating, fiery, and watery in nature and will automatically challenge rigid structures when it encounters them.

My whole earth pilgrimage was an initiation into meeting the Mother in a deeper way and learning her hidden mysteries. I had started to remember lifetimes of being in her service. As I discovered the magnitude of her power, I also discovered my own. The many gifts she so generously shared with me forever pushed the boundaries of what I thought was possible and what I assumed I was capable of. The miraculous was constantly present; all it took was to meet her with an open heart and a curious mind.

Almost two years into this sacred pilgrimage and earth school, my husband and I were guided back to Europe: to Glastonbury, UK, more specifically. Also known as Avalon, it is a powerful earth temple, considered by many to be the heart chakra of the planet. On this potent land where Mary Magdalene has lived and shared her sacred ministry, my earth ministry as a priestess of the Magdalene was born. Very soon after we landed there, Mary Magdalene asked me to stay: she wanted to initiate me into her mysteries, and she asked me to tend to the temple of Avalon. Although part of me wanted to keep travelling, I also felt a certainty that it was my dharma to honour her request and learn from her. Thus, my initiation into the ways of the Magdalene and the lineage of the rose began. I received activations from her and was asked to do certain practices to awaken the energetic structure, signature, and wisdom of the rose within— opening my physical and energy body to increase my capacity to hold Shekinah (also known as the holy spirit or the feminine aspect of God). As I progressed in my initiation, the presence of the holy spirit within grew. I could feel the inner shifts but didn't yet understand how it would affect my external reality. There was a fire and a strength that was seeded within me, and Mary Magdalene started inhabiting my inner space more and more. Her energy merged with mine, and I started seeing and understanding things from her perspective in addition to my own. As her presence within me grew, I came more into my true self, and my soul's light radiated outward stronger. This amplification was perceived on the outside and had some immediate results. On the one hand, women started to feel drawn to me as a teacher, and a community of Magdalene initiates and sisters naturally started forming. On the other hand, my presence started triggering the men around me. My spiritual world was expanding while simultaneously, my marriage started falling apart. The story of eternal and unconditional love we had written for ourselves started unravelling as Mary Magdalene and Avalon started revealing hidden layers of resistance and wounding. The purification process that was initiated when we said yes to moving to Glastonbury took us into the depths of our being. It was beautiful as much as it was brutal; no stone was left unturned, and no hidden pocket of pain or trauma was unaddressed. The integration of the frequency of the rose required that I not hold onto anything—no identification to victimhood or trauma, no identification to glory or inner thresholds of accomplishment. I was asked to open all my petals to allow holy spirit to move through me freely.

For my husband, this process proved to be too painful—the light streaming in revealed pockets of trauma that he chose to not relive or address, and he started doing the opposite: withdrawing more and more, increasingly feeling that he didn't have a place next to me anymore. It became painful for him to be around me, as it was for others who were working or living with me—because the energy of the Magdalene working through me cut like a sword through the illusions that people were desperately trying to uphold. He tried to hold on for a long time out of love for me, but his being darkened more and more, and he spiralled into deeper, more intense states of being. It was as if we were living in two different realities—he was stuck in a hell realm.

Although my life wasn't easy—the feeling of being abandoned by the masculine was very painful—I still felt very blessed by the increasing presence of the rose and everything unfolding in my life through her presence. I felt powerless, faced with his inability and seeming unwillingness to face and vanquish his demons. I tried everything to build a bridge between us, to salvage the crumbling structure of our relationship, but to no avail. I waited for a long time for him to find his way back—too long in hindsight—because I loved him and because we had catalysed so much opening for each other and had written such a strong odyssey together. I just couldn't resolve myself to give up after everything we had experienced together. I had literally brought him back from the dead; we had channelled together for the first time, and we experienced and saw things that many people will never experience that are thought to be impossible.

For a while, the vortex that was created between us was a vortex of the miraculous, opening possibilities and timelines of the extraordinary. We magnetised incredible people, experiences, and things into our lives. But after two years in Glastonbury, I had to admit that this energy was no longer present and that he had unconsciously chosen a path of destruction. The darkness within him felt cornered, and it started lashing out. The trauma would turn into venom, mostly directed towards himself, but more and more often towards the world and people around us as well. He felt under siege from the world, but the war was raging within, not without. Our relationship was gradually hollowed out. Every low point we hit drained a bit more of its life force, and it became a shell of what it once was. We drifted apart: we slept in separate bedrooms in the end because I could no longer rest in the vicinity of his energy field. It was a long and painful process to accept that no number of words, love, attention, encouragement, threats, withdrawal, or pleading on my end was able to change his trajectory.

It became very clear that I had a choice to make. I could either stay in the relationship, slowly lose all my energy, and risk not continuing with the Magdalene teachings because I would no longer have the energetic capacity to hold the transmission. Or, I could leave him and honour my dharma, retrieve my energy, and redirect it to where it was most purposeful and could still make a difference. Making the choice to leave him broke my heart. It was a great teaching that I couldn't save the person closest to me from his demons, and it continues to be a learning to this day.

This whole period of unravelling felt like a path of crucifixion—at the same time, I was revealed unto myself, and my dharma locked in. I experienced the hardest times of my life; my heart was broken, and I was betrayed by very close friends and business partners. Leaving my husband was the final test in my initiation: having to choose between my service to the divine or my relationship. In the end, choosing Mary Magdalene really came down to choosing myself and my integrity of being, offering myself the love and respect others couldn't offer me because of their wounding, not because of unwillingness.

Since our separation, I've been able to heal and regain my energy, and the path of the Magdalene has anchored and expressed itself through me even stronger. I am fully devoted to sharing what she has to offer because I see how needed her transmission is. She held my hand through a portal of death and shepherded me to the other side into a full, uncompromising commitment to life in all its splendour. This is what she is facilitating for the collective, as well.

She is shifting our paradigm by resurrecting humanity. Mary Magdalene shows up as an energy of radical truth: much like the sword of the divine mother, she cuts through the illusions we hold to bring us back to the truth of who we are. She breaks down all the walls within that block our life force from flowing freely.

As a priestess of resurrection, Mary Magdalene shows us the parts of ourselves that are morbid and stagnant. Parts of our lives where life force is no longer circulating, places where we are out of alignment. She reveals these patterns of contraction so we can release them. She confronts us with death so we can choose life. She opens the rigid structures within our mind, consciousness, energy body, physical body, and even our DNA structure. She releases the light codes contained within our DNA, trapped in structures of (trans-generational) conditioned behaviour and patterns. Once we start to transition back to who we are and where we are meant to be in life, a fluid of light is released from the base of the spine, bringing our inner tree of life back to life. This essence is the breath of life. It is present in all living beings, animates the universe, generates flowers, and creates mountains and rivers. It is an immensely powerful, beautiful current of life that has shaped our world and has the potential to change it, as well—rapidly and profoundly. It emanates from the world's power places, the planet's pulse points anchored in the wisdom of the rose, the Magdalene, and the Shekinah as the breath of life.

And now, it is beginning to radiate through the awakened wombs of priestesses, women, and sisters attuned to the voice and wisdom of the land. They are summoning the Earth's kundalini energy to dissolve the rigid, patriarchal paradigm that humanity has imposed upon the surface, guiding us back to the planet's original architecture of light—the sacred geometrical template of the Golden Rose, the foundation of our naturally harmonious and abundant world. As our earth has grown through many eras and stages of evolution, the Magdalenes are now being called forward to anoint humanity into the most holy of sacraments: the Hieros Gamos—the divine marriage rite—that will once again reunite the heart of humanity with the heart of the planet and the heart of the universe.

Mary Magdalene wants you to fall in love with life and feel that the whole universe is reciprocating that love. She guides you on a path of divine union so you can know the kind of love that she shared with Yeshua and be transformed through it. Magdalene is knocking on the door of your heart. Will you let her in?

Anaïs Theyskens

Anaïs Theyskens is a priestess of the Magdalene. Her life's work is devoted to sharing the gnosis of the rose and the lost mystery teachings of Mary Magdalene as one of the most powerful and ancient paths towards wholeness and harmony for our time. She has been initiated into the druid lineage in Brittany and has received the teachings of the Path of the Magdalene as a channelled transmission directly from Mary Magdalene at the sacred sites of Avalon (Glastonbury, UK), an earth temple and sanctuary she has been in devoted service to for more than eight years. With the earth as her guru, she has been guided to different power places in the world, receiving visions about the true story of humanity and perceiving threads of wisdom to guide us back to coherence.

She weaves the teachings and wisdom of the Celtic druid lineage with the devotional lineage of the Magdalene, tracing all the way back through the mystery schools of Sumer and Ancient Egypt to the academies of light of Atlantis and Lumeria. She has been teaching courses on the ritual arts, mythology, cosmology, and archetypal work of those spiritual traditions for more than 15 years.

Anaïs seeks to resurrect the heart of humanity by helping people remember their divine heritage and purpose as guardians of this earth dedicated to creating a more beautiful and loving reality for our collective. Today she stewards an international community of students dedicated to the path of the divine mother and the Christ-rose wisdom path and organises the yearly Sacred Magdalene festival in Glastonbury, as well as being involved in the organisation of the Heart of the Rose women's festival dedicated to sharing the different approaches to Rose-teachings and -medicine in Kent, UK. All of her work is an expression of the sacred mystery school initiation of Hieros Gamos or the divine union rites as practiced by Mary Magdalene and Yeshua and the different lineages that inspired them.

Learn more:
www.pathofthemagdalene.com
https://www.instagram.com/anaismagdalenepriestess
https://www.youtube.com/@pathofthemagdalene

SACRED GIFT

A Workshop on Divine Love—A Celebration

A celebration of divine love inspired by the sacred love shared by Mary Magdalene and Yeshua, an awakening of the codes of divine union within.

A journey of love accompanied by mystical Sufi poetry, a heart-opening rose meditation, energetic activation of the codes of divine union, a share on the meaning of mystical union, inner divine union, and sacred love. Includes integrating practices to continue the journey of blossoming to love afterwards.

Access here*:
https://www.pathofthemagdalene.academy/offers/o8ZLicHg

*Enter this coupon code at checkout to receive the workshop for free: **MAGDALENEANTHOLOGY**

CHAPTER 28

WHO IS YOUR TRUTH FOR?

A Journey of Embodiment with a Magdalene

by Elisha Tichelle

"During the road of trials a woman transcends the limits of her conditioning. It is a particularly harrowing time, an adventure fraught with fears, tears, and trauma."
—*Maureen Murdock*

Deeper into the cave I move. The air feels thick, heavy, and damp. *I do not like being this deep in caves,* I think to myself. I know I am dreaming, but I can feel this in my body as if I were awake, so I am uncertain why there isn't fear of being so deep in the darkness of a cave following a shadowy figure with a small light. I just know I need to keep going.

We arrive at a more prominent space after walking on a downward-sloping path. It is an open room of sorts. There are people around the room, though I can barely make out their shapes, so I don't know exactly how many people there are. The crackling, dancing light of a small fire at the center of the space cuts through the darkness and casts shifting shapes through the air. I feel and hear the sounds of something like humming. It's not quite humming, but I can't quite grasp it. Loud enough to be heard and felt but also elusive, it seems to be coming from all directions and flickering like the flames. *Maybe the fire is singing,* I think. I wonder if I am supposed to know what to do. Fear, confusion, and awkwardness are all vying for awareness.

"Sit here," I hear someone say as I notice cushions around the fire. I do as I am instructed. As I fold onto the cushion, I look around the space more. There isn't much more I can make out except that I see piercing eyes studying me across the small fire. I try not to squirm and hold the gaze. She seems shrouded, but her presence is palpable—I feel exposed to the bones. After long moments, when I am about to ask what is happening, the piercing eyes across the fire turn and nod to the side where someone is waiting. They move quickly forward, and several bodies surround the fire. With a whoosh of wind, they douse the fire. The flames cease, and I suck in my breath. The already dark cave becomes infinitely more so. The voice, like the humming, seems to come from every direction. "Now," She says in a slow, vibrant tone, "you will see."

I wake in a sweat. Sitting straight up in my bed, I realize it's still night. The dream clings to me. This recurring dream has continued for the last few nights, but I've never been plunged into the dark like this. I am not great in small, cramped spaces, especially deep in the earth, so that part of the dream was enough. And how am I supposed to see if the light is gone? Each time I have the dream, it feels so real. More like memory than something just playing out in the mind. Which just makes me more frustrated. *Say it straight;* I grouse to nobody before sighing dejectedly and lying back down. I hope that I'm finished with the cave for the night. I hope I can make it another day, feeling the pressure of being adrift and cornered simultaneously. I hope I don't run out of the small amount of hope I am surviving on.

The next night, I am determined to be more prepared for my nightly sojourn into the cave. I anoint with mugwort and sip chamomile tea before bed. I write what I remember about the dream and what I am curious about. I pray out loud with deep breaths, "Okay, Goddess, just tell me what I need to know." It is the recalcitrant and somewhat defeated prayer of a child who has lost her way but is desperate to cling to her control. This child, after all, has no time for a breakdown. But I also fear that if something doesn't change, I will be in for more than a breakdown.

Before I sleep, I place a bundle of herbs wrapped in cheesecloth and tied with a red thread under my pillow. I also leave a small nightlight on. If I am going to be plunged into the dark "there," I decide to keep a light "here." I don't know how long I have been asleep before I awake into the dream—climbing into the cave, following the figure with the small light, hearing the sound of the strange humming, and arriving at Her. I retake my place sitting at the fire. I am less awkward this time. And more fearful. Not because of the cave or the dark. No, I am afraid of what I might have to know. Those piercing eyes seem to have a bit more sparkle from the flames. No nod this time. So I look over to the side and see the awaiting figure. I am almost sure I see a smile as the figures in the room collectively shift to circle the fire. Then, the darkness takes over. "Now," She says in a slow, vibrant tone, "you will see." I fight the fear that wants to push me back to the surface. "See what?" I ask in a trembling voice. "Truth," She says. "Truth is waiting for you." She begins to laugh, and it sounds like tinkling bells. It is her laughter that carries me back. I have not mastered the fear. But I met it.

It's Friday morning, a few weeks later, and I awaken with the weirdest sensation of being wrapped inside stiff cotton. Feeling a strange impulse of knowing in my belly, I grab my phone and see several missed calls from work. That's pretty strange, especially so early in the morning. I am traveling, so maybe I forgot to do something, or information is needed from me; I am thinking this as I put the phone to my ear and call the office back. "Have you seen it?" the secretary says. This is a confusing start to a conversation, but I don't get a chance to ask what she means before she continues, her voice speeding up and pitching higher. "It's on national news. It's everywhere." She is starting to alarm me, and even though I am not quite sure what we are talking about, I am pretty sure I know who has created whatever problem we have.

"You're mentioned. It's a lot. This is crazy. How can they print this without checking the facts? Are you okay?"

Her words keep coming as I put the phone on speaker and follow the link she texts me. And I see it. All the ugliness I have been dodging and swimming against for four years in print. The article is full of lies and salaciousness. I lose all feeling and feel everything at once. "Shit" is the only word in my vocabulary. I slowly tumble inside of myself until the inevitable loop and waves of shame begin to engulf me.

What will people think of me?
How could this be happening?
What am I going to do?
Is my life over and my career ruined?

Yet even as the thoughts tumble, stumble, and loop around, I feel something beating beneath them—a soft and fierce cry, like a war cry of reclamation. I will not lose myself here. I will not untether from my truth.

"That's right, Daughter," I hear Her voice echo inside me. "But is your truth for you or them? Will you trust your truth even if nobody else believes it?"

The Journey Deepens

We are often well into an initiation process before we recognize it as such. It is often not until the end of the journey that we look back and understand the scope of the experience. Of course, the more aware we are of cycles, initiatory paths, and our journey, the more present we can be throughout the process.

In the case of my wild ride through the initiation of embodying my truth, I was only partially aware of the initiation but had no awareness of the purpose or scope of what I was moving through or why. I was asking for growth without being open to the process. I wanted the journey's outcome without having to experience its messy discombobulation. I was saying *yes* and *no* in the same breath. I was all in and completely gripping into my patterns of control. I wanted to surrender and had no understanding of how to let go.

The descent took years. But the initiatory journey was catapulted to the forefront of my life through the catalyzation of a lawsuit and public slandering. My slow descent to the underworld became a slide I could no longer control.

My Relationship with the Magdalene

The dreams in the cave were not my first encounter with the Magdalene. While they coincided with a profound awakening into the remembrance of being a priestess, I already wore Her symbol of the Camargue Cross, inked in red on my wrist. For me, Magdalene is more than just an archetype or historical character. She is Mother, Sister, Guide, Initiator, and one to whom my heart is devoted. Her dynamic presence made an imprint on me as a child, and when I began to awaken to myself as priestess, Her guidance carried me through the deep initiatory path of learning to embody my truth. In fact, from my childhood, Her story and the activation of remembrance it brought forth in me put my life on a path I continued to follow.

The first experience I recall with the Magdalene was as a young girl when I heard her story shared at church in a Sunday School lesson. I remember hearing the story of Jesus coming to the house of two sisters, Mary and Martha. They are to have a special dinner. While Martha prepares the meal and takes care of the house, Mary comes with a jar of expensive oil and pours it on Jesus's feet. This expensive oil is supposedly as much as someone's salary and is carried in a fancy jar. I found those details intriguing, but the next part of the story stopped me. The story continues by sharing that Mary breaks open the precious jar of expensive oil and then uses her hair to spread the oil all over Jesus's feet. This story captures and enthralls me; I become enraptured by the images and the aliveness they make me feel.

This was the second time in my life that I had what I would later start to call *my knowings*. And what I knew through my thrall of this story was *I am that. That is me. I am one who does this—this jar-breaking, oil-sharing, body-spreading thing.* Her story brought me alive through the visceral sensuousness of it. I could smell the oil and feel the hair. I could sense the movement. I could almost hear a faint reverb of voice and music. It evoked both knowing and longing of how I wanted to move in the world. I wanted the aliveness that I felt in the story. I craved it in a way I had never craved in my short life. *I will do that,* I thought. *I will anoint the feet and move my body and be ME!*

It wasn't that I thought I was Mary Magdalene reincarnated. The knowing was a transmission of remembrance about the oil, the body, and ultimately, about aliveness. This was my breadcrumb. Nothing about it was logical, but I was young enough, wise enough, open enough, and brash enough to believe myself. I knew my truth. And I never questioned. Well, at least not until much later.

I was also deeply fascinated by—and resonated with—the pushback and ridicule Mary faced from her sister and the other disciples for her act. The demonstration of being moved by love and devotion was so full of wildness and beauty, and I didn't understand why others would take issue with that. But the response also confirmed my experiences of being asked to "please not do or be like that." The experiences of rejection felt familiar and ongoing. From the messages I was getting from a variety of people and situations, *calm down, don't be so emotional, be a little less excited, you can't do it that way, you need to follow the rules, that's not how we do it…* pushback was seemingly constant. And I was definitely developing the idea that to be me, I would need to carry a chip on my shoulder and fight for my place.

Later, I learned from reading Mary's own gospel that the anointing at dinner was not the only time her devotion and service rubbed male disciples the wrong way. Yet, even after that discovery, it took me years to realize that I could follow her example from the *Gospel of Mary*—to offer myself vulnerably, tenderly, and fully while embodying my truth—without over-armoring myself in moments of challenge. It took a dark night journey into the underworld to finally uncouple the remembrance that had budded in childhood from the layers of defensiveness that had formed to protect it. That journey revealed a painful paradox: I had unknowingly locked it away in my attempt to shield my truth.

Who Is Your Truth For?

The Magdalene had asked me this as lies were being spread, and I feared drowning under their weight. My curiosity and exploration of this question helped me understand another aspect of the ongoing historical treatment of Mary Magdalene. In the beginning, I did know who my truth was for—everyone, I assumed. The Truth and speaking my truth was how I got heard, held my ground, and demanded my worth, right?

It didn't bother me (though it seemed a hot button for others around me) that Mary was [deemed] a prostitute who needed demons cast out of her. Those aspects did nothing to dim my knowing that She was my model, my blueprint, and my wayshower of truth. I wasn't worried if that meant I needed to become a prostitute (of course, I didn't understand exactly what it meant, just that it was "bad" and good Christian girls would never...). I was good with it if it led me to the jar of oil and an aliveness full of love and devotion.

I was also not concerned in the least with needing to have my demons cast out. In many ways, it seemed like an efficient and effective path. Perhaps then I wouldn't worry about being bad and being sent to hell for punishment for all the ways I was not doing it like I should be, which was still a seemingly constant refrain from the authority figures in my life. I just continued being captivated by the deep resonance of knowing that I would arrive into the level of aliveness she was showing me if I stayed true to myself.

But I found it fascinating that there was so much drama and rhetoric around the sinning "demon-filled" prostitute and the one who was not believed to have first seen the risen Yeshua. Of course, growing up, I had no clue about the dominant socio-political power dynamics at play in the treatment of the story or even how the bible was assembled. So, my understanding may have been simplistic, but I also did not consider how Mary felt about how she was portrayed and reviled. But the bullying and vilification I was experiencing gave me a new perspective. And, seeing the effect it had on how I saw and felt about myself, I marveled at how this must have been and continued to be for Her.

In this experience of being slandered, I had a massive epiphany that I had been wielding my truth like a weapon rather than receiving it as a resource and anchor. I had been willing to shout it to get it "out there," but in actuality, many places within me were hollow and malnourished. I needed to learn how to hold my truth "in here," especially when there was no space for the truth. It doesn't dawn on you that nobody will ask for your story or want to listen to the truth in these crazy situations. The need to control the narrative, cover legal bases, and protect the money while operating from business as usual was very much the focus. The entirety of my legal instruction and coaching was to load all my emails onto a hard drive and say nothing to reporters. I was never once asked about all I had endured at the hands of this woman, why she seemed hell-bent on destroying my reputation, and even if I had done any of the horrible things she was saying. To make matters worse, my longtime boss—someone dear to me, almost like a second father—had been with me through all the chaos, hiring and firing this woman. But he retired just a month before the lawsuit, leaving me to navigate the storm alone. I felt utterly alone and completely silenced.

Who is your truth for?

This question would pop into my mind over and over again. I would contemplate and journal, learning to listen more deeply than ever before. Am I going to waver in my own truth because of other people's stories? Is it enough to know who I am, even if no one ever asks—*Is this true? Is this my truth? Is this truth at all?* And like river water moving continuously and swiftly over stones, polishing and smoothing them, it worked me until I was on my own ground in my own body. I met the grief and anger of being silenced. I held my neglected, unsupported inner child who had developed and lived with the protections of perfectionism, professionalism, and ambition as ways to make sure she would be seen, heard, and safe, only to be left here in the rubble. I met the frightened and exiled aspects that remembered being kicked out, punished, and even killed for truth and not relinquishing it.

The dreams with Magdalene continued throughout this time, as did many encounters through visions in journey space and ceremony. This became the most profound mystery school training I had ever had—the intensity of my external world creating the alchemical chrism for my sacred reckoning.

Plot Twist: Embracing the Path that Initiation Opens for You

Before this trying time, my priestessing, leading of pilgrimages, and spiritual mentorship work was my "side job" passion project. A few ceremonies and calls fit in here and there, with pilgrimages occurring in the summer between semesters. I was on the executive administrative path. My trajectory had been to become a program head and then a department head; I was the school's associate director at the time. My next move was to try for an associate deanship and then into the Vice Provost's office, where I could finally do some good to change the educational situation. The lawsuit and the four years of bullying that preceded it were just enough destabilization that my well-orchestrated and highly controlled plan wasn't as enticing as it had once been.

It didn't start out as a major pivot or big decision. It was a series of small choices that gradually led me to align with my soul's work. I began to embody these new levels in all areas of my life, and opportunities beyond the ivory tower of academia started to flow in. I never had a dramatic moment of realization that it was time to start a business. In the year following the bullying, but before the lawsuit, I already felt a stirring within me. The tide was already shifting. My passion project of priestessing was thriving, and the circles and pilgrimages I led were invigorating for both me and the participants.

Over the summer, while teaching a creative process course in Ireland, I noticed the young students struggling with the pressure of deciding where to focus their creativity. "Take the pressure off. Just decide for now. There will be other times to decide," I advised them wisely. Then, with a touch of humor, I added, "I am still deciding what I want to be when I grow up."

This playful statement served as a disruptive reminder that I could indeed let go of the old ways. I was still incorporating some "Martha-ing" aspects, trying to present my work in a palatable, edgy yet recognizable format. Fully embracing the "Mary" approach meant confronting my tendencies to please others and outsource authority. This was the journey of healing and reclamation that the lawsuit offered.

Coming alive requires moving through the death portal as we rebirth ourselves. For me, this death was an ongoing wake-up out of a dream. Slowly, I returned to my senses, not just in a perfunctory way but in a profound, inhabiting way that brings deep embodiment. The power of our embodiment is that it allows us to be in the truth of our story—the truth of our own experience—even when other people's stories of us are different. We locate ourselves from our own ground. As I followed this path, what looked like a left-hand turn from the outside was the most organic baby step on the inside.

The rebirthing process is about returning to our inner blueprint, which has always existed but has been clouded by conditioning, belief systems, and experiences that have caught us in a loop. The unfolding into your embodiment shows you who you are as you die to the ideas of yourself, whether your own or those of other people or societies.

Embodiment is the process of living through an inner sensory map of your own innate aliveness that easily accesses your intuition and higher intelligence. Embodiment, though, is an ongoing process of continuously waking into self and integrating essence into form. It is what it is to be resurrected or second-born into the body.

> *"You must awaken while in this body, for everything exists in it: resurrect in this life."*
>
> **—The Gospel of Philip**

The heroine's mystical journey is to come home to herself through this rebirthing process and to fully seat her Soul in this body, in this life. It is a journey she must make over and over again. This path is one of integration, melding, forming, releasing, and emerging into being-ness. It is a beautiful and also painful spiral.

Healing doesn't happen in the absence of clear, compassionate witnessing, but in my case, so much of the witnessing was in being witnessed and loved by the Magdalene. Her witnessing and guidance allowed grace to wash through, clearing the blocks and irrigating the wounds as She guided me to reclaim my wholeness.

Returning to the dark cave of my dreams, I now understand that the extinguishing of the fire was not an end, but a profound beginning. In that deep, enveloping darkness, stripped of external light and validation, I unearthed the power and light within myself. The Magdalene's promise reverberated: "Now… you will see." And indeed, I did. I beheld the truth of my own embodied experience, the vibrant aliveness that had been whispering to me since childhood. The winding path through shadows and trials led me back to that initial spark of knowing, the oil-sharing essence of my soul.

I stand resolute on solid ground, no longer fearing the darkness but embracing it as an essential part of the journey. I am here, fully alive, radiating the light that I discovered within the depths, just as the Magdalene foretold. The darkness has become a canvas upon which my inner light paints its brilliance, transforming fear into a beacon of hope and truth. The cool air now feels invigorating, the scent of the earth a reminder of my connection to all that is. The echoes of my journey resonate within me, a symphony of discovery and transformation. I carry the medicines of descent, remembrance, and holy reckoning in my alabaster jar. I am she who lives in service to Her.

Elisha Tichelle

Elisha Tichelle is a sorceress, mystic, and oracle living on Florida's Emerald Coast. Following a 20-year career as a somatic researcher and professor, Elisha now integrates depth nervous system healing with the mystical arts to evolve consciousness through our body. Over the last decade, Elisha's facilitation has guided hundreds of one-on-one clients to new depths of mastery and embodiment and given thousands of students new experiences of knowing themselves on a soul level.

Elisha is the "behind the scenes" priestess and oracle to some of the world's most successful and well-known coaches and leaders. Through training programs and masterminds, Elisha guides visionaries, leaders, and heart-centered entrepreneurs to heal their nervous system, access their intuition, and let their sacred medicine become their legacy. Elisha is here to help you expand the human journey by accessing the full potential of your soul's knowing.

Learn more:
https://linktr.ee/elisha_halpin
https://elishahalpin.com

Attuning to the Heart of the Rose
A Free Magdalene Meditation + Energy Activation

This is a sacred audio transmission for the woman ready to come home to her body, her voice, and her divinity.

Access here:
https://elishatichelle.lpages.co/magdalenemeditation

CHAPTER 29

MY VOICE IS MEDICINE

by Connie Viglietti

I remember
The vibration of my song
Sound
Widens the portal
For gnosis rekindled
Spikenard sparks senses
Heightened
Light the flame
The watchtower torch
I am here now
The lineage bearer
Weaving my voice, my touch, my heart
Remember HER holy name is
My holy name

I lay naked on the massage table. Five inches of mattress foam held me while two anointing priestesses covered my body with blankets. The weight of each gemstone in the palms of my hands, on my heart, and my third eye centered me while the eye pillow blocking the afternoon California sun completed the preparation. This was the third holy anointing I had received that week.

The tuning fork's song flooded my senses, and the rapture that followed startled me. So much so that I felt edgy when their buzz faded. I longed to be saturated in their resonance for an eternity. The aroma of the oils exploded into my being. They seemed to be familiar friends.

My body met the oily touch with ecstasy and trust. I could not drink in the scent fast enough. Each oil's signature scent transported me to another time and place.

Sisters healed my body, spirit, and energy with a blend of sound, scent, and touch infused with their incredible love. Their love channeled from the heavens, from the Great Mother, through the Magdalene and the high priestess lineage that we once embodied thousands of years ago.

As I allowed myself to receive and relax, trauma left its hiding places. The heaviness carried in this lifetime, and the grief and sorrow endured from past lives slipped away. I had never experienced anything like this.

The Myrrophores anointing me shared psychic visions of my past lives as a beggar, opera singer, and mother superior. Receiving their mystical attunement left a healing impact that unraveled both instantly and over the coming weeks of processing and integration.

Each playback I experienced behind the eye pillow offered liberation, whether or not I understood the impression. The memories being recalled were clearing away energetic debris. This fascinated me. The first memory that taught me this was happening was when I was whisked to a moment in my childhood when I felt left behind because of a jealous friend. On the table, I wept at the thought of that moment, and like a flash, the emotion faded and disappeared. The tension that built up in my right hip vanished. I had no idea I was carrying that jealousy in my body! But I was so thankful it was gone.

Another moment of release struck when extreme sadness and anguish washed over me. I wept softly, my heart broken. As the tears flowed and my devastated cries escaped, I had no understanding of *why*. After the anointing, my beloved mentor Diana asked me if I had ever miscarried and that she felt my sadness as she touched the right side of my womb. She had no idea that I had experienced this! I was speechless that we could match the experience on the table to my miscarriage. How truly healing to be witnessed in my sadness all these years later. The truth is, I never processed that miscarriage. I was blessed to be pregnant the next cycle with my daughter, so I didn't make time to be with the loss.

My sisters held me with each release and wiped every tear. We even laughed together when the moment held hilarity. Plenty of real and funny moments come up in healing sessions. I made the occasional weird sound and got snot everywhere through my tears! The joy existed in the pain.

Each wave of remembrance took on an energy of its own. It was quite remarkable. All the versions of myself that I hadn't yet met, that I never had a chance to explore beyond my inner knowing, were right there *with me*.

And then, there it was: a daggering betrayal that had followed me into this lifetime physically and emotionally. My body felt strange and shifted as if it were preparing me. My throat felt tight. The position of my neck intolerably screamed for my attention. I snapped.

I pushed away the pillow under my head. My neck and shoulders needed to be free. I felt my body temperature drop to a teeth-chattering cold. The ladies quickly tended to me, covered my tense body with more blankets, and held me. They knew something was leaving my system.

And then it happened. I saw a woman running towards me, lunging at my throat. She choked me through tears and rage. I screamed as I've never screamed before. It was the burning times, and even though I didn't recognize her, I knew she was a beloved, trusted sister. And she was choking me to my death because of who I was: a healer. My heart was breaking into a million pieces. How could she do this to me?! The shrill that emerged from my voice surely cleared the hateful act from that lifetime through all eternity.

I was instantly transported back to the table, in the present moment, where I connected with the sadness around the scar tissue on my vocal fold. Could these two memories, one of this lifetime and one of the past, be connected? As I came back into my body more and more, I felt the betrayal, the pain and sadness, and the vocal injury were no longer alive within me.

I experienced vocal injuries in my late teens and early twenties. I had the life-changing opportunity to study music theatre at Elon University with the most amazing teachers and classmates who have become lifelong friends. It was a soul appointment moment—we were all meant to be there together, of that I am sure.

Year after year, my cherished voice teacher urged me to get my vocal cords scoped. The breathy quality of my voice, with too much air escaping, signaled something she believed I shouldn't ignore. I often lost my voice if I sang too much or when stress took over. I underwent multiple scopes, but no injury was ever detected.

The summer before my senior year, I had a wonderful summer stock season playing Miss Hannigan in *Annie* and Lucy in *Jekyll & Hyde*. By the final performance of the season, my voice was so strained and exhausted that I had no choice but to seek a second opinion. Some research led me to Philadelphia to see Gloria Estefan's doctor, Dr. Robert Sataloff. I will never forget his blessed name. It was there we discovered scar tissue on my left vocal fold. This scar tissue created a bump that allowed air to escape, creating the breathy quality my voice teacher detected from the beginning.

During the visit with Dr. Sataloff, his technicians painfully measured the electrical activity of my laryngeal musculature. To do this, they inserted a small needle into the vocal cord muscles through the skin of my neck. That was the first time I cried that day. Terrified, I lay there frozen, feeling as though I was being choked or stabbed. Yet, it wasn't physical pain—it was energetic and emotional. The results showed the left side of my voice box/vocal fold was working only at 80%.

This felt like a devastating blow as I entered my senior year, dreaming of a career in performance. I opted out of surgery. I feared what might become of my voice should a mistake occur. Instead, I chose physical therapy and worked my tail off that semester to soothe the scar tissue. My voice became stronger, and I found fresh vocal freedom in the steadiness of my training and therapies. It felt so healing to have so much support around me.

Yet, even with all the work in the world and getting my voice into the best-sounding shape, knowing that scar tissue existed in the most vulnerable place in my body left a scar on my confidence.

I continued pursuing a performing career, but along the way, I made choices that helped me ignore the pain of the story I kept replaying: my voice wasn't strong enough to handle eight shows a week on Broadway. I would never make a living as a professional singer. My voice was damaged, and because of that, I would never reach my full potential.

Each "no" at an audition or callback felt like another log thrown onto the fire of my unworthiness. I grew exhausted from not sparkling and shining in the ways I desired. So, I walked away, searching to carve out a new path.

But no matter which path you choose, when you have a gift—a soul-deep connection like singing was for me—it never truly leaves you. The gift will keep calling you home, whispering to you when you wake in the morning, and softly calling your name as you close your eyes at night. It will nudge you, beg you to practice, and long to be in touch with you. Because it's not just a gift; it's your medicine for the world.

How can I possibly describe the feeling that comes over me when I express myself through my voice? Sometimes, she comes from the womb of my soul like a shooting star sounds out of my heart. Sometimes, she is a balm to my sadness, singing through tears to soothe a throbbing pain. Sometimes, she is the seductress, my desires released through my breathy sound. My sound is mine and mine alone. It is my communion with the divine. She is with me, and I am her.

My voice was raw from the screams released on the anointing table. My exhausted body surrendered into stillness and let go. A single tear rolled down my cheek. I was here now—fully present in this lifetime. Sadness crept in, wrapping itself around the memory of my vocal injury and the neglect I had shown my gift. I had cast her aside, made her an outcast. I made her believe she wasn't good enough. I doubted her sound, her shape, her movement—*her power to heal*.

I lay there with loving hands anointing me with oil and tending to my broken heart. The heartache was fleeting, though, because then my awareness turned to the wonder at the recognition of my friend who had ended my life. I knew who she was in this life! What was I meant to do with this knowledge? My mind wanted to move me to anger and revenge, but my heart quickly let it go. There was only love for her and forgiveness for the past and the wrongs done in this lifetime. The healing was instantaneous—and so curious. It was as if everything healed for us across all timelines in that one single moment. This moment, I would discover in the coming weeks, opened up my voice and cleared out the cobwebs of my broken confidence. It also healed the anger I possessed toward this old friend of mine. How profound.

The tuning forks were back, and a handheld singing bowl washed away and cleared my field as the angels sang from the speaker. This music was so full and alive in me. Typically, I connected deeply with prayerful music like mantras or Gregorian chant. But this time, it was women's voices that soared—like crystal wine glasses singing under a water-dipped finger circling the rim—whirling and twirling in my ear. Transported to another place and time, my voice and heartbreak mended.

I sat up from the anointing table with a newly upgraded lens to see the world. My body felt renewed, my spirit fortified. No chains choked my voice, and

I was curious to test this newfound confidence. I sat there, covered in sacred oil, looking around the room in wonder at the gorgeous goddesses surfacing from their own journeys. Women draped in robes of light and wrapped in soft flannel sheets were being fed berries and chocolate—dripping with beauty and sensual peace. We sprawled across sheepskin rugs, limbs intertwined, hair twirling through fingers. *Do I look like that?* I wondered. *Wow.*

A warm, tingling sensation filled me as I remembered my place within the Sisterhood of the Rose lineage. The conscious heartbeat of this sacred sisterhood is alive and thriving within the Rosa Mystica Mystery School, brought to life by Diana Dubrow and Elayne Kalila Doughty. I was surrounded by incredible women, all of us learning the ancient art of anointing from our master teachers. We were held in a container of safety, bathed in adoration for one another and the immense power each of us carried.

Mary Magdalene belonged to this sacred lineage, and in her presence, forgotten pieces of me came online. I stood in the spotlight again, this time allowing the women to fully see me in my truth. I was received with open hearts, just as I witnessed their glory. The palpable love in that space was something I desired so deeply to carry with me—to infuse into my work as a healer. And from that experience, I remembered.

Spring turned to summer, and I returned to my life with a sense of curiosity and a lightness of spirit. I dove into the opportunity to sing at my cousin's wedding and noticed something very different about my singing voice. Where there had once been tension, my voice now spun higher notes with ease. I found vocal freedom in a way I'm not sure had ever existed before. I attributed this newfound ease to the release and healing I received on the anointing table.

I confided in my mother and father, sharing my remarkable experience. They listened with love and open minds, as they always have when it comes to matters of my heart. When my gorgeous cousin Maria met her groom walking down the aisle under a majestic tree-covered setting, my voice rang through the summer air and danced my love from my heart to hers. It wasn't a perfect performance. But my voice was free. And I thoroughly enjoyed sharing my gift.

My father walked by me during cocktail hour and whispered in my ear: "Wow, Con, you weren't kidding. Your voice IS different. That was wonderful."

Being witnessed by my parents felt incredible, and I took it as a sign to keep going, to keep singing, to keep bringing the healing medicine that is my voice out into the world.

I continue to sing every chance I get. I sing along with the grocery store playlist and wake my children up in the morning in song. I sing with the women who attend my women's circles to amplify the fact that our voices are stronger together. I sing to my clients on my anointing table to help move energy and restore love. My voice is a tool. When I recognize its power and listen deeply to how the Magdalene inspires me to use it, it is potential medicine for those willing to receive it. May it be a reminder of their unique song.

I am a lighthouse. I know how to pour love from my eyes and a song from my heart. I know how to embrace you and hold you. I will encourage you to take the risk toward your wildest dream because only when we take that chance do we truly live. I am the emotion bubbling up. *You are not alone,* she says. *I am with you.* Her words hold hands with the messages that Yeshua's lips spoke because their union was a practice. Together, they explored the unseen and the power and technologies our bodies possess. They walked a different path. They were true to their teachings—the ultimate scene partners.

The Magdalene never lets me forget. The frequency of love and the codes carried by the Magdalene consciousness gently call to us, pinging our hearts again and again until we finally listen. Over the years, I've learned that the dream and the way we share our gifts are not only allowed to evolve but must shapeshift and grow, expanding with us as we walk this path.

She's always been with me. She was the voice carrying my voice as I sang with my grandmother, standing on the back of the kitchen chair, belting out *Five Foot Two*. Oh, the shakti that flowed through us! She carried my voice in choirs, where I learned about the power that harmonies hold. She's there with women as they connect to their power in the birth portal. She is in the loving touch of anointing. She's the fire in my belly when I question, "Where are all the women?" in the Catholic Church. Her deep, holy rage is mine, rattling my bones at the injustices in our society today.

Magdalene, as an anointing high priestess, Yeshua's holy cohort, his partner in these divine mysteries, and the one He loved the most, is a full body remembrance. I knew there was more to her story. There is no way that Yeshua's messages of love and his teachings would cut out the magick of women. Deepening into Mary Magdalene's frequency felt like the chains around my heart and throat were lifted, allowing a long-forgotten knowing to be restored. I recognize myself in the stories of her that surface all around me.

I dipped my fingers into the bowl of oil, feeling the cool, sacred blend drip into my palms. As the aroma rose to meet me, I was transported. As I slid my hands together, a wave of arousal washed over me, catching me off guard. As my senses fully attuned to the magick of the moment—the magick that women create—my spirits lifted. The aroma, the gliding oil, the presence of women healing women in that holy room—it was all an act of love, a living embodiment of the Mother's unconditional, steady, and devoted love. It was a remembrance, ancient and eternal.

I had found my way home. Sound filled the chapel-turned-ancient temple: singing bowls and tuning forks chimed, cries of sorrow, shrieks of pain, the joy of climactic ecstasy, and the soft whimpers of discovering what safe, loving, respected, pleasurable touch could exude.

My hands knew exactly what to do. There was a startling confidence. I was timid in moments to ensure I was honoring my beloved Diana's exact form, but then, I'd done this thousands of times before throughout many lifetimes. I tenderly touched my sister from another lifetime so she felt my love. I went on slowly applying the oil to her body, between her toes, her feet, the backs of her knees, and the small of her back. I massaged her womb, her ribs, and her heart space. I coated her throat and third eye with the most exquisite oils with every ounce of presence I could offer her. I held her when her body shuddered in fear. I wailed with her as she sat up and wept for reasons she may or may not have known. I held sacred and profound space for her to find and explore healing. And together, we created a field of courage and love. Together, we remembered.

I love being who I am in this body in this lifetime. I love being able to connect with the people who cross my path. I am so lucky to be alive in a time when I feel mostly safe calling myself what I am: a priestess who walks the way of the Magdalene. My voice rings out, singing my truth for others to witness and receive—inviting healing, inspiration, and the discovery of their own soul's gifts. May it empower them to express their essence fully in this lifetime.

Sing your song!
It's time to tell your story,
Reclaim the vision of your dream
Let go of your worry
The truth will reign forever more
We are the ones, we are the ones that we've been waiting for

IN HER NAME I AM LOVE
IN HER NAME I WALK AS LOVE

The one heart beats
Fall into the pocket,
feel her rhythm move your hips
tune in, rock it
Let down your hair, let out a mighty roar
We are the ones we've been waiting for

IN HER NAME I AM LOVE
IN HER NAME I WALK AS LOVE

Call in the lovers by battalions
(We are the ones we've been waiting for)
Anoint your holy body temple
(We are the ones we've been waiting for)
Hold the line, walk in truth
(We are the ones we've been waiting for)
We are, we are the ones that we've been waiting for

Connie Viglietti

Connie Viglietti is an intuitive healer, channel, and scent priestess devoted to guiding women home to themselves. With deep presence and a gift for holding sacred space, she blends creativity, voice, and a safe container to support transformation and healing.

A woman of many passions, she draws from her experience as a yoga and meditation teacher, birth worker, wellness coach, and performer to weave a rich tapestry of embodied insight and soul-centered care. Her work is rooted in ritual, connection, and the remembrance of who we truly are. Through 1:1 sessions, women's circles, retreats, and her signature line of holy anointing oils, Harmonia Anointing Oils, women soften, sing, laugh, and rise together in unity.

Poetry and song lyrics in her formative years sparked her passion for putting the pen to the page. Connie enjoys writing about the magical moments of living life to the fullest. She sang in a duo as a finalist in the *Great American Duet Sing-Off* episode of *A Prairie Home Companion with Garrison Keillor.* Performing for 4 million listeners and taking home the Ray Markland Award for being the most fun to work with was an opportunity of a lifetime!

Learn more about Connie's healing sessions, sacred vessels, and her line of anointing oils, Harmonia Anointing Oils, at:

www.connieviglietti.com
www.instagram.com/connie_viglietti

SACRED GIFT

Vocal Heart Transmission—"Walk as Love"

It is a blessing and a thrill to walk this sacred path together. From my heart to yours, I would love to gift you the heart transmission at the end of my chapter, which came to me in song. I offer "Walk as Love" as a gift, so that we may sing together and lift our voices. May we all be inspired by the presence and devotion of Mary Magdalene. This song is a remembrance. A prayer. A call to return to love.

May Her love move through this song and meet you exactly where you are.

Access here:
http://www.connieviglietti.com/mufreegift

CHAPTER 30

Magdalene Maverick

The Art of Achieving Wild Success Through Divine Love

by Rose Wilder

"She who knows her worth changes the world with her presence."

A Divine Invitation

As an abduction survivor, my relationship with trust, power, and divine guidance was forged in the crucible of darkness that few others have experienced. My miracle, and I choose that word intentionally, lies in how I emerged from those shadowed hours with an unbreakable bond to the holy family, especially Mary Magdalene and Yeshua. This connection hasn't merely aided my healing; it has transformed my entire understanding of success, purpose, and divine calling.

What emerged from those depths was an unshakable resilience, the nurturing presence of divine motherhood, and the untamed spirit of a maverick that now illuminates everything I create. And beloved sister, if these words have found their way to you in this sacred moment, know that our souls were meant to connect in this divine intersection of time and purpose.

You see, when life forces you to rebuild your entire sense of self from the ground up, you develop an extraordinary gift: pristine clarity about what truly matters amid the cacophony of "shoulds" that bombard us daily. And here's a truth that might make your wild heart dance: those conventional success formulas they're selling you—the endless hustle, the rise-and-grind mentality, the social media hamster wheel—your soul has known all along that there's another path entirely. I call this the "Magdalene Maverick" way.

[Pulls chair closer and pats the seat beside her with a knowing smile.]

Come closer, beloved. Let's speak heart-to-heart, priestess-to-priestess about what professional success actually means when you're walking the Magdalene path. Because here is what I have discovered through my own journey and witnessed in countless sisters who've joined me: What the mainstream business world labels as our "weaknesses" or "limitations" are actually our most powerful gifts when illuminated by divine love and purpose.

Mary Magdalene, the Apostle to the Apostles, was the first to witness the risen Christ. Some dismissed her as delusional, yet she stood unwaveringly in her truth. Her direct experience superseded what others claimed was possible. And precious one, this is precisely the invitation I extend to you: a way of creating abundance that may seem utterly radical to the outside world yet feels like returning home to your most authentic self.

The Sacred Rewiring of Success

Let me offer you something that I hope will feel like a warm embrace for your entrepreneurial soul:

- Your sensitivity is not something to overcome—it's your most potent business superpower.
- Your tears are not signs of weakness—they're alchemical waters of transformation.
- Your yearning for deep connection isn't "inefficient"—it's your greatest business asset.
- Your inner knowing isn't secondary to expert advice—it's your primary divine compass.
- Your boundaries aren't obstacles to growth—they're the sacred container for your abundance.

When you attune to your inner guidance as your sovereign advisor, you access wisdom that transcends what any external expert could provide. This intimate communion with your divine compass becomes your North Star, especially when navigating decisions about your soul's work. As you honor the boundaries that this inner wisdom reveals, you are not merely protecting your energy. You are creating the alchemical vessel where your greatest abundance is born. This sacred transmutation happens naturally when you place your own truth above all external voices, allowing your unique medicine to flow unobstructed into a world desperately waiting for it.

The Magdalene Business Revolution: Success on Sacred Terms

Do you know what sometimes makes me burst into laughter? Imagining Mary Magdalene confronted with modern business advice. Can you picture her scrolling through reels about "crushing your goals" or "10x-ing your income"? *[Winks knowingly.]* This woman who remained at the tomb when others fled, who proclaimed her truth when doubters scoffed, would surely remind us to honor our deepest knowing, even when conventional wisdom screams otherwise.

What I have discovered through years of Magdalene's mentorship is that authentic success bears little resemblance to the glossy images we're sold. My most profound business breakthrough? When I completely unplugged from all social media. *[Gasps dramatically.]* Yes, total business heresy, according to conventional wisdom! Yet here's what manifested...

I began prioritizing genuine soul connections, the kind where divine feminine wisdom flows freely between hearts. Each client interaction became a sacred ritual rather than a transaction. And contrary to what business "experts" predicted, my practice didn't merely survive; it flourished beyond my wildest dreams. Because here's the truth they don't teach in business school: your greatest power lies in being unapologetically, radiantly yourself.

Remember, precious one, that we are here to embody both human vulnerability and divine power simultaneously. Perfect in our exquisite imperfection.

Sister, here's what I wish someone had whispered to me years ago: every single quality that makes you feel "too much" for conventional spaces is actually your most magnetic gift in the marketplace of souls.

Your ability to sense energetic undercurrents? That's your divine client alignment system. Your expansive, compassionate heart? That's your unique value proposition. Your need for sacred rest and replenishment? There's your sustainable business model for generations of impact.

The Seven Sacred Principles of Magdalene Success

I am thrilled to share with you what I call the "Seven Sacred Principles for Magdalene Success." These guiding tenets emerged from years of deep communion with Magdalene wisdom and have completely transformed how I approach business and abundance.

1. Sacred Worth

This principle stirs my soul to its depths whenever I connect with it. Consider how Mary Magdalene stepped into her power as a spiritual teacher in her own right. In an era when women's testimony held no legal validity, she became known as the Apostle to the Apostles. She never diminished her spiritual authority or dimmed her radiance. When she taught, she did so with absolute conviction in her divine calling. When she spoke, she carried the certainty of one who knows her inherent value.

I have witnessed so many modern priestesses suffering today, undercharging, overgiving, apologizing for their rates, yet your gifts are just as sacred as Magdalene's. I learned this lesson through countless painful cycles of saying yes to discount requests until I was energetically bankrupt.

Now I understand: owning your worth isn't just for your benefit. It's about honoring the Magdalene lineage and divine feminine wisdom flowing through you. Just as Mary Magdalene stood firmly in her spiritual authority during a time of fierce patriarchal dominance, you, too, can stand unwavering in the value of your unique gifts, wisdom, and sacred work.

> *"Yeshua and the ministry were supported by Mary Magdalene,*
> *whose resources were used to support Yeshua."*
> **(Inspired by Luke 8:2-3)**

By embodying your worth, you illuminate the path for countless sisters waiting for permission to do the same. Your prosperity becomes a beacon showing what's possible.

2. Divine Timing

This principle revolutionized everything for me, beloved. Mary Magdalene embodied divine timing at its most profound: She awakened at the tomb while others slept and waited in darkness for the perfect moment of revelation. She neither rushed the resurrection nor forced the mystery. She simply showed up fully and remained present until sacred timing unfolded.

In my business, this has meant trusting the quiet seasons instead of panicking, honoring the divine "no" that precedes the sacred "yes." I have watched countless sisters strain and hustle themselves into exhaustion, but I have discovered that our greatest abundance arrives through divine patience, not forced action. It's about attuning to the sacred rhythms of creation, which yield all treasures in their perfect season. When I fully surrendered to divine timing, opportunities began flowing in ways I could never have engineered through strategic planning alone.

3. Authentic Power

Prepare yourself for this truth, magnificent one, because it will transform everything. Remember when Mary Magdalene stood unwavering in her testimony when no one, not even the other disciples, believed her account of the resurrection? That's authentic power. Not power over others, but power sourced from within. She didn't try to persuade, defend, or explain. She simply knew what she knew and spoke her truth calmly and confidently.

I have watched this principle work miracles in my business and with my clients. The magic manifests when we stop forcing our message into someone else's formula and instead speak our individual truth. I still remember the first time I publicly challenged the "hustle harder" narrative; my hands trembled as I shared my message. But the response was overwhelming, countless women had been silently waiting for permission to create success differently.

The world doesn't merely need your voice, precious one. It needs your unique perspective, your particular way of seeing and being. Your truth isn't just a nice addition; it's essential medicine for this moment. When you summon the courage to speak your truth, just as Mary Magdalene did, your words become liberation for others.

4. Sacred Circle

Mary Magdalene existed within a sacred circle of connection, and so do you. You're here to forge soul-deep bonds through your work, not surface-level "networking," but profound connections that bring clarity and support to everyone they touch. When I stopped trying to reach "the masses" and instead nurtured my sacred circle, everything transformed. Your true community recognizes your heart; they celebrate your victories and hold space for your evolution.

5. Divine Flow

Oh, sister, this principle revolutionized my entire approach to business! Mary Magdalene understood divine flow intimately. She knew when to speak, when to hold silence, when to step forward, and when to retreat. In your business, this means honoring your natural rhythms. Some seasons call for vibrant expansion, while others require deep rooting and rest. Both are equally sacred, equally necessary for sustainable abundance.

6. Sacred Service

Consider how Mary Magdalene ministered from her abundance (Luke 8:3), offering her resources, presence, and influence in service to the greater vision. This principle teaches us to align our service with our soul's purpose. It's not about depleting yourself; it's about giving generously, without overgiving, so that your presence becomes a blessing everywhere you go. Your energy becomes naturally magnetic. I intuitively recognized this truth, yet earlier in my journey, I tried the conventional approach, the exhausting way. Now, I understand that our well-being isn't optional; it's the prerequisite for our greatest contribution.

7. Magnetic Presence

This final principle embodies living your truth so completely that your soul-aligned clients naturally gravitate toward you. Mary Magdalene didn't chase followers; she was so anchored in her truth that people were magnetized to her radiance. I have learned to embody both the divine feminine wisdom flowing through me and the divine masculine structure that brings vision into form.

All these principles emerged from my intimate communion with Magdalene wisdom and my own healing journey. They aren't mere business strategies; they are invitations to a completely new paradigm of abundance that honors the sacred calling within you. *[Gently squeezes your hand.]*

Why I Abandoned Hustle Culture (and why you might consider it, too) *[wink wink]*

Here is the revolutionary truth: Authentic success is not defined by social media metrics or external validation; it blossoms when we follow our divine guidance rather than chasing approval from online business gurus. Here is what my professional reality looks like now:

- Some weeks, I work 3 hours; others, I work 30.
- I take random weekdays off for sacred rest whenever my spirit requires it.
- My content emerges from divine inspiration, not contrived content calendars.
- I implicitly trust my intuition about client relationships.

- I have released comparison and impostor syndrome.
- I have reclaimed precious time that no amount of money could buy.
- I have cultivated abundant calm and inner peace that radiates through everything I create.

Do you know what brings me the greatest joy in my work? Witnessing spiritual sisters step into their full divine worth and abundance. Whether they're attending one of my "Seeds of Abundance" talks or experiencing profound transformation in our "Luminary Abundance" membership or holding monthly temple space together in our Spiritual Practitioners membership, each journey is uniquely sacred and divinely orchestrated.

I have watched these teachings transform lives in countless ways as we explore Magdalene mysteries together, creating sustainable, soul-aligned practices. Through my high-touch work, I have witnessed extraordinary maverick spirits elevate their relationship with abundance, success, and freedom as they dismantle outdated paradigms while building lives and businesses aligned with their divine vision.

The most magical part? Once these teachings take root, I see my private clients, powerful spiritual leaders and change-makers, applying these principles to discover their unique expression of abundance. Celestial wisdom, after all, is Mary Magdalene's greatest teaching: that each of us carries a unique light, a particular medicine, and a different way of expressing timeless truths.

Divine Business Practices for the Modern Magdalene Maverick

You know what still brings tears of gratitude to my eyes? The way divine guidance arrives in the most unexpected moments.

Like when I was struggling with pricing my offerings, feeling those ancient unworthiness wounds resurfacing. One morning in meditation, I felt Mary Magdalene's presence so strongly it took my breath away. Suddenly, I remembered her alabaster jar and received a profound teaching that changed everything.

The Alabaster Jar Principle in Practice:

- Anoint your workspace with sacred intention each morning.
- Price your services from a place of inherent sacred worth.
- Create a transcendent experience for each client.
- Honor the energetic exchange in every transaction.

Let me share a story that illustrates this principle, beloved. Years ago, divine guidance prompted me to completely reimagine my client welcome process. Rather than standard automated emails, I created what I call "The Sacred Abundance Temple Welcome." New clients or alumni receive a beautifully curated package containing:

- A handwritten blessing note.
- A small vial of consecrated rose oil.
- A specially selected quartz crystal attuned to their energy.
- Sacred success rituals to support their journey.
- Fresh roses whenever possible!

Is it more investment than standard onboarding, closing, or promoting? Absolutely. Has it been worth it? Beyond measure. The miraculous connections, referrals, and transformations that have flowed from this practice have been nothing short of alchemical.

[Moves closer, takes your hands in hers.]

Magdalene Money Mysteries and Your Sacred Abundance

Beloved visionary, let's illuminate a truth that Mary Magdalene embodied perfectly: spiritual power and material prosperity are divine partners, not opposing forces. While many modern spiritual leaders struggle with charging for their gifts, Mary Magdalene shows us another way.

Remember the alabaster jar containing precious spikenard? That sacred offering was worth an entire year's wages! Yet Mary Magdalene approached with absolute certainty in its value and purpose. She didn't diminish its worth. She didn't offer a discount. She simply knew the perfect alignment between spiritual offering and material value.

When you find yourself undercharging, overgiving, or caught in endless cycles of discounts and energy-draining exchanges, return to this powerful image. Envision Mary Magdalene standing in her truth, holding her valuable offering with complete confidence. This is your birthright, too, to know the worth of your spiritual gifts and to exchange them in perfect sacred balance.

Breaking the Poverty Vows

Let's address the magnificent elephant in the temple: the persistent myth that spiritual gifts must be given freely without fair exchange. Beloved, at some point, many of us unconsciously made what I call "poverty vows" in our spiritual work. We internalized false teachings about service and sacrifice. Yet, consider how Mary Magdalene actually lived:

- She was a woman of independent means and sovereign power.
- She funded Yeshua's ministry from her abundance.
- She possessed valuable sacred instruments and substances.
- She moved through the world freely, supported by her resources.

Pause and truly absorb this revelation. The woman closest to Yeshua, who understood his teachings most profoundly, wasn't living in lack or limitation; she embodied purposeful prosperity in service to her divine mission!

When we release our unconscious poverty vows and embrace sacred abundance, we honor the authentic Magdalene tradition. Take a moment to craft your own wealth vows, sacred promises to yourself that affirm your divine right to prosperity. Write from your heart: "I vow to receive abundance as my spiritual birthright," "I commit to honoring my gifts through aligned exchange," or "I promise to use my prosperity to amplify my sacred mission." These new commitments replace the unconscious poverty agreements that have limited your impact and well-being.

Whenever that old programming around charging for your gifts begins resurfacing, try this prayer, offered in deep communion with the Magdalene:

Prayer: The Blessing of Magdalene's Success

Our Beloved Magdalene,
Help me remember my sacred worth.
Let me receive as gracefully as I give.
May my prosperity be a light for others.
May my abundance create more good for all.
Thank you for showing me how to be both spiritual and prosperous,
Both in service and abundantly supported in return.
Guide us as we revolutionize success through divine love.
Strengthen us to trust our knowing,
Honor our worth,
And serve from our radiant overflow.
Let our work be a blessing,
Our success a beacon,
And our prosperity an ever-expanding blessing for all.
In divine love, so it is.

The Magdalene's Invitation to Your Wild Heart

This journey together has been so deliciously sacred, and now, beloved sister, as we complete our time together, I invite you into a powerful embodiment practice. Place one hand on your heart center and one hand on your sacred womb space. Breathe deeply into this connection and recognize you are the living continuation of Mary Magdalene's lineage in our time.

That wild, untamed, abundant maverick heart of yours that refuses to accept the conventional "shoulds" of success… that exquisite sensitivity someone once labeled "too much,"… that profound longing for connection that transcends meaningless metrics… these are not burdens to overcome, they are your most potent superpowers.

You were called to this path for a divine purpose. The world needs your voice, your energy, your unique combination of gifts—the special medicine that only you can offer. And yes, you absolutely deserve to be compensated abundantly for sharing these sacred gifts! Hold fast to the alabaster jar, precious one, and remember the woman who knew her inestimable worth.

In those moments when the noise of conventional business advice becomes overwhelming, when you feel pulled to follow the crowd instead of your inner guidance, return to these Magdalene teachings. Light your sacred candle. Attune to your Magdalene wisdom. Listen to the gentle whispers of your soul. Your success doesn't need to mirror anyone else's. It only needs to resonate with your deepest truth.

You are not walking this path alone. Every time you stand in your worth, establish a sacred boundary, trust your divine timing, or choose depth over hustle, you walk in the footsteps of an ancient lineage of sacred maverick women who dared to forge a different path. And you journey alongside me and all your modern Magdalene sisters who are choosing this revolutionary way of being.

[Rises to embrace you with unconditional love.]

Take these practices. Embody them. Make them uniquely yours. May they support you in creating success that feels like returning to your most authentic self. And remember, magnificent one: your sensitivity is your superpower, your depth is your differentiation, and the wisdom of your heart is your most trusted business advisor.

May your success illuminate the path for others. Let your abundance flow and bless our world.

You are witnessed, you are held, and you are so deeply loved. Until we meet again, let your light radiate without dimming.

With holy maverick love and rose-scented blessings, remember, beloved, we aren't merely building businesses; we're creating sacred vessels for divine love to flow through us into a world that desperately needs it. Every client connection, every offering, every expression of your gifts is an opportunity to emanate your light. You are blessed, and the Magdalene walks with you—always.

> *"Every woman who stands in her worth illuminates the path for others to discover their own light."*
> **—Ancient Magdalene Teaching**

Rose Wilder

With an alabaster jar in one hand and wildfire in her heart, Rose Wilder stands as an abduction survivor transformed into a prosperity priestess. Walking the Magdalene path with sovereign certainty, she has alchemized her deepest wounds into divine gifts that now illuminate the way for thousands.

Her journey from trauma to transcendence wasn't merely a healing path—it became her soul's revolutionary purpose. As founder of Inner Light Collective and a Professional Priestess in the Magdalene Rose tradition, Rose guides spiritual mavericks who refuse to dim their radiance or discount their worth in a world obsessed with hustle culture.

When you have had to rebuild your entire sense of safety, you develop extraordinary discernment: the ability to recognize what's truly life-giving amidst the noise. This clarity has guided Rose to create multiple thriving businesses, including a healing center, day spa, and professional product line—all while being a Mother to her six beautiful children. She lives with her beloved on her sanctuary farm nestled in the Pacific Northwest mountains.

What distinguishes Rose's approach is her rare integration of seemingly opposite worlds: pragmatic business expertise and mystical Magdalene wisdom. As Creator of Abundance Keys and an Energetic Blueprint Mentor, she helps women decondition from conventional success paradigms that exhaust rather than enliven. Her clients learn to anchor their business decisions in their own divine knowing, establishing sacred boundaries while cultivating magnetic abundance that flows from alignment rather than hustle.

Those who work with Rose discover not just a mentor but a devoted priestess who holds space for their complete awakening. Through her guidance, women across the globe have reclaimed their divine birthright of prosperity, building businesses that honor both their spiritual gifts and material sovereignty.

Learn more:
https://www.luminaryilc.com
rose@innerlightcollective.org

Alabaster Jar Collection: Sacred Magdalene Treasures for the Divine Maverick

"She who knows her worth changes the world with her presence."

The Alabaster Jar Collection awaits you, a carefully curated sanctuary of sacred offerings that I've poured my heart and soul into creating. Just as Mary Magdalene approached with her precious spikenard, knowing its inestimable worth and divine purpose, I offer these treasures with absolute certainty in their value to your journey.

- **Sacred Magdalene Meditations**—Experience the transformative power of divine communion through exclusive guided meditations. One channeled through my own connection to the Magdalene wisdom, and another sacred journey guided by my sister-priestess Natasha. These are not ordinary meditations, precious one, they are energetic doorways into the Magdalene temple spaces where your most authentic self awaits.

- **Private Sanctuary Invitation**—*[Whispers with a wink.]* Say goodbye to algorithm-driven connections and step into our private Magdalene Maverick sanctuary, completely off social media. This sacred space is where holy maverick sisters gather to share their wildest visions, deepest questions, and most radiant celebrations, all held in the unshakable container of divine feminine wisdom.

But wait, magnificent one, the magic doesn't end there! Can you feel the delicious anticipation? Over the next seven months, your inbox will become a portal for divine abundance as I unveil a new sacred treasure each month. Each revelation will arrive like an alabaster jar of precious spikenard, carrying exactly the medicine your maverick heart needs in that moment. Claim your Alabaster Jar Collection now and begin your eight-month journey of divine abundance revelations. Let these sacred treasures illuminate your path to wild success through divine love.

Access here:
www.luminaryilc.com/magdaleneunveiled

Visit us at floweroflifepress.com

www.ingramcontent.com/pod-product-compliance
Lightning Source LLC
Chambersburg PA
CBHW022058150426
43195CB00008B/183